WRITERS
AS
READERS

THE ILLUSTRATOR

A graduate from Central Saint Martins with a degree in graphic design, Yehrin Tong creates illusory, eye-boggling, hypnotic patterns and typographic illustrations. Her tessellating mathematical motifs, optical illusions and meticulous detail has encompassed ad campaigns on print and screen, installations and editorial illustrations as well as graphics for fashion prints and embroideries. Yehrin's work is complex, beautiful and intricate. She has won the V&A Book Cover Illustration Award and is a winner of AIGA's 50 books | 50 covers of 2016.

WRITERS

AS

READERS

A CELEBRATION OF
VIRAGO MODERN CLASSICS

VIRAGO

First published in Great Britain in 2018 by Virago Press

1 3 5 7 9 10 8 6 4 2

This collection copyright © Virago Press 2018

Pages 407–8 constitute an extension to this copyright page.

A CIP catalogue record for this book
is available from the British Library.

ISBN 978-0-349-00862-2

Typeset in Goudy by M Rules
Printed and bound in Great Britain by
Clays Ltd, St Ives plc

Papers used by Virago are from well-managed forests
and other responsible sources.

Virago Press
An imprint of
Little, Brown Book Group
Carmelite House
50 Victoria Embankment
London EC4Y 0DZ

An Hachette UK Company
www.hachette.co.uk

www.virago.co.uk

CONTENTS

INTRODUCTION

Forty years ago, the Virago Modern Classics list was created by Carmen Callil, and it's not an overstatement to say that it changed literary history. Launching with Antonia White's elegant, devastating autobiographical novel *Frost in May*, the list's aim was, and is, to celebrate women writers and to demonstrate the existence of a female tradition in literature. Published with distinctive green spines and introductions by some of the best contemporary writers, it attracted an enthusiastic, dedicated following, which continues today. Four decades later, our ethos hasn't changed: we are still discovering books by women, to inspire, challenge and delight. One might say life is just beginning.

If women's stories aren't published in all their variety, their voices are silenced, and only part of human experience – in both the historical and the imaginative landscapes – is represented. Vera Brittain recognised this when she wrote *Testament of Youth*: 'Any picture of the war years is incomplete which omits those aspects that mainly concerned women.' Today it seems astonishing that her searing memoir, a monumental bestseller in 1933 and now regarded as integral to the canon of First World War literature, had been all but wiped from the public's consciousness until it was republished by Virago in 1978.

The Virago Modern Classics list redrew the literary map to expose what had been hidden from view, providing a counterbalance to the existing male-dominated perspective. Many of the books had been unavailable for decades, but that certainly wasn't due to lack of literary merit – or, I would argue, how could Ernest Hemingway have been in print, but not Willa Cather? A platform that values the female experience as equal to the male is crucial: storytelling is central to what it is to be human, and giving a voice to generations of important but neglected women writers benefits everyone. History is incomplete without them, and readers miss out on the pleasure of discovering their female literary heritage.

One only needs to consider the writers published in the first few years of the list's existence to realise how essential it was: Elizabeth Taylor, Rebecca West, Edith Wharton, Willa Cather, Charlotte Perkins Gilman, Rosamond Lehmann, Stevie Smith, Radclyffe Hall and Sylvia Townsend Warner. I have always taken the availability of these writers for granted, but back then Virago, a fledgling list, was the only publisher issuing them. Antonia White and Rosamond Lehmann were still living and delighted at their 'reincarnation' (as Lehmann put it), and readers were thrilled to rediscover their novels.

The list has always been a uniquely collaborative enterprise, with authors, agents and readers suggesting long-lost favourites to resurrect. In this anthology of forty introductions from the past four decades, we celebrate some of the many women and men who, from the list's inception, have shared their knowledge, insights and enthusiasm to endorse books that deserve once again to be read. I only wish we could have included more.

Introductions act as personal recommendations to readers. You may not have heard of Sylvia Townsend Warner, but if Sarah Waters tells you 'she's certainly one of the most shamefully under-read great British authors of the past hundred years', it might persuade you to try her. When Sandi Toksvig says that *Confessions of a Failed Southern Lady* by Florence King 'ought to be printed with a mechanism for turning down the volume of the reader' as it contains 'some of the best comic writing ever put down on paper', you'll want to be let in on the joke. When Diana Athill introduces *The Diary of 'Helena Morley'*, beautifully translated by the poet Elizabeth Bishop, she enthuses, 'I love the book ... her writing carries us away out of our own lives into hers, so different, so surprising, often so funny and always, because of her company, so enjoyable.' How can you deny yourself this little-known Brazilian classic a moment longer?

As well as endorsing a work ('Perhaps this introduction can act like a friend enthusing over her favourite book and urging you to read it. Why should you? Why is Frame's work so good?' – Michèle Roberts), an introduction should enhance your reading experience, whether that's by informing you about a writer's life, her other works, or the historical context in which the book was written. Or it may be a deeply personal appreciation.

The books that we read and love, especially when young, shape us, help us to forge our identity, and let us know that we are not alone. A number of the writers in this collection introduce books that were seismic discoveries for their younger selves:

I had never read anything like it before. I hadn't known it was possible to write in such a clean, insouciant style ... It was one of those moments ... when the world suddenly shifts on its axis and everything looks sharp with potential – Maggie O'Farrell on *The Yellow Wallpaper*

Gay politics and the tortuous fight for dignity and equality are inextricably linked in my mind to my first reading of Mary Renault – Simon Russell Beale on *The Charioteer*

At fourteen I couldn't find words (or words I liked) for the marvellous feeling of recognition that came with these characters who had my hair, my eyes, my skin ... These forms of identification are so natural to white readers – Zadie Smith on *Their Eyes Were Watching God*

It is the introducer's role to offer a new perspective; to unseat your assumptions; to make you see familiar books in a new light. You might not agree that *Valley of the Dolls*, that juicy, record-breaking sixties bestseller, is 'a brave, bold, angry and, yes, definitely a feminist book', but Julie Burchill makes a good case for it. What writer could better open your eyes to the fairy-tale heritage of *Jane Eyre* than Angela Carter? This is also a poignant piece, as Carter's early death would follow just two years after she wrote 'there is a tender embarrassment about rereading *Jane Eyre* in the middle age; one wants the world to be kind, not to Jane, but to the girl who invented Jane, and, in doing so, set out so vividly her hopes and fears and longings on the page ... If she had not died so young, the course of English fiction would have been utterly different. Anything would have been possible.'

Just as painters study early masters, discovering their own unique style in the process, so writers hone their craft by reading widely and analytically. There is a thread of inspiration and influence that can be traced across generations of storytellers, exemplified here in the introductions of Beryl Bainbridge, who introduces Emily Brontë, and Linda Grant, who introduces Bainbridge's early work. The Brontës, and Emily in particular, were enthralled by the folktales told to them by their house-keeper, Tabby, and those wild stories influenced *Wuthering Heights*. Bainbridge alludes to this, and admires Brontë's style: the 'almost casual confidence of a writer of genius telling a superb story'. In her introduction, we go on a pilgrimage with her, trundling in a fifties snub-nosed car, to Haworth Parsonage, so she can get closer to the writer she loved.

In Linda Grant's introduction to Bainbridge, she recalls the first time she met Beryl, whom she 'had been reading since [her] early twenties'. She perfectly describes her novels as having 'a black heart ... in a comic chest', and the esteem in which she holds Bainbridge is tangible: 'She was *sui generis*, one of the greatest.' And so, when Grant dissects soap plotlines with Bainbridge while chugging down Turnpike Lane in a minibus, we can follow a thread that leads back to a Yorkshire servant entrancing her charges with stories by the parsonage fire. The female literary tradition is perfectly encapsulated here.

I hope, as you dip into these pages, you will encounter a writer you've never heard of or a book you've never read – whether Muriel Spark's first novel or Barbara Pym's last; whether the diary of a Brazilian schoolgirl or the memoir of a wartime nurse. In viewing familiar books through another reader's eyes, I hope you will revisit old favourites and see them anew, alive to new interpretations. And I hope, that in continuing to champion voices from the past, we will help provide inspiration for the writers of the future.

Donna Coonan
Editorial Director, Virago Modern Classics

MARGARET DRABBLE
ON
JANE AUSTEN

Pride and Prejudice (1813)

First Virago edition 1989

Jane Austen was born in Hampshire in 1775. Her novels, *Sense and Sensibility, Pride and Prejudice, Mansfield Park, Emma, Persuasion* and *Northanger Abbey*, earned her a place as one of the best known and best loved writers in English literature. She died in 1817. In 2017 she was chosen to appear on the ten-pound note.

Margaret Drabble was born in Sheffield in 1939 and was educated at Newnham College, Cambridge. She is the author of nineteen novels, including *A Summer Bird-Cage, The Millstone, The Peppered Moth, The Red Queen, The Sea Lady, The Pure Gold Baby* and *The Dark Flood Rises*. She has also written biographies and screenplays, and was the editor of the *Oxford Companion to English Literature*. She was appointed CBE in 1980, and made DBE in the 2008 honours list. She was also awarded the 2011 Golden PEN Award for a Lifetime's Distinguished Service to Literature.

She is married to the biographer Michael Holroyd.

Jane Austen characterised *Pride and Prejudice* in a famous letter to her sister Cassandra as 'rather too light, and bright, and sparkling; it wants shade; it wants to be stretched out here and there with a long chapter of sense, if it could be had; if not, of solemn specious nonsense, about something unconnected with the story; an essay on writing, a critique on Walter Scott, or the history of Buonaparte'.* Her readers have not felt the lack of tedious digressions, and it has remained one of her most popular works. It is an astonishing accomplishment for a young woman of twenty-one, and on each rereading one can only discover new subtleties, new ironies. Unlike her other early novels, *Northanger Abbey* and *Sense and Sensibility*, it has an extraordinary poise and coherence of subject and style, and although it is indeed bright and sparkling, it by no means lacks shades of meaning. The brilliance with which 'sense' is unobtrusively subsumed in plot continues to compel admiration. The elegance of this performance is almost beyond praise.

After such a panegyric, there might seem to be little more to be said about this most accessible and entertaining of novels. And yet it is a book which we are likely to find very different

* Letter 14 February 1813, *Jane Austen's Letters to her Sister Cassandra and others*, Collected and edited by R. W. Chapman, 2 vols, Clarendon Press, Oxford, 1932.

on a third from on a first reading. This is perhaps appropriate, as the book's original title was 'First Impressions', and one of its themes is the way in which a hasty judgement can mislead. But before turning to variant interpretations and finer shades, let us look at the admiring consensus of those early readers who found it 'agreeable', 'entertaining', 'interesting', and 'finely written', and who unite in a praise of its realistic portrayal of characters of 'middling' rank. Annabella Milbanke (later Lady Byron) wrote to her mother in 1813 (the year of publication) that she found it,

> a very superior work. It depends not on any of the common resources or novel writers, no drownings, no conflagrations, nor runaway horses, nor lapdogs and parrots, nor chambermaids and milliners, nor rencontres and disguises. I really think it is the *most probable* I have ever read. It is not a crying book, but the interest is very strong ... I wish much to know who is the author or *ess* as I am told.

This warm response is echoed (with a little more judicious condescension) by Sir Walter Scott, who in 1815 found it 'a very pretty thing. No dark passages; no secret chambers; no wind-howlings in long gallerie; no drops of blood upon a rusty dagger – things that should now be left to ladies' maids and sentimental washerwomen.'* (Scott read the novel at least three times, and on his third reading humbly noted in his *Journal* 'The Big Bow-wow strain I can do myself like any now going, but the exquisite touch which renders ordinary commonplace things and

* H. J. C. Grierson (ed.), *Wako Scott's Letters*, 12 vols, Constable & Co., London, 1932–7.

characters interesting from the truth of the description and the sentiment is denied to me.'*)

One notes that both these early admirers select for special praise the 'ordinariness' of the plot, and contrast it with the sentimental improbabilities and Gothic horrors of much popular fiction (of which Scott himself, as he admits, was often guilty). This draws our attention to the fact that unlike her other early works, *Sense and Sensibility* and *Northanger Abbey* (and also her juvenilia), *Pride and Prejudice* has no strong elements of parody or burlesque. It is charged with satirical references, but it does not depend on its relation to any imported or inherited framework. It is, very confidently, itself: a domestic novel of manners and marriage set in and near a small country town somewhere around the turn of the century. The interest rises principally from following the relationships of two couples, that of the amiable Jane Bennet with the pleasant Mr Bingley, and that of the witty Elizabeth Bennet with the proud and wealthy Mr Darcy. Many obstacles (provided principally by the vulgarity of several members of the Bennet family) delay the final happy ending, and entertainment is provided by a fine cast of minor characters (Mr Collins, Lady Catherine de Bourgh, Sir William Lucas). But the principal plot is matrimony, and the principal mode is comic.

On a first reading, what perhaps strikes one most is the wonderfully sure touch with which Jane Austen handles her heroine Elizabeth and in particular her passages with Mr Darcy. In Elizabeth, she allows herself all the uncensored freedom of wit that she felt obliged to repress in later works, and the result is some of the best repartee in fiction. Critics have rightly compared

* J. G. Tail (ed.), *Walter Scott's Journal,* 14 March 1826, 3 vols, Oliver and Boyd, London, 1950.

the relationship of Elizabeth and Darcy to that of those other embattled couples, Benedict and Beatrice in *Much Ado About Nothing* and Mirabell and Millamant in Congreve's *The Way of the World*. There is something theatrical in the way they view themselves – both, in different ways, are keenly interested in their impact upon an audience, and it is revealing to note that towards the end (Chapter 50), Elizabeth regrets her imagined loss of Darcy as the loss of an opportunity to 'teach the admiring multitude what connubial felicity really was'.

We have little doubt, from their first meeting, that they will finally be brought together, for the convention of violent antipathy that turns to love is almost as strong as the convention of love at first sight, and there is already something sexually provocative in Darcy's manner of dismissing Elizabeth as a dance partner: 'She is tolerable; but not handsome enough to tempt *me*,' he says, in her hearing, and the remark acts upon Elizabeth, subconsciously, as a challenge. She may not intend to attract him, indeed she declares herself indifferent and hostile to him, but he has caught her attention, and she means at least to put him in his place. The development of their mutual attraction is beautifully traced: Darcy's proposal (as grotesque in its own way as that of Mr Collins) is one of the high points of the novel, but there are many other lesser moments of creative tension between the two which indicate their long-term compatibility – as, for example, the interesting dialogue at Rosings in which Elizabeth audaciously challenges Darcy with his initial rudeness to her, and tells him he too could learn to 'converse easily' if only he would practise. His replies are as challenging as her attack: the balance between them is finely judged and both hold their own.

Perhaps one of the secrets of the novel's lasting appeal lies in its portrayal of a well-matched couple. There is no trimming, no half measure here. One really does not doubt that Elizabeth and Darcy will be happy together. As Brigid Brophy* has commented, although the novel's 'decorous prose and seemly narrative never makes an explicit reference to sexual intercourse', Jane Austen has nevertheless 'metaphorically depicted it' in the sexual dialectic and interpenetration of their dialogues. But when she goes on to say that they have also been damaged, humbled and 'ruthlessly chopped' by one another, she surely overstates the case: one of the delights of this novel is that its hero and heroine are allowed to learn without too much suffering or humiliation, and far from having to cut themselves down to size to enter the Procrustean bed of marriage, they are given one another *and* the riches of Pemberley. A fairy-tale ending, but one justified by the sexual radiance that shines from the protagonists. If anyone ever has a chance to make a good marriage, these two have.

And in her other relationships, Elizabeth also shines. Her fondness for her sister Jane, her spirited rejoinders to Miss Bingley, her instant (and correct) appraisal of Mr Collins, her loyal friendship to Charlotte Lucas – all show her in an amiable light. Unlike Elinor Dashwood, she is not too wise – she is taken in very easily by Mr Wickham – but she has a quick resilience and an easiness of temper that make her able to cut her losses very quickly. She is half-disposed to find herself half in love with the apparently eligible thirty-year-old Colonel Fitzwilliam, but when he warns her that as a younger son he cannot afford to marry, she quickly swallows what must have been a moment of real mortification for a dowerless girl and with some courage teases him about 'the usual price of an Earl's younger son'. After this, her main instinct is to put him at his ease for having made her uncomfortable. She

* Introduction to *Pride and Prejudice*, Pan, London, 1967.

shows a similar generosity in more serious circumstances when she says 'with a good-humoured smile' to Wickham (who is foolishly insisting on his own version of Darcy's conduct), 'Come, Mr Wickham, we are brother and sister, you know. Do not let us quarrel about the past. In future, I hope we shall always be of one mind.' And she holds out her hand to him, which he kisses 'with affectionate gallantry' and much embarrassment. We know that Jane Austen herself felt a peculiar fondness for her heroine (whom she claimed with only a touch of self-mockery to consider 'as delightful a creature as ever appeared in print'), and can only be grateful that, exceptionally, she allowed her a free rein as well as a bright future.

If the brightness and sparkle of the central characters account for the book's appeal on its first impression, perhaps we do not need to look further. But it has other satisfactions, and other shades. The neatness of the plot and its expert articulation have been justly admired: there are none of the uneasy shifts of focus or hasty tying or cutting of Gordian knots that mark and mar the other two early novels. Nothing here is superfluous or implausible; the story unfolds with a pleasing mixture of suspense and foreknowledge, and it fulfils all its own expectations. The shocks and surprises all make sense: when Lydia runs off with Wickham, we are surprised only that we had not seen it coming, and Darcy's explanations of his past conduct are far more convincing than the more lurid revelations of Colonel Brandon's in *Sense and Sensibility*. Almost all the characters are given space and identity, and even those who appear very sketchily, such as the indolent Mr Hurst or the pleasant Colonel Fitzwilliam, are integrated into and play an important role in both plot and social atmosphere. Compare the treatment of Kitty Bennet with that of Margaret Dashwood, the youngest sister in *Sense and Sensibility*. Margaret as an individual hardly exists and has little real function in the novel, whereas Kitty, although the most shadowy of the five Bennet girls, has more than a merely supernumerary role (though that, of course, is important, as numbers are of the essence here). She echoes Lydia, she imitates Lydia, she is fretful because she cannot follow Lydia; her very lack of character is her character, and she adds considerably to the interplay of family dynamics. Austen understood sibling rivalry very well, and here, in this small portrait, offers another dimension of it.

The novel has also been highly praised for its accurate portrayal of social customs, but it is here that we come to one of its more controversial aspects. Some readers really deeply dislike the society in which Austen's works are so firmly grounded: much ado about nothing indeed is the accusation, and what about the French Revolution and the Napoleonic wars? Have soldiers nothing better to do than to flirt with young women, play whist and lottery, and seduce the daughters of tradesmen? Come to that, has *nobody* anything better to do? And on inspection, it does appear that many of the novel's characters do remarkably little. Bingley shoots and gives parties and admits to not reading very much; Mr Hurst plays cards and falls asleep; even Mr Collins, who has a proper job, seems to spend most of his time watching the road for carriages or eating at Rosings. Wickham's military duties do not seem to be very onerous. Darcy, it is true, is shown as a responsible landowner admired by his housekeeper, tenants and servants, but he too has a great deal of leisure. Mr Gardiner is in trade in the city, but we see and hear next to nothing of him at work. The women, of course, are not expected to employ themselves except at the piano: Mrs Bennet is proud of the fact that her daughters (unlike Charlotte Lucas) do not have to busy themselves in the kitchen, as she has a first-rate cook. Various maids feature, almost subliminally, in the text – Jane and Elizabeth are 'helped on' with their gowns and have their hair dressed by a non-speaking part called Sarah.

The most mysterious figure, in terms of employment, is Mr Bennet himself, the head of this large all-female household. We are told the circumstances of the entail which means that his considerable property will pass on his death not to his wife or any of his daughters but to Mr Collins. He is of no profession: he is a gentleman. He shoots, and we know he has scholarly interests, for he spends much time in his library (and resents being pursued there by Mr Collins), but we suspect that he is fond of his library partly because it is a refuge from his wife, and there is no evidence that he has written even as much as a small monograph. He is unhappily married, having been unwisely carried away by his 'first impressions' of the sexually attractive Mrs Bennet, who after many efforts has failed to produce an heir. (In those days, of course, it was not known that it is the male input that determines a baby's sex.) He is fond of Jane, and fond of Elizabeth to the point of what would now be called 'favouritism': the rest of his family he tends to ridicule. He has retreated from the world (as, some have suggested, did Austen herself) into an ironic distance, yet he is also imprudent, for he spends his whole income and comes to regret that he has put nothing away 'for the better provision of his children, and of his wife, if she survived him'. He is thus a negligent father, whose responsibility for what happens to Lydia is judged heavy: Darcy (damningly) finds him occasionally guilty of 'want of propriety' – in other words, not quite a gentleman.

Yet at a first reading, most find him much more attractive and judge him less harshly than his wife. This was certainly my own first response on reading the novel in the 1950s, and indeed tended then to be the received opinion. He is genuinely witty and intelligent: his sardonic remarks seem a fitting commentary on the vacuity of much of the social life in which he is reluctantly obliged to engage, and his view that 'we live, but to make sport for our neighbours, and laugh at them in our turn' may seem close to that of his author, and therefore to be condoned by her. I recall my indignation when asked to reassess him as a father, and consider whether Austen herself did not find him wanting.

On rereading one sees that she does indeed imply criticism of his negligence as a father, and recognises that his eccentricities are a hindrance to the matrimonial prospects of his daughters. Nevertheless, she relishes his ironic wit and clearly enjoys wreaking through his voice a little irresponsible revenge on the bores and fools of the neighbourhood. Nineteenth-century critics tended to view him indulgently, as a 'recluse' and an 'eccentric'. And nobody, not even Austen herself, seems to question how he actually spends his time. One might legitimately wonder if there is not as much vacuity in Mr Bennet's life as in that of his wife.

This, of course, is very much a feminist, twentieth-century perspective, and one that would have been difficult to perceive from within the society so faithfully depicted. Recent studies, predictably, have begun to produce defences of the vulgar, impossible, stupid, uncultured, embarrassing Mrs Bennet. Of course, we may now say, she was desperate to marry off her daughters: this was the 'employment' of her life, and she attacks it much more energetically than her husband does. She understands about dinners and balls and good cooking. We may wince from her pushiness and ignorance on first reading, but on the tenth are we not a little more impressed by the evidence that she runs a generous household, keeps a good table, is a good hostess? Fay Weldon, in her *Letters to Alice on First Reading Jane Austen*, comments that in her 'politeness warred . . . with desperation':* desperation often won. Mary Evans, in a characteristic 1980s revisionist statement, comments that she has generally been regarded 'as one of the more absurd and comic figures of English fiction', but asks us to consider that,

> if Mrs Bennet is slightly crazy, then perhaps she is so because she perceives, more clearly than her husband, the possible fate of her daughters if they do not marry . . . Given that she has five daughters, it is little wonder that at times Mrs Bennet is less than rational.†

A non-revisionist would point out the strong evidence that Mrs Bennet's zeal and indelicacy damage her own best interests, and that therefore she cannot be condoned even as an anxious mother. One might also point to her more serious lack of judgement over the Lydia–Wickham affair, which could, without the intervention of Darcy, have ended very badly (and expensively) for all the Bennets. Yet there still remain points on the credit side. Nobody, surely, could object to her volte-face over the acceptability of Darcy as a son-in-law, for here she is merely echoing Elizabeth's own behaviour, and indeed there is something sympathetic and generous (if not exactly sensible) in her desire to dislike the important Mr Darcy as strongly as she is given to believe her daughters do. Her chagrin when Lady Lucas boasts of the marriage of Charlotte is similarly venial. And she is on at least one occasion credited with the voice of pure maternal common sense. When one of the young Lucas boys cries out that if he were

* Michael Joseph, London, 1984.
† *Jane Austen and the State*, Tavistock Publications, London, 1987.

as rich as Mr Darcy, he would 'keep a pack of foxhounds, and drink a bottle of wine every day', Mrs Bennet replies 'Then you would drink a great deal more than you ought . . . and if I were to see you at it I should take away your bottle directly.' There is something endearingly normal about this remark which the subsequent sentence does nothing to dispel – 'The boy protested that she should not; she continued to declare that she would, and the argument ended only with the visit.' The informality, the easy good nature of Mrs Bennet's manner may plunge frequently into silliness or soar into absurd pretension when she feels herself outclassed by her company, but she is not always absurd.

The fact that her characters can be plausibly interpreted against her own intentions and in the light of the vagaries of sociology and history is a tribute to Austen's powers of mimesis. She creates and manifests Mr and Mrs Bennet: we bring to them our own feminist, post-feminist (and post-Marxist) insights. In this case the possible variant readings do not indicate an uncertainty of artistic purpose or an internal conflict, as they may in *Sense and Sensibility*. On the contrary, the roundness and the wholeness of the portraits is what gives them shade and depth. In the Lukácsian sense, Austen, like Balzac, portrays her own society so faithfully that she preserves it as a valid object for later historical analysis.

The case of the unfortunate Mary Bennet is slightly different, and any objections one may have to this portrait are drawn strictly from outside the text. Jane Austen's intentions are clear enough: Mary, the plain middle daughter, does not represent learning or intelligence or wisdom or a critique of the deficiencies of female education, she represents hollow pedantry and false accomplishment. She is no George Eliot in the making, and her affectation of profundity is intended to be ridiculous. Is it illegitimate to ask what other choices she had? May one complain that Jane Austen is cruelly reinforcing the unattractive stereotype of the bluestocking, the *femme savante*? These questions are difficult to answer, and one certainly would not like to suggest that this portrait in any way unsettles the mood of the novel. But they do invite one to speculate a little on Austen's own role as a clever (and largely self-educated) woman in a society in which women who read too much ware suspected of being 'satirical'. (Lady Middleton in *Sense and Sensibility* Chapter 36, on Elinor and Marianne: 'because they were fond of reading, she fancied them satirical: perhaps without exactly knowing what it was to be satirical; but *that* did not signify. It was censure in common use, and easily given.')

If reading books invited censure, how much more so must the writing of them have done? There must have been a strong incentive for women to conceal their intellectual interests, and we see that although our heroine Elizabeth shows herself to be well-read and to have good taste in music and landscape, she does not present herself as formidably learned, and she certainly is not 'impatient for display' like Mary. Her lack of real skill at the piano (like Emma's?) is presented as endearing, as is her acknowledgement of her own limitations. We are told that 'her performance was pleasing, though by no means capital', and although she tells Darcy that she thinks she could play better if she practised more, she is only scoring a point here: her vanity, as she tells her friend Charlotte, does not take 'a musical turn'. It is interesting to note that the most artistically gifted of Austen's female characters, Jane Fairfax in *Emma*, is portrayed from a certain distance and with a certain coolness – a coolness directly connected with Emma's own slightly guilty and jealous sense of inferiority.

Of whom, one asks oneself, did Jane Austen feel jealous, and why is she so anxious to portray her heroines as 'amateurs' of the arts? What turn did her own 'vanity' take? She never attempts a portrait of a professional, although women had been making money as writers for at least a century, nor does she ever explore the dark world of female labour (as milliner, shopkeeper, opera singer, paid companion) that her contemporary Fanny Burney tackles (not very successfully, it is true) in her novel *The Wanderer* (1814). Like Virginia Woolf many generations later, she chose on the whole to describe women less gifted, intellectually less audacious, more conventional than herself. One of the reasons why *Pride and Prejudice* is such a cheerful book is that she allows Elizabeth to be both unconventional and unpunished, either for her muddy petticoats ('an abominable sort of conceited independence, a most country town indifference to decorum,' says Miss Bingley) or for her sharp opinions.

Austen's own intelligence is concealed and absorbed, in her life, in her art. We all know her nephew's famous account of her writing habits:

> [she] wrote upon small sheets of paper, which could easily be put away, or covered with a piece of blotting paper. There was, between the front door and the offices, a swing door which creaked when it was opened, but she objected to having this little inconvenience remedied, because it gave her notice when anyone was coming.*

She preferred concealment to ostentation, secrecy to display. She could no doubt with ease have treated the reader to a digression (or a parody of a digression) on the work of Walter Scott in order

* J. E. Austen-Leigh, *A Memoir of Jane Austen*, Bentley, London, 1870, and R. W. Chapman (ed.), Clarendon Press, Oxford, 1926. (Also reprinted with the text of *Persuasion*, by Penguin, London, 1965.)

to add weight to her comedy, as a Mary Bennet might have done, but she chose not to do so.

One explanation for her apparent assumption of female modesty is that she was trying through it to avert ridicule and criticism for 'over-reaching'. Marilyn Butler seems to endorse this possibility, when she claims that Austen

> represents women's abilities and aspirations as they manifest themselves in speech, and the verbal characteristics of her heroines include some striking negations: restraint, deference, inarticulacy, an absence of reference to events, books and ideas. The women she allows to speak out form the largest single group of her minor characters – her female fools.*

While recognising the application of both halves of this judgement to some of Austen's heroines and fools – for example, Fanny Price and Mrs Bennet herself – we note at once that Elizabeth is certainly not marked by 'restraint, deference and inarticulacy', but rather by their reverse. And one might suggest that Elizabeth's lack of overt references to 'books and ideas' is, precisely, one of the novel's strengths. The other two early novels are if anything too bookish, too dependent on their reaction from earlier literary genres: conspicuous intertextuality like the references to *The Mysteries of Udolpho* in *Northanger Abbey* may be entertaining, and may indeed have a semi-serious purpose, but the novel's play with literary convention is far less original than the seamless and apparently realistic texture of *Pride and Prejudice*. It is always easier to imitate other books than life itself.

An equally plausible explanation of the discreet absence of

* *Jane Austen and the War of Ideas*, Introduction, Clarendon Press, Oxford, 1987.

intellectual display from her works might lie in the fact that her confidence was such that she felt she did not need to bother with it. She had no need to strain after effects, to insist on her own importance, to demonstrate her superiority. She knew her own worth, and she was sure of her subject matter, something more like arrogance than modesty dictated her tone. Catherine, in *Northanger Abbey*, confesses to Henry and Eleanor Tilney that she is not fond of history, although she reads a little as a duty, for there are 'quarrels of popes and kings, with wars and pestilences, in every page; the men are all so good for nothing, and hardly any women at all – it is very tiresome: and yet I often think it odd that it should be so dull, for a great deal of it must be invention'. This *faux-naif* commentary has a great deal of double-edged shrewdness in it, and could well be argued to hint at Austen's dismissal of some of the pretensions of male culture and scholarship. Male critics this century have made extravagant claims for Austen's own possible reading habits – what did she make of Locke and Hume, what were her opinions of French and German philosophy and history? – but far more striking is her evident (and historically justified) faith in the enduring interest and originality of her own chosen ground and subject matter, where one may find plenty of women, and men who are neither popes nor kings. This faith is in itself a form of audacity.

Not all women have shared her faith in the domestic novel. Charlotte Brontë, in a celebrated attack (in a letter to G. H. Lewes),* complained that *Pride and Prejudice* is

an accurate daguerreotyped portrait of a commonplace face:
a carefully fenced, highly cultivated garden, with neat borders

---

* 12 January 1848, Clement K. Shorter (ed.), *The Brontës: Life and Letters*, Hodder & Stoughton, London, 1908.

and delicate flowers: but no glance of a bright, vivid physiog-
nomy, no open country, no fresh air ... I should hardly like
to live with her ladies and gentlemen, in their elegant but
confined houses.

Thus speaks a post-Romantic and a writer who certainly risked
making a fool of herself by different forms of daring. Many
have echoed her complaints, but more (including myself) have
endorsed the general view that this novel is one of the great
original works of fiction. Reginald Farrar, in the *Quarterly Review*
of 1917, called it 'the greatest miracle of English Literature'. One
recalls Annabella Milbanke's praise of it as the 'most probable'
novel she had ever read. What kind of genius is it that can produce a probable miracle? The originality and brilliance of this
performance – at such an age, at any age – go beyond the probable, and do indeed partake of the miraculous.

ANGELA CARTER
ON
CHARLOTTE BRONTË

Jane Eyre (1847)

First Virago edition 1990

Charlotte Brontë was born in Yorkshire in 1816 and became a teacher and governess. In 1842 she travelled to Brussels to study languages. As well as publishing poetry with her sisters Emily and Anne, she wrote four novels: *The Professor, Jane Eyre, Shirley* and *Villette*. She died in 1855.

Angela Carter was one of Britain's most original writers, highly acclaimed for her novels, short stories and journalism. *The Magic Toyshop* won the John Llewellyn Rhys Prize in 1968 and *Several Perceptions* won the Somerset Maugham Prize in 1969. More novels followed as well as her 1977 translation of the fairy tales of Charles Perrault. Angela Carter's last novel was the much-lauded *Wise Children*, published in 1991. Her death in 1992 at the age of fifty-one 'robbed the English literary scene of one of its most vivacious and compelling voices' (*Independent*).

In 1847, a young woman of genius, vexed at publishers' rejections of *The Professor*, the first novel she had completed, on the grounds that it 'lacked colour' and was too short, sat down to give the reading public exactly what she had been told they wanted – something 'wild, wonderful and thrilling', in three volumes. Rarely, if ever, has such a strategy proved so successful. The young woman's name was Charlotte Brontë and the novel she produced, *Jane Eyre*, is still, after a century and a half, 'wild, wonderful and thrilling'. It remains the most durable of melodramas, angry, sexy, a little crazy, a perennial bestseller – one of the oddest novels ever written, a delirious romance replete with elements of pure fairy tale, given its extraordinary edge by the sheer emotional intelligence of the writer, the exceptional sophistication of her heart.

Charlotte Brontë lived during one of the greatest periods of social change in English history. In all her novels, she is attempting to describe a way of living that had never existed before and had come into being with the unprecedented social and economic upheavals of England in the early industrial revolution. Jane Eyre herself is the prototype Charlotte Brontë heroine – a woman on her own for whose behaviour there are no guidelines. This woman is not only capable of earning her own living but must and needs to do so; for her, therefore, love is a means of existential definition, an exploration of the potentials of her self, rather than the means of induction into the contingent existence of the married woman, as it had been for the previous heroines of the bourgeois novel.

I don't think for one moment that Charlotte Brontë knew she was doing this, precisely. When she wrote *Jane Eyre*, she thought she was writing a love story; but in order for Charlotte Brontë, with her precise configuration of class background and personal history, to write a love story, she had, first of all, to perform an analysis of the operation of erotic attraction upon a young woman who is not rich nor beautiful but, all the same, due to her background and education, free to choose what she does with her life.

The clarity and strength of Charlotte Brontë's perception of her heroine's struggle for love is extraordinary. Yet, of all the great novels in the world, *Jane Eyre* veers the closest towards trash. Elizabeth Rigby, writing in the *Quarterly Review*, 1848, makes the exact point that the novel combines 'such genuine power with such horrid taste'. She went on, a touch petulantly: 'the popularity of *Jane Eyre* is a proof how deeply the love of the illegitimate romance is implanted in our nature'. In order to do something new, in order to describe a way of being that had no existing language to describe it, Charlotte Brontë reverted, to a large extent, to pre-bourgeois forms. *Jane Eyre* is the classic formulation of the romance narrative, with its mysteries of parentage, lost relatives miraculously recovered, stolen letters, betrayal, deceit – and it fuses elements of two ancient fairy tales, *Bluebeard*, specifically referred to in the text when Thornfield Hall is compared to Bluebeard's castle, and *Beauty and the Beast*, plus a titillating hint of *Cinderella*. The archaic sub-literary forms of romance and fairy tale are so close to dreaming they lend themselves readily to psychoanalytic interpretation. Episodes such as that in which Rochester's mad wife rips apart the veil he has bought Jane to wear at his second, bigamous wedding have the delirium of Freudian dream language. As a result, *Jane Eyre* is a peculiarly unsettling blend of penetrating psychological realism, of violent and intuitive feminism, of a surprisingly firm sociological grasp, and of the utterly non-realistic apparatus of psycho-sexual fantasy – irresistible passion, madness, violent death, dream, telepathic communication.

The latter element is so pronounced that it gives the novel a good deal in common, not with *Emma* or *Middlemarch*, but with certain enormously influential, sub-literary texts in which nineteenth-century England discussed in images those aspects of unprecedented experience for which words could not, yet, be found: Mary Shelley's *Frankenstein*, Bram Stoker's *Dracula*. 'There are times when reality becomes too complex for Oral Communication,' says the computer in Jean-Luc Godard's 1967 movie, *Alphaville*, 'but Legend gives it a form by which it pervades the whole world.' *Jane Eyre* has this quality of legend and, like *Frankenstein* and *Dracula*, has proved infinitely translatable into other media: stage, screen, radio. I first encountered *Jane Eyre* in a comic-strip version. The text easily secretes other versions of itself; one of them, Jean Rhys's *Wide Sargasso Sea*, restores the first Mrs Rochester, Jane's predecessor, to the centre of the narrative. One of the great bestsellers of the mid-twentieth century, Daphne du Maurier's *Rebecca*, shamelessly reduplicated the plot of *Jane Eyre*, and went on to have the same kind of vigorous trans-media after-life.

Nevertheless, if Jane Eyre arrives, like Bluebeard's wife or Beauty, at an old, dark house, whose ugly/beautiful master nourishes a fatal secret, she arrives there not as a result of marriage or magic, but as the result of an advertisement she herself had placed in a newspaper. She has come to earn her own living and the fairy-tale heroine, as she travels to the abode of secrets and the place of initiation, is fully aware of her own social mobility, which is specifically the product of history. 'Let the worst come to the worst,' she ponders, 'I can advertise again.'

Jane is only pretending to be a heroine of romance or fairy tale. She may act out the Gothic role of 'woman in peril' for a while at Thornfield Hall, when she is menaced by her lover's first wife, but, when things become intolerable, she leaves. She might be trapped by her desires, but she is never trapped by her circumstances. She is, in terms of social and literary history, not a romance figure at all but a precursor of the rootless urban intelligentsia who, seventy years later, will take the fictional form of the Brangwen sisters in D. H. Lawrence's *Women in Love*. Like the Brangwen sisters, and like Lucy Snowe in *Villette*, Jane Eyre must earn her living by teaching. There is no other 'respectable' option, except writing fiction, and, since Jane is a character in a piece of fiction, she would give the game away if she resorted to that. When Jane sets out on her journey to her new place of employment, she says things that no woman in fiction has ever said before:

> It is a very strange sensation to inexperienced youth to feel itself quite alone in the world; cut adrift from every connection, uncertain whether the port to which it is bound can be reached, and prevented by many impediments from returning to that it has quitted. The charm of adventure sweetens that sensation, the glow of pride warms it; but then the throb of fear disturbs it . . .

Independence is not a piece of cake. But, for Jane, it is essential. It isn't surprising to find her saying:

Nobody knows how many rebellions, besides political rebellions, ferment in the masses of life which people earth. Women
are supposed to be very calm generally; but women feel just as
men feel; they need exercise for their faculties, and a field for
their efforts, as much as their brothers do . . .

The history of Charlotte Brontë and her family has itself been
the subject of much fiction and speculation, as if it, too, were the
stuff of legend. Certainly, the six Brontë children seem to have
tried hard to be ordinary, but could not help making a hash of
it. The Reverend Patrick Brontë, their father, may have passed
his life as the 'perpetual curate' of Haworth Parsonage, near
Keighley, in Yorkshire, but he early exhibited that discontent
with the everyday that marked out the clan when he celebrated
his arrival in England from his native Ireland by changing his
spelling from Brunty. (The umlaut is a master stroke.) Of all of
them, he repressed the discontent the best, which may be why he
lived the longest, outliving his last surviving child, Charlotte, by
six years, to die at the age of eighty-four in 1861; Charlotte died
in 1855, at thirty-nine years old.

From childhood, the Brontë children knew there were no
such things as happy endings. Cancer claimed Mrs Maria Brontë
in 1821, when Charlotte was five. The two eldest daughters,
Maria and Elizabeth, died at the school Charlotte Brontë barely
fictionalised in *Jane Eyre* as Lowood. (Charlotte claimed Maria
as the prototype of Jane's unnaturally self-abnegating friend,
Helen Burns.)

Charlotte, Emily, Branwell, the only boy, and Anne lived to
grow up. The family home at Haworth was close to both the
majestic landscape of the Yorkshire moors but also to the newly
built, sombre milltowns surrounding Leeds; their life was not

as isolated as might be supposed. They read voraciously and extremely widely. Their father does not appear to have censored their reading at all.

From an early age, they amused themselves by writing stories and poems. After a failed attempt to set up a school following the period Charlotte and Emily spent in Brussels in 1842, studying French, Charlotte persuaded her sisters to publish an anthology of their poetry under the sexually indeterminate names, Currer, Ellis and Acton Bell. Charlotte wrote that they 'did not like to declare ourselves women, because ... we had a vague impression that authoresses are liable to be looked on with prejudice'. That's an elegant piece of irony, especially since there have been persistent attempts to attribute not only *Wuthering Heights*, Emily Brontë's great novel, to the authorship of Branwell Brontë, but virtually the entire oeuvre of all the other sisters too. Branwell, in fact, possessed little literary talent but, alone of them exhibited signs of a genuine talent for physical excess that might have passed unnoticed at the time of *Tom Jones* but dissipated itself in drink and scandal at Haworth Parsonage.

Jane Eyre was published under the name of Currer Bell in 1847 and was an immediate and smashing success. It was followed, successfully, by *Shirley* in 1849 but Charlotte Brontë can have taken little pleasure in her growing fame; Branwell, Emily and Anne all died of tuberculosis between September 1848 and May 1849. The unusually closely knit and self-sufficient family was gone. Charlotte and her father lived on together. In 1853, she published *Villette*, one of the most Balzacian of English novels, a neurotic romance that uses fantastic and grotesque effects sparingly to heighten an emotionally exacerbated realism in a most striking way. In 1854, Charlotte Brontë finally ceased to rebuff the advances of her father's curates, who had been proposing to her in relays all her adult life, and married the most persistent, the Reverend Arthur Nicholls, in 1854. Less than a year later, she was dead, possibly from tuberculosis, possibly from complications of pregnancy.

Few lives have been more unrelievedly tragic. It is salutory to discover that her novels, for all their stormy emotionalism, their troubling atmosphere of psycho-drama, their sense of a life lived on the edge of the nerves, are also full of fun, and of a wonderfully sensuous response to landscape, music, painting and to the small, domestic pleasures of a warm fire, hot tea, the smell of fresh-baked bread.

There is also a spirit of defiance always at large. It is an oddly alarmed defiance; Charlotte Brontë's frail yet indomitable heroines burn with injustice, then collapse with nervous exhaustion after they have passionately made their point. All the same, Matthew Arnold put his finger on it when he expostulated that her mind 'contains nothing but hunger, rebellion, and rage'. As orphaned children, as Englishwomen abroad, as wandering beggars, as governesses, as lovers, Charlotte Brontë's heroines do not know their place. They suffer from a cosmic insecurity that starts in the nursery. Their childhoods are full of pain.

The first relation with the family, the elementary institutions of authority, is often distorted or displaced. After the infant Jane suffers a kind of fit, or seizure, while being punished by her Aunt Reed, the local apothecary is sent for: 'I felt an inexpressible relief, a soothing conviction of protection and security, when I knew there was a stranger in the room.'

Aunt Reed's husband, who might have protected her, is dead. Jane's own father is long dead. When she is befriended by the Rivers family, they are freshly in mourning for their father. *Jane Eyre* is a novel full of dead fathers. As if to pre-empt the possibility of his own demise, Mr Rochester himself staunchly denies paternity – he refuses to accept little Adèle Varens, daughter of a former mistress, as his own child, causing Jane to cry out protectively:

> 'Adèle is not answerable for either her mother's faults or yours;
> I have a regard for her, and now that I know she is, in a sense,
> parentless – forsaken by her mother and disowned by you, sir –
> I shall cling closer to her than before.'

The question of whether Rochester actually *is* Adèle's father is left interestingly moot. But something curious happens at the end of the novel: after Rochester has been blinded and maimed, we are left with the image of himself and Jane, a grizzled, ageing, blind man, led by the hand by a young girl (Jane is young enough to be his daughter). Suddenly, astonishingly, they look like Oedipus and Antigone, having ascended to the very highest level of mythic resonance. (Charlotte hastily restores the sight in one of his eyes before the first child of the union is born, and that is an interesting thing for her to do, too.) Jane has transformed Rochester into a father. Her mediation lets him live.

Jane Eyre begins, magnificently, with a clarion call for the rights of children. Jane, at ten years old, squares up to her Aunt Reed, who has signally failed to care for the orphaned child left in her charge.

> 'I will never call you aunt again as long as I live; I will never
> come to see you when I am grown up; and if any one asks me
> how I liked you, and how you treated me, I will say the very
> thought of you makes me sick, and that you treated me with
> miserable cruelty.'

No child in fiction ever stood up for itself like that before. Burning with injustice, the infant Jane, true child of the romantic period, demands love as a right: 'You think I have no feelings, and that I can live without one bit of love or kindness; but I cannot live so.'

Indeed, she specifies love as a precondition of existence. And not love in a vacuum, love as a selfless, unreciprocated devotion, either. There isn't a trace of selfless devotion anywhere in *Jane Eyre*, unless it is the selfless devotion of the missionary, St John Rivers, to himself. After all, it is very easy to love, and may be done in private without inconveniencing the object of one's affections in the least; that is the way that plain, clever parson's daughters are supposed to do it, anyway. But Jane *wants to be loved*, as if, without reciprocity, love can't exist. This is why, towards the end of the novel, she will reject St John Rivers's proposal of marriage although he has half-mesmerised her into subservience to him. She rejects him because he doesn't love her. It is as simple as that.

It is also exhilarating, almost endearing, to note that, in spite of the sentimental pietism which Charlotte Brontë falls back on almost as a form of self-defence against her genuinely transgressive impulses, she can also – see the entire treatment of Blanche Ingram, Jane's alleged rival for Mr Rochester's affections – be something of a bitch.

Although the sober *The Professor*, published posthumously in 1857, was the first novel that Charlotte Brontë completed, it is *Jane Eyre* that exhibits all the profligate imagination we associate with youth. However much it may have been written with a bitter ambition for fame foremost in the author's mind, the novel remains firmly rooted in the furious dreams of a passionate young woman whose life never quite matched up to her own capacity for experience. It is the author's unfulfilled desire that makes *Jane Eyre* so haunting.

The writing that the Brontë children had engaged in since childhood was of a very particular kind. They spent their adolescence constructing together a comprehensive alternative to the post-Romantic world of steam engine and mill chimney they were doomed to inhabit. Charlotte and Branwell chronicled a territory they named Angria; Anne and Emily constructed the history of the island of Gondal. This alternative universe 'with its emperors and its seas, with its minerals and its birds and its fish', just like the encyclopaedic other world in Borges's marvellous story, 'Tlön, Uqbar, Orbis Tertius', was so intensely imagined that sometimes its landscapes and inhabitants pushed aside the real ones that surrounded their creators:

> Never shall I, Charlotte Brontë, forget ... how distinctly I, sitting in the school-room at Roe-Head, saw the Duke of Zamorna ... his black horse turned loose grazing among the heather, the moonlight so mild and exquisitely tranquil, sleeping upon that vast and vacant road ... I was quite gone. I had really utterly forgot where I was and all the gloom and cheerlessness of my situation. I felt myself breathing quick and short as I beheld the Duke lifting up his sable crest, which undulated as the plume of a hearse waves to the wind ...*

At nineteen, Charlotte Brontë had lost her heart to a creature of her own invention, the irresistibly seductive, sexually generous Duke of Zamorna, a Byronic *homme fatal* untouched

---

* *The Poems of Charlotte Brontë and Patrick Branwell Brontë*, ed. T. J. Wise and J. A. Symington, Blackwell, Oxford, 1934.

by irony. It is easy to say that real life never could have lived up to this, that Charlotte Brontë's wonderfully discontented art comes out of a kind of Bovaryism, a bookish virgin's yearning for a kind of significance that experience rarely, if ever, provides. Jane Eyre, before her discontent is made glorious summer by the charismatic Rochester, who himself bears some resemblance to the Duke of Zamorna, often allows herself to: 'open my inward ear to a tale that was never ended – a tale my imagination created, and narrated continuously, quickened with all of incident, life, fire, feeling, that I desired and had not in my actual existence'.

But Charlotte Brontë *did* possess a sophistication, a temperament, that could, perhaps, be equalled by her immediate family, but by precious few other Englishmen and women of the period. Thackeray, whom she admired, patronised her, 'The poor little woman of genius! the fiery little eager brave tremulous homely-faced creature!' he said, as if passion was, by rights, the perquisite only of those blessed with conventional good looks. But Europe was full of artists exhibiting the same temperament as Charlotte Brontë – Berlioz, Delacroix, de Musset. Charlotte Brontë herself admired George Sand. Yet she went to Brussels to study French, not Paris, and her Protestantism, which can amount to fanaticism, springs into operation as soon as she arrives in a Catholic country, as if to protect herself from *giving herself away*. Charlotte Brontë's fiction inhabits the space between passion and repression. She knows she must not have the thing she wants; she also knows it will be restored to her in her dreams.

What would have happened if Charlotte Brontë really had met Byron? Although I doubt a spark would have flared between those two; Claire Clairmont and Lady Caroline Lamb had taught Byron to steer clear of women of passion. But Shelley, now . . .

Byron and Shelley were dead and gone by the time Charlotte Brontë was growing up in those dour, northern schoolrooms. Yet those James Deans of the Romantic period burned their images of beauty, genius and freedom on the minds of more than a generation. If the Byronic hero contributed in no small measure to the character of Edward Fairfax de Rochester, the man whom Jane habitually, in masochistic ecstasy, calls 'my master', he also contributed towards the ambitions of the young woman who invented Rochester.

But there is more to it than that. Mr Rochester's name irresistibly recalls that of the great libertine poet of the Restoration, the Earl of Rochester – the 'de' is as elegant a touch as the umlaut in Brontë – and he is evidently libido personified. Not only is his a history of sexual licence but he is also consistently identified with fire and warmth just as Jane's other suitor, St John Rivers, is associated with coldness and marble.

If Rochester is libido personified, then libido is genderless. He is not only the object of Jane's desire, but the *objectification* of Jane's desire. *Jane Eyre* is the story of this young woman's desire and how she learns to name it. Name it, and tame it. Charlotte Brontë cuts him down to size – literally so. Rochester loses a hand and an eye as well as his first wife, that swollen, raging, purple-skinned part of himself, before Charlotte Brontë finally consents to mate him to Jane. In taming him, Charlotte is also taming Jane, domesticating her passions, banishing the Duke of Zamorna from the family hearth forever.

If Rochester is the id, however, then St John Rivers is the super-ego. The second of Jane's suitors, this chaste and austere clergyman, attracts less attention than Mr Rochester and his unconventional ménage (which comprises not only a deranged wife but a putative daughter). But he represents the opposite pole to Rochester; Rochester is love and St John Rivers marriage. He is the super-ego. And he is monstrous.

When Jane finds refuge with Rivers's sisters at Moor House after she has fled Thornfield Hall, St John himself arrives as the perfect antidote to the squalor and mess of passion. Indeed, he is the antidote to the squalor and mess of life itself. There is an element of sadism in Rochester's emotional teasing of Jane, in the bizarre episode where he dresses up as a gypsy woman and quizzes her about her secrets, for example. But St John Rivers is a different kind of sadist, one who regards his lust for domination as a God-given right.

Rochester is a libertine but, worse than that, a cad, as well. He exhibits his caddishness not only because of his actual treatment of the first Mrs Rochester, but – as Jane is quick to note – because of the way he talks about her. It should be said that Jane is wise not to trust Rochester. She exhibits an exemplary perceptiveness, and, indeed, an exemplary female solidarity in her refusal to trust him. When Rochester finally confesses the truth about the existence of his hated but legal and living wife, Jane says, reasonably and also honourably, that the poor woman 'cannot help being mad'.

'If you were mad, do you think I should hate you?'
'I do indeed, sir.'

One cannot imagine Emma Bovary, in a similar situation, saying that. Some things about life you can't learn from books. Jane Eyre may burn with the longing for love, but that does not prevent her from making a bleak, clear-eyed appraisal of the realities of the situation. Rochester invites her to live with him in the South of France, not as his wife but as a companion; she turns down that offer with alacrity. She speculates that, when he is tired of her, he will dismiss her and, after that, talk about her in the contemptuous way he has told her about his other women. 'I now hate the recollection of the time I passed with Céline, Giacinta, and Clara.' Yet he must have told each one of them he loved her, once upon a time, and Charlotte Brontë cannot think of a good reason why a libertine and sensualist like Rochester, who has fixed upon tiny, plain, uncanny-looking Jane because of her difference, should not, one day, some day, want a difference from that difference.

The fire burns his wife and burns his home and disfigures him and, after that, he ceases to be a cad and becomes . . . something else. A husband. A father, He loses the shaggy grandeur with which unfulfilled desire has dowered him. There is a dying fall, a sadness, to the last chapter, the one that begins so famously: 'Reader, I married him.' Marriage is not the point of their relationship, after all.

St John Rivers is worse than a cad; he is a prig. Turning his back on his own sensual response to the beautiful heiress Rosamond Oliver he concentrates all his energies on subjugating Jane, indeed, on killing her spirit. He succeeds in inspiring her with his enthusiasm for the mission field, although he seems the very type of missionary who, one hopes, will end in the pot. He virtually forces her to learn Hindustani. ('Rivers taught you Hindostanee?' says Rochester, when he and Jane are reunited, echoing the incredulity of the reader.) His intention is to bully this young woman into marriage. He says to her one of the nastiest things a fictional man ever said to a fictional woman: 'God and nature intended you for a missionary's wife.' Jane would gladly accompany him to India as a companion; she foresees none of the same problems that would have arisen had she accompanied

Rochester to Marseilles. But St John Rivers will admit of no such impropriety. He will marry her, without – and Charlotte Brontë is perfectly explicit about it – any kind of sexual feeling for Jane on his part, almost as if to mortify his flesh.

Yet Jane knows he would feel it necessary, once they were married, to perform his duty as a husband. She is fully aware of what this would entail and the prospect freezes her blood. She describes her idea of what their married life would be in a passage of crystalline perceptiveness:

'... yet, if forced to be his wife, I can imagine the possibility of conceiving an inevitable, strange, torturing kind of love for him, because he is so talented; and there is often a certain heroic grandeur in his look, manner and conversation. In that case, my lot would become unspeakably wretched. He would not want me to love him; and if I showed the feeling, he would make me sensible that it was a superfluity, unrequired by him, unbecoming in me.'

The clarity and strength of Charlotte Brontë's observation and sensitivity is astonishing. She uses melodrama and excess to say what otherwise could not be said. Yet *Jane Eyre* remains an intensely personal novel, with a quality of private reverie about it, of a young girl's erotic reverie, that disguises itself as romantic dreaming to evade discovery and self-censorship. There is a tender embarrassment about rereading *Jane Eyre* in the middle age; one wants the world to be kind, not to Jane, but to the girl who invented Jane, and, in doing so, set out so vividly her hopes and fears and longings on the page. We know the world was not particularly kind to her, that fame came mixed with grief and death. And her achievement is singular; in *Jane Eyre* she endowed a modern heroine, a young woman not dissimilar from Teresa Hawkins in Christina Stead's *For Love Alone*, not dissimilar from the early heroines of Doris Lessing, with the power and force, the extra-dimensional quality, of a legendary being. If she had not died so young, the course of English fiction would have been utterly different. Anything would have been possible.

BERYL BAINBRIDGE
ON
EMILY BRONTË

Wuthering Heights (1847)

First Virago edition 1990

Emily Brontë was born in Yorkshire in 1818, the younger sister of Charlotte Brontë. She worked as a teacher and a governess, and wrote poetry. Her only novel, *Wuthering Heights*, was published in 1847 and is generally regarded as one of the masterpieces of English literature. She died in 1848.

Beryl Bainbridge wrote eighteen novels, two travel books and five plays for stage and television. Shortlisted for the Booker Prize five times, she won literary awards including the Whitbread Prize and Author of the Year at the British Book Awards. She died in July 2010. In 2011 the Booker Prize Foundation created a special prize, the Man Booker Best of Beryl, which was won by *Master Georgie.*

It is possible both to enjoy and to appreciate a novel without knowing anything about its author, but if a particular text has struck more than an ordinary response in the reader – we all know someone who would have us believe that one book or another has actually changed their lives – then it is interesting to know something of the writer's background. Not only interesting, but enlightening.

It is no accident that the models in paintings by artists as diverse as Rembrandt and Francis Bacon – whether portrayed as fractured popes, or staalmeesters of Amsterdam – all bear a certain resemblance to the artist who painted them. Over and over, artists illuminate themselves.

Writers are no different. The larger-than-life characters who strut the pages of the works of Charles Dickens, grimacing, gesturing, spouting comical phrases, mirror what would appear to have been the theatrical, flamboyant personality of their creator, just as the doomed protagonists of *Crime and Punishment* and *The Possessed* would seem to reflect the gloomy introspection of Dostoevsky.

There is nothing mystical in this identification. When Catherine Earnshaw, momentarily dazzled by the courtship of Edgar Linton and attempting to put into words the chasm existing between her feelings for him and for Heathcliff, cries out to Nelly Dean: 'Nelly, I *am* Heathcliff', her creator, Emily Brontë, is speaking no more than the truth. The writer, much like the rest of us, can never get away from self. Imagination, endlessly puzzled over by literary critics and often mistakenly regarded as something an individual is born with, similar to blue eyes or red hair, is surely nothing more than a collection of acquired memories, a ragbag of half-remembered phrases, views from windows, sentences from forgotten books, whispers on the stairs, glimpses of pictures hung on a wall.

Emily Brontë, fourth daughter of the six children of Maria Branwell of Penzance and Patrick Brontë of Ireland, was born at Thornton, Yorkshire, on 30 July 1818. When she was two the family moved to the Parsonage at Haworth, that then pestilent village to the north of the West Riding – small wonder that its inhabitants' average age at death was twenty-five, for it was later found to have been built on a cesspit.

One could say that the house, which stood next to the graveyard, was nothing if not handy for funerals. Mrs Brontë died the year after Emily's birth, and four years later, within a month of each other, the two eldest children, Maria and Elizabeth, were dead of tuberculosis.

For the next six years the surviving children remained at home, relying on one another both for company and for stimulation. They read avariciously (Bunyan, Shakespeare, Byron, the *Leeds Mercury*, *Blackwood's Magazine*, the fables of Aesop), they drew, they pressed flowers, brought home wounded birds, walked across the moors, eavesdropped in the cobbled High Street on the women gossiping at the corner. At night, around the fire, they listened to stories, half myth, half fact, told by Tabby, the family servant: tales of unrequited love, revenge and bitter feuds; of workers, terrified of losing their daily bread, smashing newfangled machinery in the textile mills beside the streams; of men who had lost limbs by cannonball at the Battle of Waterloo; of slum children, every bit as wild as Heathcliff, press-ganged from the hellholes of Manchester and Liverpool to work at the looms for fourteen hours a day; of the preacher, Wesley, who had travelled the country raging against sin.

One evening, returning from a visit to Leeds, Mr Brontë brought home a box of toy soldiers for his son, Branwell. The contents of that Pandora's box catapulted his children into writing. Each chose a wooden figure and gave it a name. Branwell's favourite was called Buonaparte, Charlotte's the Duke of Wellington, Anne's Waiting-boy. Emily named hers Gravey. The soldiers were collectively known as the Young Men, or sometimes the Twelves, and they lived in the imaginary kingdom of the Great Glass Town Confederacy, peopled with writers and generals, publishers and scoundrels. In time, Emily and Anne invented a separate kingdom and called it Gondal. The children already thought of books not as rare objects manufactured by strange beings but as commodities anyone could fashion. Mr Brontë was the published author of some rather feeble poems, and copies of these slender volumes stood on a shelf in the parlour. The stories and poems of Glass Town and Gondal were written on doll-sized sheets of paper, the leaves stitched together to make miniature books. Emily continued to pen such stories all her life, and although *Wuthering Heights* is undoubtedly a work of genius it would be selling her short to pretend that she had not served a long apprenticeship.

The story of *Wuthering Heights*, if one disregards the masterly construction, is simple, and concerns the fortunes of two families: the Earnshaws, who live at Wuthering Heights, and the Lintons, who reside at Thrushcross Grange. Mr Earnshaw, father of Cathy and Hindley, goes on business to Liverpool and brings back the 'gipsy brat', the catalyst Heathcliff, 'a dirty, ragged black-haired child; big enough both to walk and talk … yet, when it was set on its feet, it only stared round, and repeated over and over again some gibberish, that nobody could understand'. Heathcliff's arrival serves the same function as the box of toy soldiers brought home by Mr Brontë. Nothing can ever be the same again.

Both Catherine and Mr Earnshaw prefer Heathcliff to Hindley, who grows savage through rejection. Cathy meets Edgar Linton, who asks her to marry him, and Heathcliff, overhearing only some of her conversation with Nelly Dean, that part in which she confides she has accepted him, leaves Wuthering Heights. If he had listened but a moment longer, if he had not been deafened by the blood pounding in his ears, he would have heard Catherine's concluding words:

'It would degrade me to marry Heathcliff now; so he shall never know now how I love him: and that, not because he's handsome, Nelly, but because he's more myself than I am. Whatever our souls are made of, his and mine are the same; and Linton's is as different as a moonbeam from lightning, or frost from fire.'

Cathy marries Linton, and Heathcliff, having become wealthy by some unspecified means, returns to take his revenge on both the Earnshaws and the Lintons. Cathy tormented by her love for him, falls ill. Poor Nelly Dean, scandalized by her feverish ravings, has a hard time confining her to bed. She is forever leaning out of the window to look across the moor in the direction of Wuthering Heights, now owned by Heathcliff:

There was no moon, and everything beneath lay in misty darkness: not a light gleamed from any house, far or near – all had been extinguished long ago; and those at Wuthering Heights were never visible – still she asserted she caught their shining.

'Look!' she cried eagerly, 'that's my room with the candle in it, and the trees swaying before it; and the other candle is in Joseph's garret ... He's waiting till I come home that he may lock the gate. Well, he'll wait a while yet. It's a rough journey, and a sad heart to travel it; and we must pass by Gimmerton Kirk, to go that journey! We've braved its ghosts often together, and dared each other to stand among the graves and ask them to come. But, Heathcliff, if I dare you now, will you venture? If you do, I'll keep you. I'll not lie there by myself: they may bury me twelve feet deep, and throw the church down over me, but I won't rest till you are with me. I never will!"

Some months afterwards, following a runaway marriage with Edgar Linton's sister Isabella, Heathcliff does indeed venture. There is a shocking scene – risky by any standards, let alone by the conventions of the time – in which Heathcliff forces his way into Thrushcross Grange and, in front of her outraged husband, clasps Cathy in his arms, gnashing his teeth and foaming like a mad dog at all who try to take her from him. Cathy dies a few hours later, after giving birth to a daughter, Catherine.

If Heathcliff's manners and demeanour were somewhat less than refined while Cathy still lived, her death turns him into the Devil incarnate. He is repeatedly knocking people to the ground, setting the dogs on unfortunate visitors, threatening to strangle anyone who happens to cross his path.

It is not a happy household. Cathy's brother, the wretched

Hindley, now dispossessed of his property and a hopeless drunk, still lives at Wuthering Heights with *his* son, Hareton. Hareton, unable to read or write and brutally beaten by both Heathcliff and Hindley whenever the fancy takes them, occupies himself in hanging puppies from the backs of chairs. Then there is young Linton, Heathcliff's son by Isabella, fetched back home on the death of his mother who, showing amazing common sense, had run away from Heathcliff twelve years before. Since he is a delicate boy, not to mention a namby-pamby, Linton's life with Father can be imagined. He manages to survive the ceremony of a shotgun wedding (almost literally) to Cathy's daughter – young Catherine is abducted and locked in an upstairs room until the vicar arrives – and then dies.

Meanwhile Heathcliff, tortured by dreams of Cathy, is starving himself into the grave. Nelly Dean finds him on his terrible deathbed, the window open to the moors:

> His eyes met mine so keen and fierce, I started; and then he seemed to smile. I could not think him dead: but his face and throat were washed with rain; the bed-clothes dripped, and he was perfectly still . . .
>
> I hasped the window; I combed his black long hair from his forehead; I tried to close his eyes: to extinguish, if possible, that frightful, life-like gaze of exultation . . .

Though it is always foolish, not to say arrogant, to guess at an author's intention, to my mind there is a deliberately hopeful ending to the novel, in that Catherine and Hareton begin to fall in love. Seeing that Hareton is neither as depraved as Hindley, nor Catherine as perverse as her mother, one can believe that they at least, unlike Catherine and Heathcliff, have a chance of happiness this side of the grave.

Much has been written about the novel in an attempt to explain its 'disturbing complexity', and much waffle talked about the powerful forces working within Emily Brontë of which 'she herself was probably not conscious'. What impertinence! I would imagine she knew, down to the last full stop of the last paragraph, exactly what she was doing. The narrative, shared between the outsider Lockwood and Nelly Dean, gives the story its unshakeable foundation. For the rest, its 'complexity' amounts to nothing more and nothing less than the supreme, almost casual confidence of a writer of genius telling a superb story. All her life, from the back windows of the Parsonage, she had seen the coffins being carried to the graveside. She had suffered the loss of her own mother, two sisters, and watched her brother drink himself to death. She had been fiercely independent and a solitary by disposition, and her descriptions of landscape, of weather, of emotions, are 'significant' only in that she perceived herself as part of the natural world. That is not to say that she conformed and came to terms with life – rather that she understood its purpose and, wrestling with language, gloriously and triumphantly turned her feelings into words.

Wuthering Heights was the only novel she wrote. In 1847 her sister Anne had just completed *Agnes Grey*; both books were published in the one volume, their authors paying £50 for the privilege. Charlotte Brontë's *Jane Eyre* had appeared in print two months earlier and was an immediate success. *Wuthering Heights* was generally thought to be the outpourings of a 'dogged, morose and brutal mind'. Its author died a year later.

I first visited Haworth Parsonage forty-odd years ago, one of a group of actors from the Liverpool Playhouse who had recently been to a matinée of the film *Wuthering Heights*, starring Merle

Oberon and Laurence Olivier. We had all been reduced to tears by Heathcliff's awesome declaration of passion on hearing of Catherine's death:

> 'Catherine Earnshaw, may you not rest as long as I am living! You said I killed you – haunt me, then! The murdered *do* haunt their murderers, I believe. I know that ghosts *have* wandered on earth. Be with me always – take any form – drive me mad! only *do* not leave me in this abyss, where I cannot find you! . . . I *cannot* live without my life! I *cannot* live without my soul!'

We drove in snub-nosed cars to Haworth, under a sky fitting tight as a saucepan lid. Though the Parsonage had been added to after the death of the Brontë family, there was as yet no Gift Shoppe tacked on to the side, nor had the road in front been turned into a parking area.

Studying the original plans of the house, we were all bothered by the sleeping arrangements. There were only three bedrooms, unless one counted the couch in the parlour on which both Emily and Charlotte had died. Emily had been seven when the two eldest Brontë sisters, dying of consumption, had been fetched home from the Cowan Bridge School for clergy's daughters. That still left four children, one of whom was male, Mr Brontë, Aunt Branwell – the hatchet-faced spinster sister of his dead wife – and Tabitha Aykroyd, the widow woman who for thirty years devotedly cooked and cleaned for them. Anne could have slept with the aunt, Charlotte and Emily together, and Tabby could have been housed in the village. But what about Branwell and Mr Brontë? It was quite possible these two might have shared the same bed when Branwell was small, but what happened later, when he was grown and in the habit of staggering home drunk from the Black Bull? Perhaps he just curled up on a convenient grave in the back yard.

We admired the little books containing the stories of Gondal. We gazed at the engraving hung in the hall of John Martin's *Belshazzar's Feast*; at the portrait of his sisters painted by Branwell with himself rubbed out. We stood on the stairs reverently stroking the grandfather clock which Mr Brontë had wound up every night before retiring to bed, until we saw the notice which said it wasn't the same clock but one like it. Through a glass case I read a page of a book open at an unflattering description of Emily. She had apparently been small of stature, with a frizzy fringe, bad teeth, a flat chest and a poor complexion. She had nice eyes, though.

We went outside and walked along the narrow path that led through fields to the moors beyond the house. The sky had lifted and larks swooped above the bracken. One of us tried to scratch C loves H on a lump of rock with a penknife, but the blade broke.

It was now a bright afternoon but I would rather it had been a dark evening, threatening thunder. I thought of the last-but-one page of *Wuthering Heights*, when Lockwood encounters the shepherd boy:

> . . . he was crying terribly, and I supposed the lambs were skittish, and would not be guided.
>
> 'What's the matter, my little man?' I asked.
>
> 'They's Heathcliff and a woman yonder, under t'nab,' he blubbered, 'un Aw darnut pass 'em.'

We took one last look at Emily's name engraved on the tombstone in the churchyard. One of the actors recited some lines written under the pen name of Ellis Bell:

Death, that struck when I was most confiding . . .

Cold in the earth – and the deep snow piled above
        thee . . .

He comes with western winds, with evening's
        wandering airs,
With that clear dusk of heaven that brings the thickest
        stars . . .

Then we left her and went home.

MAGGIE O'FARRELL
ON
CHARLOTTE PERKINS GILMAN

The Yellow Wallpaper (1892)

First Virago edition 1981

Charlotte Perkins Gilman was born in 1860. She was a writer of non-fiction and poetry, an editor and feminist theorist, and most of her work is about the status and oppression of women. *The Yellow Wallpaper* was published in 1892 and a book of verse, *In This Our World*, was published in the following year. Between 1895 and 1900 she lectured and produced the bulk of her work that centred on the oppression of women, including *Women and Economics* and *Herland*. She is often considered America's leading feminist intellectual of the early twentieth century. She died in 1935.

Maggie O'Farrell is the author of seven novels: *After You'd Gone, My Lover's Lover, The Distance Between Us* (Somerset Maugham Award), *The Vanishing Act of Esme Lennox, The Hand that First Held Mine* (Costa Novel Award), *Instructions for a Heatwave*, (shortlisted for the Costa Novel Award) and *This Must Be the Place* (also shortlisted for the Costa Novel Award). In 2017 she published a memoir, *I Am, I Am, I Am*. She lives in Edinburgh.

At the close of the nineteenth century, a Boston physician was so enraged by the publication of a certain story that he wrote the following complaint: 'The story can hardly, it would seem, give pleasure to any reader ... such literature contains deadly peril. Should such stories be allowed to pass without severest censure?'

It's a pretty powerful claim, that a work of literature places the reader in danger or 'deadly peril'. There is, of course, no shortage of books that have in the past been labelled dangerous, but usually for reasons of morality. There aren't many that have been considered capable of robbing you of your mental stability, even your life, as the Boston doctor is suggesting.

The story that got him in such a lather was Charlotte Perkins Gilman's *The Yellow Wallpaper*. First published in the *New England Magazine* in 1892, it is an account by a nameless young woman of a summer spent in a large country house. She is, she tells you on the first page, 'sick' with a 'temporary nervous depression – a slight hysterical tendency'. Her husband, a doctor, confines her to a top-floor room to rest: '[I] am absolutely forbidden to "work" until I am well again. Personally, I disagree with their ideas. Personally, I believe that congenial work, with excitement and change, would do me good. But what is one to do?'

In that last clause, you have the crux, the terrible essence of the story. The answer is that there is nothing for her to do. Kept from 'society and stimulus', denied the freedom to write (she must hide any pages from the watchful eyes of her husband and her sister-in-law), forbidden any kind of mental activity at all, she is quite literally bored out of her mind. Slowly suffocating under the wrong kind of care, she is forced to dwell on the only things in front of her: the room; the grim bars on the windows; the bed, screwed to the floor; and the peculiar repetitions of the patterned, yellow wallpaper.

I can clearly remember the first time I encountered *The Yellow Wallpaper*. I was sixteen and I had asked for *The Oxford Book of Gothic Tales* as a Christmas present. It was, I think, the first hardback I'd ever owned. It came with a dark, winter-green cover, decorated with ivy, and a dim painting of a woman surrounded by gloom and poppies.

It was late on Christmas night, a storm was hurling itself off the sea, and I settled down in bed with my new book. I read Wadham, Poe, Hawthorne, and just as I was about to shut the book and go to sleep, I noticed this opening sentence: 'It is very seldom that mere ordinary people like John and myself secure ancestral halls for the summer.'

Something in that frank, intimate, urgent voice must have struck me, because I read on. And when I got to the end and raised my head, I remember being amazed to find myself back in my own life, in the present, not in the top floor of an old house, the floor littered by torn hunks of sulphurous yellow wallpaper.

I had never read anything like it before. I hadn't known it was possible to write in such a clean, insouciant style; I hadn't known it was possible to write about oppression, illness, madness, marriage. It was one of those moments you often have as a teenager, when the world suddenly shifts on its axis and everything looks sharp with potential.

I learned later, when I studied *The Yellow Wallpaper* as an undergraduate, that it is a closely autobiographical work, and that the writing of it was fuelled by indignation at the treatment Gilman herself received under the doctor who is directly named – as a threat to the narrator – in the text.

Gilman was born Charlotte Anna Perkins on 3rd July 1860 in Connecticut, to Mary and Frederic Beecher Perkins (Harriet Beecher Stowe, author of *Uncle Tom's Cabin*, was her great aunt). Her childhood appears to have been a strange, insecure one. She had an older brother, Thomas Adie, but there were two other siblings who died in infancy. In her autobiography, Gilman makes the devastating claim that as a little girl, her mother only showed her affection when she thought she was asleep.

Mary Perkins was told by a doctor that if she had more children she might die; soon after this, Frederic left. With no means of financial support, Mary Perkins and her two children were left in poverty, condemned to the existence of poor relations, moving from the house of one sympathetic relative to the next.

In 1878, aged eighteen, Charlotte began attending the Rhode Island School of Design, supporting herself by making trade cards. In 1884, she married the artist Charles Walter Stetson; the marriage proved to be a fraught one and would, unusually for the time, end in divorce. Gilman had a child with Stetson, Katharine Beecher Stetson, whose birth prompted a severe bout of what would now be diagnosed as post-natal depression.

Motherhood did not sit easily with Gilman. Her autobiography reveals that she felt no happiness holding her baby, only pain. In 1887, after what Gilman herself describes as 'a severe and continuous nervous breakdown tending to melancholia – and beyond', she consulted the expert Dr Silas Weir Mitchell. He diagnosed

nervous exhaustion or neurasthenia (a catch-all diagnosis popular
at the time) and prescribed the rest cure. This was a controversial
treatment that Weir Mitchell pioneered and favoured above all
others. Its tenets were complete bed rest, total isolation from
family and friends, and overfeeding on a diet rich in dairy produce
to increase fat on the body. The patient was forbidden to leave
her bed, read, write, sew, talk or feed herself.

Just typing that list makes me shudder in horror. And worse
is to come, because Gilman survived a month under Weir
Mitchell and was sent home with the following instructions: 'live
as domestic a life as possible. Have your child with you all the
time . . . Lie down an hour after each meal. Have but two hours'
intellectual life a day. And never touch pen, brush or pencil as
long as you live.'

For a woman of Gilman's intelligence and drive, it can only be
imagined what torture such a 'life' was. She tried to follow Weir
Michell's advice, but the result of this unliveable situation was a
near collapse – and *The Yellow Wallpaper*.

Despite its utter control, its exquisite poise, *The Yellow
Wallpaper* is an angry story. You can feel the fury crackling off the
page, driving each carefully chosen word; you sense it inhabiting
the white spaces around the text. But it is a righteous, directed,
measured anger. Gilman goes after Weir Mitchell with a single-
minded focus, and every paragraph, every full stop, every line of
dialogue dismantles him and his treatments, bit by precise bit.

In an article she later wrote for her magazine, *The Forerunner*,
entitled 'Why I Wrote *The Yellow Wallpaper*' she explains that
the rest cure brought her 'so near the borderline of utter mental
ruin that I could see over'. She attributes her recovery to casting
'the noted specialist's advice to the winds' and going to work
again. That work was *The Yellow Wallpaper*, a copy of which she

sent 'to the physician who so nearly drove me mad. He never acknowledged it.'

The article goes on to record her delight and pride that the story 'has, to my knowledge, saved one woman from a similar fate – so terrifying her family that they let her out into normal activity and she recovered'. And that 'many years later I was told that the great specialist had admitted to friends of his that he had altered his treatment of neurasthenia since reading *The Yellow Wallpaper*.' This was never corroborated by Weir Mitchell who, unsurprisingly, refused to be drawn on the subject. But for an anecdote, it has the unmistakable ring of truth. I myself would pay untold sums for a time machine so that I could go back to Weir Mitchell's study, to watch his face as he read the manuscript.

To look at *The Yellow Wallpaper*, however, solely in autobiographical terms, or those of historical or medical interest, is to diminish its value. *The Yellow Wallpaper* is a great work of literature, the product of a questing, burning intellect.

The mad woman has been used as a trope for centuries by writers, but more often as a walk-on part: we are allowed short, horrifying glimpses of the mad Ophelia and the hallucinating Lady Macbeth before they are hurried to their deaths; Bertha Rochester escapes her attic prison to cause fires and havoc, and is then put back before she, too, is sent to death. What *The Yellow Wallpaper* does is give the mad woman pen and paper, and ultimately a voice of her own. We hear from her, directly and in detail.

The Yellow Wallpaper is a cry, not so much of defiance, but of demand. A demand to be heard, a demand to be understood, a demand to be acknowledged. You hear echoes of this cry in later books: in Jean Rhys's *Wide Sargasso Sea*, in Janet Frame's *An*

Angel at My Table – in particular at that moment when a writing prize saves her from an impending lobotomy. You can hear it in Sylvia Plath, in Antonia White, in Jennifer Dawson, in Susanna Kaysen. All we can do is listen.

ELIZABETH JANE HOWARD
ON
ELIZABETH VON ARNIM

Elizabeth and Her German Garden (1898)

First Virago edition 1985

Elizabeth von Arnim was born in Australia in 1866. In 1894 she and her first husband moved to Nassenheide which was wittily encapsulated in her most famous novel, *Elizabeth and Her German Garden*. The twenty-one books she then went on to write were signed 'By the author of *Elizabeth and Her German* Garden', and later simply 'By Elizabeth'. She was described by Alice Meynell as 'one of the three finest wits of her day'. She died in 1941.

Elizabeth Jane Howard was the author of fifteen highly acclaimed novels. The Cazalet Chronicles – *The Light Years, Marking Time, Confusion, Casting Off* and *All Change* – have become established as modern classics and have been adapted for television and radio. Her autobiography, *Slipstream*, was published in 2002, and in the same year she was awarded a CBE. She died in 2014.

In 1889 Henry Beauchamp took his youngest daughter May to Italy. He expected his wife to join them in a week or so when he would be able to abandon the exigencies of chaperoning a young girl and – leaving the women to their own devices – get down to some really serious sightseeing on his own – a practice to which he had become increasingly addicted since he had come from Australia and settled in Europe. Mary Annette – the family called her May – had acquitted herself well at school, where she won a prize for history, and also at the Royal College of Music, where she had won a prize for organ-playing. She was twenty-three, and had earlier been described by her father, who had only lately begun to appreciate her, as 'bright, industrious and good'.

Mr Beauchamp's sightseeing itinerary – even with a young and giddy daughter addicted to cake shops – was formidable. They visited Milan, Genoa, Pisa and finally Rome, looking at everything that was to be seen and only sat down when they took Italian lessons or paid calls upon the people to whom they had introductions. May's musical ability must have been out of the ordinary as one of the introductions was given her by Sir George Groves of the Royal College to a famous Roman musician in whose house, after calling, they spent the entire evening. 'Just as we were going to bed "Il Conte" appeared dressed up to the eyes on his way to a ball at the Quirinal Palace and staid over an hour.' (Mr Beauchamp's journal)

'Il Conte' was the German Graf Henning August von Arnim-Schlagenthin, who was travelling to get over the death of his wife and child who had died the previous year. He was immediately attracted to May, and when, a month after their meeting, he heard her playing Bach at organ recitals in the American Church in Rome, he was determined to marry her. There followed a brief, but intensely romantic courtship as von Arnim pursued the Beauchamps in Italy, in Switzerland and Germany, eventually persuading the family to take rooms in Bayreuth. Many years later Elizabeth was to write to Hugh Walpole, 'my first courted me in Bayreuth and there's not a tree within five miles that I haven't been kissed under'.

By the end of July their engagement was official: von Arnim did not want to wait long for the marriage, but he said that it was absolutely necessary for May to learn German, in order to manage the servants. She therefore spent three months in Dresden with her mother, having a lesson every day. The marriage took place the following February in London, and after a honeymoon in Paris, they settled to upper-class German life in Berlin, which for May (who at this point seems to have been translated into Elizabeth) was a period of stultifying dullness. She was homesick for England and her family: she somewhat mutinously bore three daughters in as many years (von Arnim was desperate for a son); she paid and received calls, went to and gave parties, received instruction in dress and etiquette – and languished.

Then, in 1896, she accompanied her husband on one of his regular visits to his enormous Pomeranian estate, Nassenheide, ninety miles north of Berlin. The estate was centred upon a large seventeenth-century schloss that had once been a convent and had been unoccupied for the previous twenty-five years. It was surrounded by a vast, rambling and derelict garden. The moment that she saw it, Elizabeth knew that she wanted to live there. Here was freedom and peace; a natural isolation from the soul-destroying social life of Berlin – a wilderness of beauty to be ordered and enjoyed. In spite of some difficulty in persuading von Arnim (who had spent practically all his life in cities, was fifteen years older than she and a Prussian to boot), she got his partial agreement to their living there – at least for the summer months.

Elizabeth and Her German Garden was published two years later, and opens with her account of the first blissful weeks from April to June when she was alone there, supposedly superintend-ing the painting and papering of the house, but in fact spending every waking moment in the wild garden, with its bird cherries, lilacs, wild flowers and four great clumps of pale silvery-pink peonies. Her meals of salad and bread and tea – with the occa-sional tiny pigeon to save her from starvation – were brought to her in the garden on trays, and she spent her reluctant nights alone in the old house with her door locked and a dinner bell by her as a weapon against fear.

This first book, published anonymously, was an instant success, reprinting eleven times in the first year, and with twenty-one editions printed by May 1899. It received a good press on the whole, although one reviewer grumbled that 'even the amateur gardener will be disappointed, for he will find therein no tips as to the best methods of grafting apples, or of destroying vermin ... ' and the *Spectator*, in the person of Quiller-Couch, complained that he found her 'not only selfish, but quite inhumanly so and her mind ... of that order which finds a smart self-satisfaction in proclaiming how thoroughly it is dominated by self'. The *Derby Mercury* felt sure that the anonymous author was a gentleman, 'betraying his sex by more than one sign' but on the whole *The Times* – in spite of its rather patronising attitude – conveys the most general contemporary response to the book.

> The anonymous author of *Elizabeth and Her German Garden* has written a very bright little book – genial, humorous, perhaps a little fantastic and wayward here and there, but full of bright glimpses of nature and sprightly criticisms of life. Elizabeth is the English wife of a German husband, who finds and makes for herself a delightful retreat from the banalities of life in a German provincial town by occupying and beautifying a deserted convent, the property of her husband, in one of the Baltic provinces. Her gardening experiences are somewhat primitive and unsophisticated, but this is, no doubt, only a harmless literary artifice, for the charm of the book lies not in its horticultural record, but in its personal atmosphere, its individuality of sentiment, its healthy sympathy with nature and outdoor life, its shrewd but kindly appreciations of character and social circumstance. There is a pleasant sub-acid flavour in some of Elizabeth's pages which show that she could do better if she chose; but she is seldom ungenerous except in the remarks about nurses and their ways which she puts into the mouth of her husband, and is never dull.

The book – described rather loosely as a novel – *is* an extraordinary piece of work. It has an idyllic quality; Elizabeth's joy and excitement about transforming a wilderness into a garden is seconded only by her desire simply to revel in the place – to become part of a great and continuing pastoral romance – of the seasons, the times of the day, of the weather, of all the amazing machinery of nature that provided such infinite variation. Her enthusiasm is matched by her self-confessed ignorance: she buys *ten pounds* of ipomaea seed – sows it in eleven beds and 'round nearly every tree, and then waited in great agitation for the promised paradise to appear. It did not, and I learned my first lesson.' It did not matter, she had the wild flowers – the old lawns that had become meadows filled with 'every pretty sort of weed'. The opening of the book contains the ecstasy of a release that every woman who has experienced marriage and motherhood will recognise and many will envy: the opportunity to be alone, to have space and privacy with no demands made upon her, to eat and sleep and read when she pleased, to have silence and solitude and the time to be with herself – all things that no doubt people like Quiller-Couch would regard as infra dig, selfish, unbecoming and unnecessary for a woman. But a singular aspect of this book is the author's determination to be something more than a good German wife and mother, and it is this quality, set against the more traditionally romantic hymn to nature that gives the work its unique flavour.

In the midst of the first few weeks of this solitary paradise, her husband arrives to rebuke her for not having written. She says that she has been too happy to think of writing. This, unsurprisingly, does not reassure him – he thinks it extraordinary that she should be happy in his absence and the absence of the children. She shows him her beloved lilacs and he remarks that they badly need pruning, she offers him her salad and toast supper 'but nothing appeased that Man of Wrath, and he said he would go straight back to the neglected family'. Henceforward, in her book, he is known as the Man of Wrath, and her relationship with him (she was in conflict with his private as well as his formal demands) adds an original dimension to the book. There seems to be no doubt but that he was devoted to her – found her fascinating and rewarding company, and was only occasionally put out by her eccentricities – her spending her pin money on artificial manure, for instance. Her portrait of the Man of Wrath is affectionately satirical – she teases him, but he comes well out of it – she feeds the liberal, eccentric aspect of his nature, but she has the rest of him to contend with, and this she does throughout with a most daring tact.

Her children, called throughout the April, May and June baby respectively, make welcome appearances. Here is Elizabeth about the April baby and a governess.

Miss Jones cast down her eyes. She is always perpetually scenting a scene, and is always ready to bring whole batteries of discretion and tact and good taste to bear on us ... I would take my courage in both hands and ask her to go ... but, unfortunately, the April baby adores her and is sure that never was any one so beautiful before. She comes every day with fresh accounts of the splendours of her wardrobe, and feeling descriptions of her umbrellas and hats ... In common with most governesses, she has a little dark down on her upper lip, and the April baby appeared one day at dinner with her own decorated in faithful imitation, having achieved it after much struggling, with the aid of a lead pencil and unbounded love. Miss Jones put her in the corner for impertinence. I wonder why governesses are so unpleasant. The Man of Wrath says it is because they are not married ... I would add that the strain of continually having to set an example must surely be very great. It is much easier, and often more pleasant, to be a warning than an example ...

The garden is her escape from domestic duties; indeed, with the exception of the white and yellow library, the house is hardly described at all. It is the garden that is her element – the place where she can breathe and live, meditate, dream, plan and above all, read. Elizabeth was a voracious reader. Books accompanied her everywhere, and it would seem that during those early years at Nassenheide she was, perhaps unconsciously, preparing herself for her subsequent career as a writer (by the end of her life she had published twenty-two books). But even her dauntless spirit was sometimes circumscribed by the rules of her society.

I wish with all my heart I were a man, for of course the first thing I should do would be to buy a spade and go and garden, and then I should have the delight of doing everything for my flowers with my own hands and need not waste time explaining what I want done to somebody else. It is dull work giving orders and trying to describe the bright visions of one's brain to a person who has no visions and no brain, and who thinks a yellow bed should be calceolarias edged with blue.

And again ...

In the first ecstasy of having a garden all my own, and in my burning impatience to make the waste places blossom like a rose, I did one warm Sunday in last year's April during the servants' dinner hour, doubly secure from the gardener by the day and the dinner, slink out with a spade and a rake and feverishly dig a little piece of ground and break it up and sow surreptitious ipomaea, and run back very hot and guilty into the house, and get into a chair and behind a book and look languid just in time to save my reputation. And why not? It is not graceful, and it makes one hot; but it is a blessed sort of work, and if Eve had had a spade in Paradise and known what to do with it, we should not have had all that sad business with the apple.

When we consider all the skilled and fulfilled women gardeners who have flourished in this century, the frustration for poor Elizabeth is poignant.

Elizabeth was ahead of her time in that she envisaged an English garden, and what she meant by that was *not* the vast elaborate geometry of bedding plants *en parterre*, but rather a merging of cultivated plants with the wild – a blending of garden to park – an apparent carelessness that was none the less artful. E. M. Forster, who stayed at Nassenheide in 1904 as tutor to her children, in complaining about the garden unconsciously describes it rather well:

> I couldn't find it. The house appeared to be surrounded by paddock and shrubberies. Later on, some flowers – mostly pansies – came into bloom. Also rose-trees in the little whirligig of laid-out beds. But there was nothing of a show – only the lilacs effected that, and the white flowering faulbaum by which the dykes were edged. Nor did Elizabeth take any interest in flowers. The garden merged in the 'park' which was sylvan in tendency and consisted of small copses ... There was also a field in the park, over whose long grass, at the end of July, a canopy of butterflies kept waving.

And Hugh Walpole, also a tutor remarked in 1907: 'the garden is becoming beautiful in a wild rather uncouth kind of way, but it is a garden of trees rather than flowers'. These two may have been highly educated in some respects, but their expectations of a garden were fashionably commonplace compared to Elizabeth's.

She went on to write some very good novels, but *Elizabeth and Her German Garden*, its more rhapsodic passages nicely balanced by her acute and sometimes very funny perceptions about her family and friends, has a freshness, a freakish charm, an irrepressible energy that springs straight from the very source of her personality. It has also the seeds of an interesting and original exposition of the conflict between liberty and oppression that in her day it was taken for granted was the lot of women – a theme that was to occupy her in her writing life for many years to come.

A. S. BYATT
ON
WILLA CATHER

My Ántonia (1918)

First Virago edition 1980

Willa Cather was born in 1873 to a family who had farmed in Virginia for generations. She worked as a teacher and a journalist before beginning to write full-time in 1912. Her novels include *Death Comes for the Archbishop, O Pioneers!* and *The Professor's House*. Her books, poems and short stories cover a wide range of themes, but it was her evocations of the pioneering West that established her reputation as one of America's foremost writers. She died in 1947.

A. S. Byatt is a novelist, short-story writer and critic. Her novels include *Possession* (winner of the Booker Prize) and the quartet of *The Virgin in the Garden, Still Life, Babel Tower* and *A Whistling Woman,* as well as *The Shadow of the Sun, The Game, The Biographer's Tale* and *The Children's Book*. She taught at Central School of Art and Design and was Senior Lecturer in English at University College London before becoming a full-time writer in 1983. She was appointed CBE in 1990 and DBE in 1999.

'When a writer begins to work with his own material,' said Willa Cather, in a retrospective preface to her first novel, *Alexander's Bridge*, 'he has less and less choice about the moulding of it. It seems to be there of itself, already moulded ... In working with this material he finds that he need have little to do with literary devices; he comes to depend more and more on something else – the thing by which our feet find the road home on a dark night, accounting of themselves for roots and stones which we never noticed by day ... what Mr Bergson calls the wisdom of intuition, as opposed to that of intellect.' *My Ántonia* (1918), unlike *Alexander's Bridge* (1912), was written with Miss Cather's 'own material' in two senses. It was autobiographical and, with one of its predecessors, *O Pioneers!*, it made available to her the unconventional, curiously paced, apparently casual form that she was to use successfully in later, very different, researched historical novels.

Like her narrator here, Jim Burden, Willa Cather was moved from a childhood home in Virginia to a house near Red Cloud in Nebraska. She said in an interview in 1913, 'I would not know how much a child's life is bound up in the woods and hills and meadows around it, if I had not been jerked away from all these and thrown out into a country as bare as a piece of sheet iron.' Jim, looking out of the wagon on his first night's journey cannot pray because of the emptiness: 'There was nothing but land: not a

country at all, but the material out of which countries are made.'
Willa Cather, returning as she describes Jim returning, when the
land had been formed and roads built, met again Annie Pavelka,
the woman who was the direct original of Ántonia: like Jim,
she formed friendships with her old friend's many children, and
the relationships survived the novel – so much so that Annie's
husband identified himself in hospital in later life as 'the husband
of My Ántonia'.

Willa Cather wrote of the origins of the novel: 'One of the
people who interested me most as a child was the Bohemian hired
girl of one of our neighbours who was so good to me. She was one
of the truest artists I ever knew in the keenness and sensitiveness
of her enjoyments, in her love of people, in her willingness to take
pains . . . But from what point of view should I write it up? I might
give her a lover and write from his standpoint. However, I thought
my Ántonia deserved something better than the *Saturday Evening
Post* sort of stuff in her book.' She decided to write as a detached
observer, and as a young man 'because much of what I knew about
Annie came from the talks I had with young men . . . There was
enough material in that book for a lurid melodrama. But I decided
that in writing it I would dwell very lightly on those things a
novelist would ordinarily emphasise, and make up my story of the
little everyday happenings and occurrences that form the greatest
part of everyone's life and happiness.'

That last sentence sounds a little suspicious – a programme for
a bucolic idyll which, despite some critics' suspicions, My Ántonia
is not. Miss Cather had a conscious idyllic intention: Jim Burden
is discovered as a student reading Virgil's *Georgics*, which meant
a great deal to Willa Cather as student and writer. '*Primus ego in
patriam mecum . . . deducam Musas* – I'll be the first to bring the
Muses of song to my birthplace.' She took from Virgil and Walt

Whitman a sense that new art could be made of describing the undescribed. And she set herself, very consciously, to avoid conventional novel forms:

'My *Ántonia*, for instance, is just the other side of the rug, the pattern that is supposed not to count in a story. In it there is no love affair, no courtship, no marriage, no broken heart, no struggle for success. I knew I'd ruin my material if I put it in the usual fictional pattern. I just used it the way I thought absolutely true.'

It is an interesting question, and not easy to answer, how the reader of a story aiming at such 'truth' can recognise whether it is, or is not, what it claims to be. What a reader like myself, whose background is urban, English and bookish, does nevertheless recognise in the narrative of My *Ántonia* is a faithful imitation of the processes of memory. What Willa Cather achieves in her series of images of Ántonia, playing as a child, observing the plough against the setting sun, dancing away her excess of energy as a girl, ploughing in a man's overcoat and boots, surrounded by children, with an aged face and a few teeth, is something different from the series of 'privileged' or epiphanic moments carefully constructed by Joyce or Forster. It is more the series of mnemonics by which a man's, or a woman's, or a writer's memory constructs his or her identity. So with the landscape, the red grass, the creek, the garden, the prairie dogs. So with the Shimerda's sod dug-out home, Jim's grandmother's kitchen with its whitewashed earth walls, Ántonia's orchard and Bohemian fruit cellar, grown and built in the wilderness. So with the significant episodes, whether tales or events: the night of the great cold, the tramp who flung himself into the threshing machine, Mr Shimerda's suicide, the story of Pavel, Peter and the wolves, Wick Cutter (a true Gothic cum 'Western' horror tale) and the birth of Ántonia's illegitimate first child. They have the odd lengths and pace of truth, depending on their nearness to the remembering mind, which is Jim's. Because this memory is his, and the story is his, the title becomes My Àntonia: as much, surely, an indication of partiality as of possession.

Critics have not always understood this. They have fussed quite unnecessarily, over whether the story was Jim's or Àntonia's, whether, if Àntonia was the 'heroine', so much space should be given to Lena Lingard (who, Maxwell Geismar misleadingly says, represents 'the frontier flesh and almost runs away with the show' whereas Àntonia is 'the frontier spirit'.) David Daiches feels that the section on the Hired Girls is structurally unsound, or can only be justified if Jim is 'fitting himself to be the ideal observer of Àntonia'. He feels also that the novel should have more effectively ended, tragically, with Àntonia betrayed and pregnant 'alone in the field in the gathering darkness', rather than being 'redeemed with a conventional happy ending'. John H. Randall III complains that Willa Cather avoids tragedy, evil, and suffering, instancing things such as the briefness of the narrative of Wick Cutter's murderous suicide (as well as its comic treatment), the paradoxical homely pleasure whilst the Burden men make the coffin for the frozen corpse of Mr Shimerda, the very indirect narration of the seduction of Àntonia and the birth of her child.

Most of these anxieties seem to me to be to do with a misunderstanding of Miss Cather's mastery of pace. The pace of the seasons and of human growth is steady: in winter things are painful, slow and hard and so is truth: in summer they are quick and warm and shifting, so that Àntonia cannot understand why the tramp, unable to find a pond with enough water to drown himself, should kill himself 'in summer . . . In threshing time, too! It's nice everywhere then.' In such a world, events form part of a very long sequence – the people's lives run from birth to death, and their surroundings are seen before and after. Mr Shimerda's death, however brief, is unforgettable – the boots considerately put aside so the blood would not damage them for use by his impoverished family, the blood spread in the cow barn and the cows returning only when it is frozen hard enough not to smell. If Jim's narrative gives more local space to the practicalities of coffin-making, the increased conversation amongst the survivors as well as the embarrassments of burying a suicide, the novel in the end places the death as a great change both for Jim and for Ántonia: the memory grows and shifts, as the memory of Mr Shimerda's longing for the Bohemia from which he is exiled expands in the prose and lives and memories of writer, narrator and Ántonia. It is proper that the birth of the illegitimate child should be told by a sympathetic 'Widow Steavens' – who also refers to 'My Ántonia'. It seems like an end, but is not, as marriage is not. Ántonia, with twelve children and domestic skills acquired both from Bohemia, Jim's grandparents and the family where she was a hired girl, is living on a different time scale. Nor, surely, is this Daiches's 'conventional happy ending', which would have been simply marriage and its concomitant emotions.

This is because Willa Cather does not exalt the fertile and domestic at the expense of everything else. She 'places' and admires the communal vitality of the immigrant 'hired girls' as opposed to the bodiless respectable young of provincial Black Hawk. But Lena Lingard's terror of family life, the eldest daughter's sense of maternity and domesticity as a loving, energy-draining trap is closer to what Miss Cather herself felt, and elsewhere expressed, than Ántonia's fecundity. Tiny Soderball's surprise 'success' on the Yukon is another use of energy and resourcefulness which is neither condemned nor admired. Jim simply notes that Tiny has lost three toes with frost-bite – and is casual about it. He also notes that 'She was like someone in whom the faculty of becoming interested is worn out.' This is not condemnation: the time for the end of Tiny's capacity came in the cold, like Mr Shimerda's. Ántonia and Jim, and Lena, for the time being survive.

Truth is very difficult, in art. In earlier tales, Willa Cather glamorised the suicide of a Bohemian fiddler by making him an 'artist', or wrote savagely and somewhat personally against the narrowness, complacencies and poverty of her world. My Ántonia is a celebration of energy, which contains, and does not evade for those who can hear, the undertow of plain knowledge that all energy fails. Miss Cather also said in the preface to Alexander's Bridge: 'A writer contrives and connives only as regards mechanical details and questions of effective presentation, always debatable. About the essential matter of his story he cannot argue this way or that: he has seen it, been enlightened about it, in flashes that are as unreasoning, often as unreasonable, as life itself.'

About debatable detail she was scrupulous indeed: only the way the story slowly works in the reader's memory can make it as certain as it seems to be that the 'essential matter' has the desired truthfulness as well.

PENELOPE LIVELY
ON
EDITH WHARTON

The Age of Innocence (1920)

First Virago edition 1982

Edith Wharton was born in 1862 in New York, and later lived in Rhode Island and France. Her first novel, *The Valley of Decision*, was published in 1902, and by 1913 she was writing at least one book a year. During the First World War she was awarded the Cross of the Legion d'Honneur and the Order of Leopold. In 1921, she became the first woman to win the Pulitzer Prize with *The Age of Innocence*; she received a Doctorate of Letters from Yale University and in 1930 she became a member of the American Academy of Arts and Letters. She died in 1937.

Penelope Lively is the author of many prize-winning novels and short-story collections for both adults and children. She was shortlisted for the Booker Prize for *The Road to Lichfield* in 1977 and *According to Mark* in 1984, and she later won the Booker Prize in 1987 for her highly acclaimed novel *Moon Tiger*. *Life in the Garden*, a memoir of her life in gardens, was published in 2017. She was appointed CBE in the 2001 New Year's honours list, and DBE in 2012.

The Age of Innocence was awarded the Pulitzer Prize in 1921, thus making Edith Wharton the first woman to be so honoured. It sold around 115,000 copies in the English-speaking world and earned its author some $70,000 dollars in its first two years. It is the novel of her maturity in which she contemplates the New York of her youth, a society now extinct and even then under threat. 'DO NEW YORK!' Henry James had urged her, back in 1902, at the beginning of their long friendship, and eventually she did. She wrote hurriedly, in the midst of personal upheavals, and she was writing to make money, for despite her wealth she felt pressed for cash; the book was published by instalments in the *Pictorial Review* amid advertisements for soap flakes and lavatory cleaners and is generally regarded as one of her best.

Edith Jones had been born in 1862 into the exclusive, entrenched and apparently immutable world of wealthy New York families, Rhinelanders and Schermerhorns, Winthrops and Roosevelts, Astors and Vanderbilts – the Four Hundred. It was a world of structured leisure, in which attendance at balls and dinners passed for occupation, in which the women devoted themselves to dress and to the maintenance of family and system and the men kept a watchful eye on the financial underpinning that made the whole process possible. It was a complacent and philistine world, but one with inflexible standards, those of 'scrupulous probity in business and private affairs' as Edith Wharton herself described them in her memoir *A Backward Glance*. This alleged probity, and offences against it, lies at the heart of *The Age of Innocence:* the sexual passion between Newland Archer, a married man, and Ellen Olenska, nonconformist and separated from her husband, threatens conventional *mores* and family security; the financial irregularities of Julius Beaufort require that he and his wife be ejected from society before they corrupt its most cherished integrities. The form of the novel allows its author to examine, with the wisdoms of hindsight, a world which was in the process of breaking up when she was a girl and which she herself rejected in any case, fleeing for the major part of her life to the fresh air of Europe.

The flight, though, was not superficially unusual. Rich New Yorkers were accustomed to frequent travel; the women needed dresses from Paris, everyone went to Italy to refresh the spirit and replenish their stock of *objets d'art*. But with Edith Wharton what had begun as a fashionable obeisance became an addiction. At twenty-three – a shy, somewhat diffident young woman – she had married Teddy Wharton. The two of them took off soon after on a prolonged Greek cruise which they could not afford. Teddy was an amiable but limited man whom Edith was to outgrow with distressing rapidity; he could not share her burgeoning literary tastes or her enthusiasm for intellectual companionship and the marriage deteriorated into irritable cohabitation until it was eventually ended by divorce in 1913. But the improvident Greek cruise had set Edith on a course that became irreversible – she was soon spending far more time in Europe than America. Meanwhile a legacy from a cousin of her grandfather's of whom she had barely heard gave her – with the trust fund she already had – an income sufficient to make her rich for the rest of her life, and Teddy disastrously dependent upon her.

It is tempting to see Edith Wharton's wealth as a character-forming factor – certainly the awkward twenty-three-year-old changed out of all recognition into the confident, furiously energetic, tempestuous woman whom Henry James called with affectionate terror 'the Firebird' and 'the Angel of Devastation'. It enabled her to indulge her restlessness, her generosity and her curiosity – migrating from capital to capital, and continent to continent, descending upon James and other cronies to sweep them off in her chauffeured limousine for prolonged and indulgent motor tours of France or Italy. It enabled her to relegate Teddy to an appendage. And yet – and this is what both surprises and compels admiration – she wrote compulsively and strenuously from the moment her first tentative literary experiments began to find publishers when she was twenty-eight. Later, she was indeed to write for money – by then her tastes and requirements had far outstripped her resources. But at the start, and for many years, she was driven by none of the pecuniary needs that dogged most of her fellow writers – notably, of course, Henry James himself. (He, indeed, thought that her money insulated her and made her to some extent insensitive.) She wrote simply because she wanted and needed to, and because it took her out of the world she wished to discard and into another, in which she could meet and talk to kindred spirits, in which she was not just another pampered and restricted young woman, but a person consorting on equal terms with those she admired and respected.

Edith Warton's reputation has undergone interesting vicissitudes. In her own lifetime, she moved from small beginnings to bestsellerdom, enjoying both wide readership and high literary esteem and enabled by her earnings to make the well-meant but grandiloquent clandestine gesture of diverting part of her own royalties from Scribners to Henry James as a hefty advance on a new novel (James was astonished, deceived and gratified). But she was always an uneven writer – her large oeuvre veers from the accomplishment of masterpieces like *Ethan Frome, The Reef, The House of Mirth* and *The Age of Innocence* to secondary works like *Hudson River Bracketed* and some of the stories. She was prolific, writing travel books, a manual on interior decoration and even a startling fragment of unpublished pornography (included as an appendix to Richard W. B. Lewis's biography). But by the end of her life, in 1937, she had fallen victim to swings in literary taste and social preoccupations – her novels were seen as old-fashioned and her concerns as elitist and of minimal interest: it was the age of Lawrence and Joyce. She was relegated to the ranks of lesser writers. In England, indeed, she remained a fairly unknown name until a recent revival of interest and the appearance of her work in paperback. Her biographer felt constrained to wonder, in the first comprehensive examination of her life and work, whether her reputation might today stand even higher if she had been a man. She has been seen, indeed, as a poor man's Henry James, a comparison that is inevitable given their relationship and her undoubted debt to his advice and criticism, with its consequent reflection in her style and approach. This, though, is both to underestimate and misinterpret her work; Edith Wharton was her own woman, and at her best she combines muscularity and dash with an individual perception and strong psychological insight.

She now has her due, with the present rehabilitation of her fiction; the large output can be seen as inevitably uneven but also as far more eclectic than has been thought and often in advance of its time. She wrote of the ambiguities of sexual conduct and expectations with great force and subtlety (most powerfully, perhaps, in *The Reef*); in *Ethan Frome* and *Summer* she showed that she could write convincingly and with feeling of the American rural working class as well as of the background from which she came. *The Fruit of the Tree* is an attempt, if not entirely successful, to address herself to the problems of industrialism. But for many of her admirers the summit of her work is the group of novels and stories in which she set herself to examine the codes and practices of that powerful and apparently impregnable group, the wealthy and patrician New York families of the late Victorian and Edwardian period: *The House of Mirth, The Age of Innocence, Old New York* and *The Custom of the Country*. Her strength was that she was able to combine the encyclopaedic knowledge of an insider with the accuracy and selective power of a fine novelist and the detachment of a highly intelligent social and historical observer. She saw that she had lived through years of galloping change, that the society of her girlhood had vanished and had been under threat at the time; she was able to analyse the nature of these changes and give fictional life to them in the form of characters like Mrs Manson Mingott, Undine Spragg, Ellen Olenska and others.

Edith Wharton herself rejected over-precise relation between life and literature: 'to introduce actual people into a novel would be exactly like gumming their snapshots into the vibrating human throng of a Guardi picture'. She did what indeed most writers have always done; she took real people and real situations and then tampered with both for her own purposes, thus transforming life into art – 'it nests the elusive, bright-winged thing, in that mysterious fourth-dimensional world which is the artist's inmost sanctuary and on the threshold of which enquiry perforce must halt'. This Jamesian flight of fancy is an uncharacteristic passage in an otherwise down-to-earth and at times positively didactic essay on *The Writing of Fiction*, in which the marriage of practical bossiness with highflown language – '[dialogue] should be reserved for the culminating moments, and regarded as the spray into which the great wave of narrative breaks in curving towards the watcher on the shore' – gives the reader an irresistible impression of her complex and bracing personality. One feels a mixture of regret and relief that she lived before the present vogue for Creative Writing Professorships; she would have revelled in the role.

But however authoritarian her views on the craft of fiction, the results are seamless. From the opening pages of *The Age of Innocence*, when young Newland Archer attends the opera (*Faust*, with an appropriateness that is undoubtedly intentional) at the Academy of Music in New York and we see through his eyes the stage and the cast of the book, we know that we are in the hands of an accomplished novelist. Not the least of her skills is the selection here of points of view: of the two central figures, Newland and Ellen Olenska, with whom he falls fatally in love, only Newland is allowed a voice; Ellen is seen always at one remove, through his eyes and those of others, and is thus given a detachment which makes her both slightly mysterious and strengthens her role as the novel's catalyst. Newland, on the other hand, by being given absolute definition of thought and action, is laid out for inspection and judgement: he has the vulnerability of exposure, while Ellen is left with privacy and silence. It is a vital distinction between the two characters who have been seen by one critic as conflicting aspects of Edith Wharton herself, the one ultimately trapped by custom and circumstance, the other a free spirit, harbinger of the future.

Newland, as the novel begins, is about to announce his engagement to May Welland, a conventional alliance with a beautiful girl from a suitable family. He loves her, but sees her, even at this early stage, with a clarity that is prescient: 'when he had gone the brief round of her he returned discouraged by the thought that all this frankness and innocence were only an artificial product'. May, indeed, can be seen as embodying in her personality all the rigidity and implacable self-righteousness of the society itself – a kind of innocence, but a dangerous and eventually self-destructive innocence. The novel falls naturally into two halves, before and after the marriage, and it is in the second half that we see the characters of both Newland and May mature and conflict. In the first part of the book, Newland himself is allowed to appear as something of an innocent, more sophisticated of course than his fiancée because he is a man and has been permitted both emotional experiences (he has had a brief affair with a married woman) and an intellectual range not available to a young woman, but nevertheless conditioned and relatively unquestioning. He views the New York of his birth and upbringing with a degree of affectionate impatience. He bows to the dictates of convention ('silver-backed brushes with his monogram in blue enamel to part his hair . . . never appearing in society without a flower . . . in his buttonhole') and accepts a world in which people move in 'an atmosphere of faint implications and pale delicacies'. But at the same time he is capable of criticism and rebellion, and it is in the second half of the novel that we see this capacity fanned into active life by his feelings for Ellen Olenska and his assessment and understanding of her situation and what it is that is being done to her by 'the tribe'. Newland's tragedy is that in the last resort he is unable to obey his own instincts: nurture triumphs over nature. Let us return, though, to May, who is a more interesting character than she immediately appears and in many ways the most Jamesian. It is towards the end of the novel that she comes into her own and a hitherto slightly negative figure emerges as positively Machiavellian. Ellen Olenska is her cousin, returned from Europe to the family fold after the collapse of a disastrous marriage to a philandering Polish count. May, initially, has been graciously kind to her and has encouraged Newland's friendly support and advice over Ellen's complex and precarious situation: should she divorce her husband? On what is she to live? But in the months after the marriage the passion between Newland and Ellen (fostered by deprivation – there are in the whole novel only four or five seminal scenes in which they are together) has become apparent to May. We never know quite how, and must assume that she is more astute and perceptive than she has appeared. And so, with stealthy adroitness, she moves to save her marriage and avert the threat to social tranquillity – the outsider cannot be allowed to strike at the heart of all that is sacrosanct, and must be ejected. The family – tacitly, as always – close ranks around her and Ellen is put under subtle pressure to return to Europe. In the final scenes between Newland and May, it is impossible not to see overtones of *The Golden Bowl* in Newland's mute and helpless anguish as he realises what is happening and that there is nothing he can do about it because to protest would be to betray himself – and Ellen.

Ellen, of course, is the pivot upon which the whole book turns. She, and her situation, are the challenge and the threat to the *status quo*. She is the renegade, the prodigal daughter who has become Europeanised and who both fascinates (the men) and repels (the women) by her cosmopolitanism, her taste for literature and art, her coolly amused view of the world of her childhood. 'I'm sure I'm dead and buried, and this dear old place is heaven,' she says to Newland at their first meeting, and from that moment he is doomed. Indeed, it is Ellen who, at the start, appears to have set her cap at him with her offhand and unconventional assumption that he will visit her – it is one of the actions whereby she is allowed to remain mysterious and unexplained. Indeed, it would be possible to construct a whole alternative interpretation of the novel in which Ellen is a scheming adventuress and May the virtuous and wronged wife (as indeed on the face of it she is). Fiction prospers upon ambiguities, and the apparent ambiguity here is one of the strengths of the novel. For Ellen is herself both victim and eventually a kind of victor.

On her return to New York, she is afforded the protection and support of her family, and especially of her grandmother, the formidable society leader Mrs Manson Mingott. They will look after their own, in the last resort; indeed, determinedly, they solicit the help of the ultimate social arbitors, the almost fossilised van der Luydens, to ensure her acceptance. But Ellen is fatally tainted; although it is she who is the innocent party in her failed marriage, she is polluted – there are even unconfirmed rumours that she has consoled herself. Here, the double standards on which that society functioned become most apparent: a woman must be blameless, but a blind eye is turned on male sexual indulgence. Initial sympathy for Ellen turns to suspicion and eventually to rejection as it is realised that she is not going to conform, that she has a freedom of mind and of spirit unacceptable in a woman, that she is no longer one of them. And it is the matriarchs who sniff her out – the custodians of tradition, of family integrity and of sexual regularity. Ellen is successfully routed; she goes back to Europe, and in doing so she becomes also the victor, escaping to the freedoms of a more expansive and imaginative society. The price, though, is her relationship with Newland Archer.

This, then, is the story – on the face of it a simple one of frustrated love. Edith Wharton's skill and success is that she has made it a parable of a time and a place. The fates of Newland and of Ellen, and indeed of May Welland, are determined by history:

they are products of their time and whatever their instincts and their inclinations, they are obliged to obey its dictation. That being said, it is not entirely without sympathy that Edith Wharton looks at late-nineteenth-century New York. There is a touch of affection as well as of astringency in her portraits of Sillerton Jackson and Lawrence Lefferts, authorities respectively on 'family' and on 'form', of Mrs Manson Mingott, cushioned by flesh, money and prestige, of the home life of the van der Luydens, who are so strangled by ancestral glory as to be almost incapable of spontaneous speech or action. And then there is the louche figure of Julius Beaufort, the banker whose dubious business dealings and eventual ruin form a secondary plot and further illustration of the lengths to which that society was prepared to go in its determination to fend off those who threatened its standards. Edith Wharton expressed her view of that world in *A Backward Glance*, reflecting with a mellowed eye in her seventies on the *mores* from which she, like Ellen, had fled in youth.

From the vantage point of the 1930s she described what she saw as its strengths as well as its weaknesses: the incorruptibility, the horror of commercial irregularity, the integrity – a view with which present-day historians of that era might in any case quarrel. Edith Wharton's picture of her own society is a restricted and a personal one and ignores entire aspects of late-nineteenth-century America; it is impossible to deny that stricture. But as one survivor's testimony of the practices of a ruling order it has a value. She saw it as a society in which wealth was still founded upon property; trade was suspected and certainly not welcome in a drawing-room. A significant offstage character in *The Age of Innocence* is Mrs Lemuel Struthers, 'the widow of Struthers's Shoepolish' who is infiltrating New York and seducing the men to her amusing but still proscribed parties: the women, more clairvoyant, see her correctly as the shape of things to come. But Edith Wharton criticised the society for its dread of innovation, its conformity, its philistinism and, perhaps most tellingly of all, for its lack of civic responsibility. These were patricians and aristocrats, but national leaders who eschewed leadership, who preferred business life to that of politics, who failed to shoulder the burdens of an expanding democratic society and paid for it in the end by being shunted to one side. She contrasted this stance with that of the British aristocracy, traditionally involved with government and therefore retaining political significance along with financial power.

But, for all her rejection of much that old New York stood for, Edith Wharton saw it also as the last link between those Americans who were 'the heirs of an old tradition of European culture which the country has now totally rejected'. Writing in the 1930s, she had come to be, herself, more at home in Europe than in America, a process started in her childhood when her father had swept the family off to Europe for years on end in order to benefit from the rent on their two houses in Manhattan and Newport. By the time she died, she had lived for far longer in Paris, Italy and England than in America; she spoke French as much as she spoke English; her friendships were cosmopolitan. But she remained essentially American, incorporating in her own outlook and personal culture that successful and perennial fusion of the Old World and the New, while her intelligence and perception enabled her to see that this was her great advantage and to make fictional use of it.

The Age of Innocence is the fruit of Edith Wharton's own cultural versatility. Written when she was fifty-seven and at a creative peak, it reflects her own life in ways that are both obvious and indirect. She was 'doing' New York, as Henry James had suggested, but she was bringing to the subject insights and observations that she would never have been able to make if she had remained within the confines of American society. She was able to see it through the eyes of both Newland Archer and of Ellen Olenska. More than that, she brought to her account of the charged and frustrated passion between Newland and Ellen her own experience of sexual and intellectual affinity – her love affair with the American journalist Morton Fullerton in her forties had been an antidote to the long sterility of her marriage. Conceived to make money, written against a background of domestic crisis and published unceremoniously in a magazine, it survives today as one of her finest works – a rich and powerful description of a vanished world, alternately witty and moving, presenting with marvellous control and range a group of characters who between them define a whole period and culture.

SARAH WATERS
ON
SYLVIA TOWNSEND WARNER

Lolly Willowes (1926)

First Virago edition 1993

Sylvia Townsend Warner was born in 1893 in Harrow. She published seven novels, four volumes of poetry, a volume of essays and eight volumes of short stories. She lived most of her adult life with her partner Valentine Ackland in Dorset and Norfolk. She died in 1978.

Sarah Waters was born in Wales in 1966. She has written six novels: *Tipping the Velvet*, *Affinity*, *Fingersmith*, *The Night Watch*, *The Little Stranger* and *The Paying Guests*, and has been shortlisted for the Man Booker Prize and the Women's Prize for Fiction. She lives in London.

When Sylvia Townsend Warner died in 1978, she left behind her a body of work of exceptional richness and variety. In a career that had lasted just over half a century she had been a talented musicologist, an admired poet, diarist and letter-writer, a political journalist, an occasional translator and biographer, a prolific short-storyist, and the author of seven remarkable novels, of which *Lolly Willowes* was the first. The intelligence of her writing has sometimes resulted in her fiction being misunderstood as 'difficult', and has perhaps lost her readers; she's certainly one of the most shamefully under-read great British authors of the past hundred years. Her reputation was re-established to a certain extent in the late 1970s, when she was first championed by the Virago Modern Classics list. It was given another boost in the '80s and '90s, which saw the publication of biographical studies by Wendy Mulford and Claire Harman, along with sensitive editions of Townsend Warner's diaries and letters. She remains, however, relatively under-appreciated – a fact that baffles, frustrates, and, I think, secretly pleases her admirers; for she's the kind of novelist who inspires an intense sense of ownership in her fans. She has a special significance for lesbian readers, thanks not so much to the content of her work (only her fourth novel, *Summer Will Show*, can really be claimed as a lesbian text) as to the example of her life, nearly forty years of which she spent in open, passionate partnership with another woman, Valentine Ackland. Both she and Ackland were writers and avid readers, and both were seriously committed to radical left-wing causes. Together they constitute a tremendously inspiring model of romantic, literary and political engagement.

Born in 1893, Sylvia Townsend Warner grew up in Harrow, close to the boys' public school where her father was a popular housemaster. An imaginative only child with a gift for words and music, she thrived in the scholarly adult atmosphere of her home, and her father's death in 1916, when she was twenty-two, she later described as having 'mutilated' her: 'It was as though I had been crippled and at the same moment realised that I must make my journey alone.' By this point, however, Townsend Warner had for several years been pursuing an affair with a married man, the much older Harrow music master, Percy Buck, and when he now became involved with an ambitious project to catalogue Tudor church music she joined him on its panel of editors. The appointment was a great stroke of luck for her, securing her a modest income and an independent life in London. She began to make friends with writers and artists, and to form links with rural Dorset, the area in which she would later make her home.

But it was a visit to the Essex marshes in 1922 that was to propel her in the direction of literature, for, surrendering herself to the odd beauty of that landscape, she experienced an epiphany – became, as Harman puts it, 'properly her own person, having been till then "the creature of whoever I was with"' – and part of this process was the discovery that 'it was possible to write poetry'. She produced poems almost feverishly after that, many of them in traditional ballad forms addressing elemental experiences: sex, toil, illness, death; she had also, with less success, begun experimenting with plays, and in 1923 she started a novel, 'The Quick and the Dead'. She soon abandoned that project, however, in order to pursue another. Having read verbatim accounts of sixteenth-century Scottish witch trials and been struck, as she described it, by the 'romance' of witchcraft for the women who became involved with it, the 'release' it represented to them from 'hard lives' and 'dull futures', it occurred to her to try out a novel on this theme, but with a contemporary setting. When her poems were accepted for publication (as *The Espalier*) in 1925, her Chatto & Windus editor Charles Prentice asked if she had any other work, and she duly sent him 'my story about a witch, that you were kind enough to say you would like to read. If you like it well enough to think it worth publishing I shall be extremely pleased. If you don't, I shan't be much surprised.' Prentice liked it very much, and brought it out early the following year.

The publication of *Lolly Willowes* established Sylvia Townsend Warner as a startling new literary talent. The novel was an instant hit with readers and with critics; it was shortlisted for the prestigious Prix Femina (won, however, by Radclyffe Hall for *Adam's Breed*), and was particularly well received in the USA, being chosen as the first Book-of-the-Month title for the brand-new American book club, and securing Townsend Warner celebrity status when she crossed the Atlantic in 1929 to become guest editor of the *New York Herald Tribune*. As late as 1965 the manuscript of *Lolly Willowes* was on display at the New York Public Library alongside handwritten works by Thackeray and Woolf. The novel had remained, in all that time, among the best-known of Townsend Warner's fictions; it had inspired musical interpretation (in the form of a sonatina by composer John Ireland), and there had been interest – never realised – in adapting it for film.

The story of Laura Willowes, a mild-mannered gentry spinster who abandons her stuffy London life in order to make her home in a village of witches, must have appealed to its first readers on all sorts of levels. For one thing, it satisfied a contemporary interest in earthy rural passions, as typified by the fiction of Mary Webb and D. H. Lawrence: Laura's journey of self-discovery at the promptings of a gamekeeperish Satan is not a million miles away from the sexual awakening of Connie Chatterley at the hands of Mellors. For another, it chimed nicely with the 1920s trend for gentle literary fantasy, recalling *Lady Into Fox* (1922) by Townsend Warner's good friend David Garnett, and anticipating works like Virginia Woolf's *Orlando* (1928) and Rebecca West's *Harriet Hume* (1929). However, the fantasy element in *Lolly Willowes* could all too easily be misinterpreted as whimsy, and though, as Harman reports, Townsend Warner to some extent encouraged this – playing up to interviewers' speculation that she herself might be a witch – an essentially light-hearted reading of the novel must have dismayed her. Even before publication she had written to Garnett to thank him for his praise of the book (he called it 'a wonderful story, with the quality of some of your poems but with much greater force'), and had added wistfully that 'Other people who have seen *Lolly* have told me that it was charming, that it was distinguished, and my mother said it was almost as good as Galsworthy. And my heart sank lower and lower, I felt as though I had tried to make a sword only to be told what a pretty pattern there was on the blade. But you have sent me a drop of blood.'

The fact is, the novel is a tough one, and to focus on its whimsical elements is to miss its satire and diminish its political force. And while it's tempting, too, to interpret the narrative biographically, to pick out the obvious parallels between Laura's experiences and Townsend Warner's – the loss of a much-loved father, the un-urban longings and solitary walks, the Road-to-Damascus moments, the acquiring of deep personal freedoms – to look more closely at *Lolly Willowes* in its particular historical context is to gain a fuller sense of the transformations to which it gestures. For Laura's decision to move to Great Mop comes in 1921, a time of turmoil and transition for Great Britain as a whole, when the aftermath of war was being felt in the form of economic crisis, a dwindling Empire, strikes and social unrest. Some of these disturbances find their way directly into the novel: they are evident, for example, in the middle-class menfolk's gloomy talk about failing investments and Socialist threats; they are there too, more subtly, in the form of the wandering cornet-player whose music drifts in from the pavement during the Willoweses' breakfast – a recurring figure in 1920s fiction, a representative of the many unemployed ex-serviceman who were reduced to busking, hawking and begging on the post-war London streets.

But the issue that the novel tackles head-on is that of gender. In the 1910s and '20s British gender mores were shaken up as never before: the war saw women taking on new jobs, gaining new responsibilities and freedoms, and though the majority of the jobs were savagely withdrawn with the return to peace, many of the liberties remained; in 1918, partly as a recognition of their contribution during the years of conflict, women were at last granted the vote. For the first decade of its life, however, the new franchise was an incomplete one, available only to women over thirty who were also householders or married to householders (which meant that single women like Laura, middle-aged but financially dependent on male relatives, remained without it); and there were still huge pressures on women to conform to social norms. The recent tragic loss of so many young male lives had inflamed existing tensions over the idea of the 'surplus woman', and with post-war anxieties about British 'racial health' prompting celebrations of family life and maternity, the spinster – a benign if dowdy figure in nineteenth-century culture – was being subtly redefined as a social problem. The popularisation of Freudian ideas about sexual repression only added to her woes, pathologising elderly virgins as chronically unfulfilled. Many novelists of the period responded to this – some, like Clemence Dane, with representations of emotionally vampiric single women which only reinforced the new stereotypes, but others, like Radclyffe Hall, Winifred Holtby and Vera Brittain, with more sensitivity to the pressures faced by ageing unmarried daughters, and more sympathy for them in their efforts to follow non-traditional paths. Two fascinating novels which particularly resemble *Lolly Willowes*, and which Townsend Warner could be said effectively to re-write, are W. B. Maxwell's *Spinster of this Parish* (1922) and F. M. Mayor's *The Rector's Daughter* (1924).

Like Townsend Warner, Maxwell and Mayor chose as their subjects unmarried women of the late-Victorian age – that is, the final generation to have assumed as a matter of course that its single daughters would remain in the family home, dutifully servicing the needs of senior relatives. Again like her, they produced novels that are intensely alive to the contrast between the unglamorous exteriors of their 'old maid' heroines and the women's actual, deeply passionate, emotional lives. But the titles of the three novels reveal a significant difference. As phrases, 'Spinster of this Parish' and 'The Rector's Daughter' testify to the ways in which women are often occluded by social and familial roles. 'Lolly Willowes', by contrast, is a statement of individuality. Laura's journey, too, is very different from that of Maxwell's and Mayor's heroines, the former of whom spends decades as the unacknowledged mistress of a celebrated explorer, and is finally rewarded by marriage to him, whilst the latter dies after a short but 'useful' life with her passionate love for a clergyman unfulfilled.

For the first half of Townsend Warner's novel Laura looks set to follow their example. A tomboy in childhood, she is soon 'subdued into young-ladyhood', and after the death of her parents she joins the London household of her unimaginative brother Henry, where she becomes spinster 'Aunt Lolly', slightly pitied, slightly patronised, but 'indispensable for Christmas Eve and birthday preparations' – an embodiment, in other words, of an old-fashioned female tradition for which her up-to-the-minute niece Fancy, who has driven lorries during the war, has a fine flapperish contempt. But Laura has depths unsuspected by her deeply conventional relatives, and with her move to Great Mop she grows ever more subversive. She quietly rejects her family. She refuses to be defined by her relationships with men. She breaches the social barriers between gentry and working people. And though she enjoys being part of the Great Mop community, her intensest pleasures are solitary ones. Again looking forward to Virginia Woolf, the novel asserts the absolute necessity of 'a room of one's own', and Laura gains a clear-sighted understanding of the combined financial and cultural interests that serve to keep women in domestic, dependent roles: 'Society, the Law, the Church, the History of Europe, the Old Testament ... the Bank of England, Prostitution, the Architect of Apsley Terrace, and half a dozen other useful props of civilisation' have robbed her of her freedom just as effectively as have her patronising London relatives. It is this analysis that informs her conversation with Satan near the end of the novel, in which she unfolds her memorable vision of women as sticks of dynamite, 'long[ing] for the concussion that may justify them'. If women, Townsend Warner implies, are denied access to power through legitimate means, they will turn instead to illegitimate methods – in this case to Satan himself, who pays them the compliment of pursuing them and then, having bagged them, performs the even more valuable service of leaving them alone.

Sylvia Townsend Warner herself, of course, was involved in an illegitimate relationship when she wrote *Lolly Willowes*: she was a decade into her affair with the older, married Percy Buck. The relationship was clearly, to some extent, an emotionally unsatisfying one; it can be tracked in her diary in the form of frustrated half-evenings, enforced separations, occasional well-mannered spats. But the affair secured her a crucial liberty from traditional female duties – from the demands of motherhood and hostessing, for example – and *Lolly Willowes* must in part, I think, be read as a statement of its pleasures, along with a warm anticipation of an unencumbered old age. But a few years after the novel's publication Townsend Warner's life would take an even less conventional turn, and with that in mind I always find it hard not to make a retrospective lesbian reading of *Lolly Willowes*, too; the narrative seems in so many ways to look ahead to its author's embracing of a kind of rural outlawry with Valentine Ackland. The very objects which kick-start Laura's new life – those glorious mop-headed chrysanthemums that she spots in a Bayswater greengrocer's, with their fleshy, deep garnet petals, over which she longs to 'stroke her hand' – hint, to me, at distinctly feminine intimacies. Significantly, their colour resurfaces in her contented evenings with her landlady Mrs Leak, when the lamplight shines 'upon the tidy room and the polished table . . . spilling pools of crimson through the flanks of the bottle of plum gin'; it also recurs, this time with an overt erotic charge, during her dance at the Witches' Sabbath with energetic village girl Emily, a strand of whose red hair comes undone and brushes across Laura's face, making her 'tingle from head to foot'. Perhaps Laura has depths unsuspected even by herself. There is a lovely echo of her experiences, anyway, in Townsend Warner's 1930 diary, which records the first morning she spent with her passionate new lover, 'lying in the hollowed tump of the Five Maries [a Dorset landmark], listening to the wind blowing over our happiness, and talking about torpedoes, and starting up at footsteps. It is so natural to be hunted, and intuitive. Feeling safe and respectable is much more of a strain.'

The lure of the unsafe was something that Sylvia Townsend Warner returned to again and again in her fiction. In her art as in her life, though entirely without sentimentality, her sympathies tended naturally to the marginal, the vulnerable, the exploited, the obscure. In *Mr Fortune's Maggot* a hapless missionary spends years on a Polynesian island, and is almost defeated by loneliness and loss of faith. *In Summer Will Show* a Victorian wife travels to revolutionary France to confront her husband's charismatic mistress, only to fall under the woman's spell herself and be drawn into the Communist struggle. *The Corner That Held Them* details the large and small dramas of life in a minor medieval convent, to produce a breathtaking vision of the richness and complexity of historical change and communal living. Lots of the preoccupations of those later novels are to be found in this early one, and Townsend Warner's never-failing talent for the perfect phrase is also much in evidence here – for example in the 'hot ginny churchyard smell' of a late-summer funeral; in the 'chairs and tables and cabinets' that 'come out blinking and forgetful from their long storage in darkness'; in the voice that is 'clear as a small bell and colourless as if time had bleached it of every human feeling save pride'. There are a great many pleasures to be had from reading *Lolly Willowes*. One of them is finding in it hints and promises of the long, inspiring career of which it was the start.

JONATHAN COE

ON

ROSAMOND LEHMANN

Dusty Answer (1927)

First Virago edition 1996

Rosamond Lehmann was born in 1901. She wrote her first novel, *Dusty Answer*, in her twenties, and her reputation was firmly established with the publication of *A Note in Music* in 1930, and the subsequent novels *Invitation to the Waltz* and *The Weather in the Streets*. She was appointed CBE in 1982 and remains one of the most distinguished novelists of the twentieth century. She died in 1990.

Jonathan Coe is the author of eleven novels and three books of non-fiction. His novels include the highly acclaimed bestsellers *What a Carve Up!*, *The House of Sleep*, *The Rotter's Club* and *Number 11*.

Rosamond Lehmann's first novel, *Dusty Answer*, was once described – quite fairly, I think – as 'this impassioned but idealistic piece of work'. It sounds at first like the condescending verdict of a male reviewer, giving the book a little verbal pat on the head before consigning it confidently to the ghetto known as 'women's fiction'; but in fact this was the author herself writing in 1967, looking back on the novel which forty years earlier had propelled her to sudden and unexpected fame.

Published in something of a literary *annus mirabilis* which also saw the appearance of *To The Lighthouse* and Elizabeth Bowen's *The Hotel, Dusty Answer* records the sentimental education of Judith Earle, the only child of an academic father and socialite mother, growing up in the seclusion of a large riverside house in the Thames Valley. The house next door is occupied, sporadically, by the Fyfe family, whose children – five cousins – drift in and out of Judith's solitary life like figures in a dream, 'mysterious and thrilling'. One of them is killed in the First World War, leaving behind a son; later, at Cambridge, Judith continues to be visited by the others, and childhood friendship starts shading into adolescent romance; but a more important relationship enters her life at this point (and a more scandalous one, for the book's contemporary readers) when she meets and falls in love with a young woman called Jennifer, the most beautiful and charismatic student in the college. None of these entanglements ends happily, but we are made to feel, at the end of the novel, that Judith has bruisingly acquired some sort of self-knowledge, even if it is the rather disillusioned and self-dramatising sort suggested by the book's epigraph.

Part One of *Dusty Answer* is a rapt, sustained flashback which trawls up fragmented memories of Judith's childhood and her all-too-occasional ventures into the Fyfes' charmed circle. Read today, of course, in the cynical climate of the postmodern era, and as Britain gropes its way towards some vague notion of classlessness, this section of the novel can pose severe problems for many readers. The conversation of the Fyfe children at times sounds almost like parody ("'Why don't you get your Mother to send you to my school?' said Mariella. 'It's ripping fun'") and Judith seems to live in an unimaginably cossetted milieu, full of book-lined drawing rooms and forelock-tugging gardeners. Given such an upbringing, it's no wonder that she comes to inhabit what Marghanita Laski – one of Rosamond Lehmann's more sympathetic readers – has called 'this intensely feminine, self-concentrated, despairing world of the heart which has welled up from one supersensitive unconscious'. The author herself, during an interview with Janet Watts in the 1980s, gave a less forgiving assessment of Judith – 'whom I think a revolting character now, soppy'.

Doubtless Judith does take a good many educational and class privileges for granted, but this is largely a reflection of Rosamond Lehmann's own background, since she too was born into a family of enviable literary and social standing. Her great-grandfather was Robert Chambers of Edinburgh, who founded Chambers Dictionary, and her grandparents were close friends of Robert Browning, Wilkie Collins and Charles Dickens. Her great-uncle, Rudolf Lehmann, was a painter, famous for portraits of these and other writers; they hung in her father's library, where Lehmann 'sat under them and felt they were my ancestors and that I'd inherited all that'. She grew up in a Thameside house in Bourne End, built by her father (a writer and Liberal MP), which is so large that it is nowadays used as a nursing home: their staff included four gardeners, two housemaids, a nurse and nursemaid, two cooks, a butler, a footman and a bootboy. Like Judith, Lehmann was privately educated, in a purpose-built pavilion at the bottom of the garden. The main point of difference between her childhood and her heroine's was that hers was not quite so solitary: she was the second of four children, all of whom would no doubt have been burdened with high expectations of future achievement.

Despite these similarities, it's impossible to read the early sections of *Dusty Answer* as simple realism. While they might offer a reasonably faithful evocation of Lehmann's own family environment, the texture of the writing is nonetheless complex, because events and impressions are presented in such a heightened, not to mention idealised, form. To understand why the author should wish to write about this not so very distant period of her life in *such* intensely nostalgic and visionary terms, we need only consider the circumstances of the book's composition. Shortly after coming down from Cambridge, and in the wake of an unhappy final-year love affair which left her broken hearted, Lehmann had married a young friend called Leslie Runciman and moved with him to Newcastle, where his family ran a shipping business. It sounds an unlikely match, now. She conceded that 'I don't think I was really in love with him, or he with me, but it was very suitable, and everyone was pleased.' This sudden relocation to the industrial North must have been a tremendous culture shock to someone brought up in the blanketing warmth of the Thames Valley. 'Newcastle,' she recalled, 'was a sort of nightmare to me. Icy cold, hideousness, trams clanking up and down outside my front door. I just couldn't believe it.' After the marriage ended, she would attempt to write about the experience – not too successfully – in her second novel *A Note in Music*, but at the time the composition of *Dusty Answer* seems to have provided a vital opportunity for escapism; and I suspect that it was precisely this abrupt plunge into a new, alien, unwelcoming context that forced Rosamond Lehmann to idealise her early life so ardently, re-inventing it as idyll. The triumphant result was that she somehow imparts a quality of universality to the kind of experience which was – even then – only available to a privileged few, describing it in language of such charged exactitude that it takes on the eerie familiarity of all our remembered childhoods:

'She saw the sky beginning to blossom with evening. The sun came out below flushed clouds and all the treetops were lit up, sombrely floating and rocking in a dark gold wash of light. Across the river the fields looked rich and wistful, brimming with sun, cut with long violet shadows. The river ran a little wildly, scattered over with fierce, fire-opal flakes. But all was softening, flattening. The clouds were drifting away, the wind was quiet now; there would be an evening as still, as carved as death.'

Contemporary reviews of *Dusty Answer*, however, concentrated less on the quality of Lehmann's writing than on what was widely perceived as her unhealthy preoccupation with sex. There were honourable exceptions to this – Alfred Noyes in the *Sunday Times*, for instance, called it 'the sort of novel Keats might have written' – but many critics appeared to regard the book (to use Rosamond Lehmann's own words) simply as 'the ravings of a nymphomaniac'. Much of the controversy centred upon a possible lesbian undercurrent in the friendship between Judith and

Jennifer, something which may be barely perceptible to modern readers: the most Lehmann seems to be insisting upon, after all, is that it's possible for two women to feel intense love for one another, and for mutual admiration of physical beauty to be an important component of this love. Watching Jennifer undress by the side of the Cam ('Her cloud of hair was vivid in the blue air. Her back was slender and strong and faultlessly moulded'), Judith whispers to herself, 'Glorious, glorious Pagan that I adore!'; but the fact that she recognises this as 'the voice . . . that could never speak out' suggests that she will never act upon her impulse, and Geraldine, the one overtly lesbian character, is emphatically presented as somehow mannish and grotesque (as is Elaine Corrigan in Lehmann's later novel, *The Echoing Grove*).

Despite this, the nation's moral guardians came down heavily on the book – something of an apogee being reached by a leading article in the *Evening Standard* headed 'The Perils of Youth', which cited both *Dusty Answer* and Alec Waugh's *The Loom of Youth* as corrupting influences on the young. 'To all these sex-ridden young men and women [Lehmann's readers, presumably] I would counsel, as the best remedy for their troubles, silence and self control,' thundered the writer. 'And I would have them remember that all their discussions will never carry them back beyond the plain unvarnished statement of Genesis, "Male and female created He them".' Rosamond Lehmann, needless to say, was 'simply horrified' to have attracted this sort of opprobrium: 'All the reviews and publicity made me feel as if I'd exposed myself nude on the platform of the Albert Hall.' In her memoir *The Swan in the Evening* she also recalls that, besides these published responses, she was inundated with letters from would-be suitors, male and female, many of them enclosing provocative photographs. One French reader even sent her a 200,000-word sequel to the novel, written in order to 'prepare me for our joint future, when he would teach me love'.

Absurd though they may seem, such reactions are not, when you read the book, inexplicable: they testify to its extraordinary emotional reality. It's not a novel to be picked up in an idle moment, for if it touches you at all it will consume you entirely, colonising and transforming your whole inner life for the time it takes to read. Rosamond Lehmann's detractors – those critics who see her as being good for little more than picking over the minutiae of the feminine consciousness – like to imagine their point proved by *Dusty Answer*, which on the surface might seem the most naive and unsophisticated of her books. Certainly it lacks any single figure of the stature of say, Sybil Jardine, the tortured matriarch of *The Ballad and the Source*, capable of drawing the events and the other characters into tight focus like some great centrifugal force; and it cannot match the combination of passionate bleakness and extreme formal and narrative ingenuity that makes *The Echoing Grove* her masterpiece. But, on a purely technical level, *Dusty Answer* already demonstrates her brilliant use of the shifting viewpoint (note how the second person singular keeps recurring in the second half of the book, at moments when Judith is feeling especially insecure and vulnerable), it contains some of her finest descriptive passages, and if it has to be regarded as an adolescent novel, at least it captures the very best of adolescence; the part which we leave behind at our peril: namely, the sense that friendship and romantic relationships will always be the most crucial testing-grounds for our standards of commitment and integrity.

A peculiar characteristic of Rosamond Lehmann's novels, finally, is their uncompromising capacity for making the reader feel *gendered*. While it would be far too simple to say that women like her and men don't, it is true that reader responses to these books tend to divide up along gender lines. Marghanita Laski, for instance, praises *Dusty Answer* on the grounds that it is 'capable of creating *in the woman reader* [my italics] an effect ... of having known, on one's own pulse, the experiences recounted, whether this was true or not'. To consider where this leaves male readers – indeed, to investigate the whole process of cross-gender identification among readers of fiction – would doubtless consume (and must already have consumed) numerous hefty volumes of literary theory: so I shall confine myself to a simpler and more personal point, which is that one of the things that appeals to *me* most strongly about Rosamond Lehmann's novels is their superb portrayals of men.

Each of the Fyfe cousins falls in love with Judith, and in each case their love turns out to be destructive and flawed: Martin, with his asexual reassurances ('Feeling safe?'), Roddy, with his callous inscrutability, and Julian, whose generosity and reckless-ness mask a fundamentally selfish temperament. In each of these characters, if we are honest (and it's the mark of good writing to make honest readers of us) most men will recognise aspects of themselves, and blush with embarrassment. I suppose that this experience, too – the thickly concentrated mixture of embar-rassment and pleasure that *Dusty Answer* provokes – is typical of adolescence: and so it seems an appropriate response to a novel which continues to enthral me, not only as an evocation of 'the mysterious enchantment of childhood' but as a powerful study of that later, more complex period when nostalgia for childhood momentarily overlaps with the dawning of adult sensibilities.

DIANA SOUHAMI
ON
RADCLYFFE HALL

The Well of Loneliness (1928)

First Virago edition 1982

Radclyffe Hall was born in 1883. She began her literary career by writing verses which were collected into five volumes of poetry. She had seven novels published, and *The Well of Loneliness* was banned on publication in 1928. Two years later she received the Eichelbergher Humane Award. She died in 1943.

Diana Souhami is the author of many widely acclaimed books and biographies including *Gluck: Her Biography* and *Selkirk's Island*, winner of the Whitbread Biography Award. *The Trials of Radclyffe Hall*, first published in 1998, was shortlisted for the James Tait Black prize for biography and won the US Lambda Literary Award. The latest edition was published in 2013. She lives in London.

An astonishing furore broke out after *The Well of Loneliness* was published in July 1928. It began with a diatribe in the *Sunday Express* by its editor James Douglas. He would, he wrote, 'rather give a healthy boy or a healthy girl a phial of prussic acid than this novel. Poison kills the body, but moral poison kills the soul.' He called for the book to be banned.

The English ruling establishment of Government and Judiciary rallied to his call. The Home Secretary, Sir William Joynson-Hicks, spent a few hours reading *The Well of Loneliness*, then declared it 'inherently obscene and gravely detrimental to the public interest'. Sir Robert Wallace, chairman of the Court that was to censor it, said it was 'more subtle, demoralising, corrosive and corruptive than anything ever written'.

Holders of high office: the Lord Chancellor, the Director of Public Prosecutions, the Chief Magistrate, the Attorney General – all knights of the realm and members of the Garrick Club – then publicly indicted the book in florid language. This *Well*, they said, would imbue thoughts of a most impure, immoral, unclean and libidinous nature in the minds of the young. It brought the name of God into corrupt passions. It glorified the vice of physical relations between women. It was 'propaganda for the practice which has long been known as Lesbianism'. It asked for toleration of the women who indulged this vice.

So horrified were the book's prosecutors, or persecutors as

Radclyffe Hall called them, at the havoc its publication might wreak on the nation's morals, they felt compelled to manipulate the law to ensure its destruction. They disallowed the usual verdict by jury, or the airing in court of any expert evidence they feared might serve the interests of Radclyffe Hall and her publisher Jonathan Cape. In a farcical trial the book was condemned as an obscene libel and 'burned in the King's furnace'.

The Well of Loneliness was censored solely because of its lesbian theme. It is an unsensational book. In contrast to the fantasies in the minds of those peers, nothing very sexy goes on in it. 'She kissed her full on the lips' and 'that night they were not divided' are as graphic as its descriptions of lesbian lovemaking get. Had the heroine, Stephen Gordon, been a man, the book would have passed into obscurity as an unremarkable piece of period fiction.

Radclyffe Hall was no stylist. Her prose is lofty and lacking in irony. She distrusted innovation in literature or art, and shunned what she saw as the modernist heresies of Edith Sitwell, Virginia Woolf, Hilda Doolittle or Gertrude Stein. In her writing she invokes the Lord with discomfiting frequency and uses words like 'betoken' and 'hath'. No title could be less gay than *The Well of Loneliness*. It invited an anonymous verse lampoon 'by several hands', *The Sink of Solitude*.

Virginia Woolf found *The Well of Loneliness* unreadable. 'The dullness of the book is such,' she wrote to a friend in November 1928, 'that any indecency may lurk there – one simply can't keep one's eyes on the page.' *Orlando*, her own virtuoso lesbian novel was published the same year to fulsome praise. About and dedicated to Vita Sackville-West, with whom she was – in her way – in love, her sexual allusions were too aerial and literary to invite scrutiny by the Home Secretary. Radclyffe Hall's subversion was that she dared to be frank with pronouns, to write, 'she [not he] kissed her full on the lips, as a lover'.

Radclyffe Hall was forty-eight when *The Well of Loneliness* was published. She and Una Troubridge (the estranged wife of an Admiral) had lived together as a married couple for a decade. 'It would appear to be clear that the authoress is herself what is known as a homosexualist, or as she prefers to describe it an "invert",' the Deputy Director of Public Prosecutions, Sir George Stephenson, wrote to the Home Secretary.

In views and manner this authoress was rather like the Old Boys who denounced her. Her clothes asserted masculine authority. She wore neckties, sapphire cufflinks and a monocle and had her hair barbered fortnightly. Early on, she dropped her given name of Marguerite and called herself John. She owned a town and country house, employed a liveried chauffeur, a secretary and resident staff. She was right wing, a patriot and a stalwart of the Catholic Church. She perceived authority and power as masculine and disliked doing business with women. It bewildered her to be branded obscene, corrupt and depraved by the social class to which she felt allegiance and by the political party she supported. She coped badly with such calumny. After her book was banned she lost confidence as a writer and vowed never again to live in England.

Her hopes had been high for her *Stephen* novel, as she at first called it. She wanted it read by schoolteachers, welfare workers, doctors, psychologists and parents. She viewed it as a pioneer work with a threefold purpose:

> To encourage inverts to face up to a hostile world in their true colours and this with dignity and courage.

To spur all classes of inverts to make good through hard work, faithful and loyal attachments and sober and useful living.

To bring normal men and women of good will to a fuller and more tolerant understanding of the inverted.

She described herself as an experienced novelist who was 'actually one of the people' about whom she was writing. These people, according to her received ideas from the vogue for 'sexology', were a 'third sex': men trapped in women's bodies. Herself dyslexic, her spelling was extraordinary and she found reading a struggle. Una Troubridge read aloud to her from *Studies in the Psychology of Sex* by Havelock Ellis and from *Psychopathia Sexualis* by Richard von Krafft-Ebing. With disconcerting ease Radclyffe Hall embraced their contentious theories about 'congenital sexual inversion'. She took such bits of their writing as appealed to her, mixed these with Catholicism, spiritualism – she was a member of the Society for Psychical Research – and oddball ideas on endocrinology, and came up with a theory of lesbian identity that has startled and dismayed readers of her classic novel down the decades.

The Well of Loneliness has aspects of pathological case history, religious parable, propaganda tract and Mills & Boon romance. To brand it obscene was ridiculous but the effect on sales from such publicity was a publisher's dream. After it was banned, every smut hound in the world wanted to read it. The fact that in Britain it could only be procured illicitly made it the more enticing. Jonathan Cape shifted the printing of it to Paris. He could not produce copies fast enough. Newspaper sellers with carts at the Gare du Nord sold it to passengers on the Golden Arrow. In the rue de Castiglione dealers bought first editions for six thousand francs and sold them for 'as high as anything you are silly enough to pay'. Sylvia Beach, who had published James Joyce's *Ulysses* in 1922, was unable to meet the torrent of orders for *The Well of Loneliness* that poured into her bookshop Shakespeare and Company in rue de l'Odéon.

Radclyffe Hall said her book was fictional over details of place and people, and only autobiographical on the 'fundamental emotions that are characteristic of the inverted'. But she included friends in the narrative without disguise. The 'brilliant' playwright Jonathan Brockett, tall, sardonic and thin, was Noël Coward, even to the bags under his eyes and 'feminine' white hands. The dilettantish writer Valérie Seymour with 'very blue, very lustrous' eyes and 'masses of thick fair hair', who rules the lesbian salon life of Paris, was the American writer Natalie Barney. And the settings for the novel are Malvern, where Radclyffe Hall lived with Una; the lesbian salons of Paris, which she visited whenever she was there; and the Canary Islands, where she went with her first partner Mabel Batten.

The moral outrage voiced about *The Well of Loneliness* was particularly British. An obscenity charge was intelligently defeated in America where publication went ahead, and in the Paris literary salons there was bewilderment as to what on earth the fuss was about.

Paris in 1928, 'the city of light', was like a different planet from London. In Paris, lesbians expressed themselves freely in life and art. Much of this freedom revolved around Natalie Barney. 'Her love affairs would fill quite three volumes, even after they had been expurgated,' Radclyffe Hall wrote of her.

Natalie did not for a moment defer to the grand old men of England. 'What do I care if they vilify me or judge me according to their prejudices?' was her heartening response to prejudice. She enjoyed extravagant affairs with beautiful women, none of whom seemed like congenital inverts, she liked lots of sex, lavish display, jewels, perfumes, clothes and theatricality, and wanted not to bind love to rules, particularly not to the rule of exclusivity. Among her lovers were the courtesan Liane de Pougy, the poet Renée Vivien, Colette, and Dolly Wilde – Oscar's niece. Her partner for fifty years, with whom she never shared a house, was the painter Romaine Brooks.

For Natalie, 'living was the first of all the arts'. She had no theory of lesbian identity. 'My queerness is not a vice, is not deliberate and harms no one,' she wrote. 'I am a lesbian. One need not hide it, nor boast of it, though being other than normal is a perilous advantage.'

Paris, with its spirit of daring, was essential to her, particularly her home at 20 rue Jacob in the sixth *arrondissement*. Friday afternoon salons there in the Grecian Temple of Friendship in her walled garden were a far cry from any Well of Loneliness. She aspired to make her salon the sapphic centre of the Western world. 'At Miss Barney's one met lesbians,' Sylvia Beach said, 'Paris ones and those only passing through town, ladies with high collars and monocles, though Miss Barney herself was so feminine.'

Natalie, known as the *Amazone* for the panache with which she daily rode a horse bareback in the Bois de Boulogne, and her lovers rejected past conventions and wrote and lived as they pleased. At her salon, in her lifestyle and in her poems and books of aphorisms she captured the essence of modernism: exuberance for the new. In London such lesbian freedom, *joie de vivre* and embracing of modernism was denied, largely due to the controlling hand of the establishment that criminalised *The Well of Loneliness*.

When books are suppressed the complexity of their subject

matter stultifies. For decades the disparagement and censorship of Radclyffe Hall's book caused a pall of embarrassment to surround same-sex relationships between women. In a more adult society the novel would have braved the way for other books on the same subject, books that reflected diversity.

Because of its content, *The Well of Loneliness* unleashed bigotry and hypocrisy. Eighty years on it is hard to believe that any reader has been corrupted by it. Society now refers more or less breezily to lesbians and gays, and the focus has shifted from breaking silence to issues of equality and lifestyle. But it remains a landmark publication, a pivotal work. There are lesbians who say that reading it changed their lives. It has featured in countless dissertations and theses on censorship, sexual politics, gender dysphasia and lesbian identity. Despite its naivety the book in its own right survives. Its courage still calls out. Acceptance of difference is never entrenched and can easily be pushed aside. *The Well of Loneliness* still invites a response from its readers to the tensions of being outside the norm – tensions painfully felt by its hero, poor Stephen Gordon.

JILLY COOPER
ON
E. M. DELAFIELD

The Diary of a Provincial Lady (1930)

First Virago edition 1984

E. M. Delafield was born in 1890. *The Diary of A Provincial Lady* began as a serial in *Time and Tide*, and made its author one of the best loved writers of the 1930s. E. M. Delafield was herself a provincial lady, whose writing combined wit and elegance with a deep interest in the lives of her class. She died in 1943.

Jilly Cooper is a journalist, author and media superstar. The author of many number one bestselling novels and twenty-five non-fiction books, she lives in Gloucestershire with her rescue greyhound, Bluebell. She was appointed OBE in 2004 for services to literature, in 2009 was awarded an honorary Doctorate of Letters by the University of Gloucestershire for her contribution to literature and services to the county, and in 2011 was awarded an honorary doctorate by Anglia Ruskin University.

I came to *The Diary of a Provincial Lady* late in life, in the early seventies, when a reader wrote to me at the *Sunday Times* reproving me for being unkind about Mary Whitehouse.

'You write much better,' she went on, 'when you stick to the domestic scene, occasionally you almost aspire to the heights of E. M. Delafield.'

Being a natural egotist, I went round the next day to our local second-hand bookshop to be told there wasn't much call for Delafield these days. A fortnight later, however, they produced *The Diary of a Provincial Lady*. With a certain lack of enthusiasm – the juxtaposition of 'Provincial' and 'Lady' having a certain fusty gentility about it – I started to read. I finished the book in one sitting, leaving the children unbathed, dogs unwalked, a husband unfed, and giving alternate cries of joy and recognition throughout. How was it that anyone living a comparatively sheltered, upper-class life of forty years ago could think and behave so exactly like me?

A week or two later an ardent American Women's Lib lady came to dinner with a very downtrodden husband called Normie, whom, she told me in stage whispers throughout the evening, she was about to divorce. She also admitted to running several other *affaires* as well. Her one horror, she added, was flying, and next day she was returning to America. Being several drinks to the good by this time, I lent her my copy of the *Provincial Lady* to comfort her on the flight. After she'd gone, I was furious with myself. She would obviously despise the book as insular, unliberated nonsense, and never bother to return it.

The next week in the *Sunday Times*, I briefly bewailed the fact that I'd mislaid my copy. A few days later a letter arrived from a schoolmistress in her eighties. The *Provincial Lady* had been her bible for years, she said, but as she had only a few months to live, she wanted to finish Proust which she hadn't yet read. Would I like her copy as a present?

In fact, shortly afterwards, my own copy was returned from America. And in an accompanying letter, the Women's Lib lady announced that she had abandoned Normie and the children and run off with another woman. But she added a PS: 'I absolutely adored the *Provincial Lady*, so like me, and isn't her MCP of a husband just like Normie!'

So there we were: a dying old lady in her eighties, a scruffy Putney journalist and an ardent American feminist, with nothing in common on the surface, yet all identifying totally with E. M. Delafield's gentle, disaster-prone, yet curiously dry-witted heroine.

Her diary, which in fact is fiction, is set in a country village, where she lives with two children, and a husband, Robert, who works as a land agent. When the story opens in November, she is planting indoor bulbs, and being dropped in on by Robert's boss, the odiously superior and crushingly insensitive Lady Boxe. Lady B. nearly sits on the bulb bowls, then goes on to point out that it is too late to plant bulbs anyway, and the best ones come from Holland. The heroine hastily replies that she feels it is her duty to buy Empire products, which she thinks is an excellent reply, until it is ruined by six-year-old Vicky rushing in saying: 'Oh, Mummie, are those the bulbs we got at Woolworths?'

From then on the bulbs become a running gag. As the days pass and new characters are introduced, the bowls are put in the cellar, moved to the attic, overwatered, underwatered, attacked by the cat, broken by Robert bringing down suitcases, and advised on by every visitor. Finally they shrivel up and die, whereupon Lady B. (who naturally has at least a dozen hyacinths flowering in her drawing-room) is told they have been sent to a sick friend in hospital.

And gradually as one reads on, despite the short sentences and the simplicity and unpretentiousness of the prose and the subject matter, one realises that here is a very subtle and deliberate talent at work, naturally satirical, with a marvellous ear for dialogue and an unerringly accurate social sense.

To understand E. M. Delafield's genius – and I do not use the word lightly – I think one must digress a little and examine the few facts known about her life. She was born Edmée Elizabeth Monica de la Pasture, in 1890. Her parents were a French count whose family escaped to England during the Revolution, and a successful novelist, Mrs Henry de la Pasture, who had a considerable influence on Ivy Compton Burnett and was much admired by Evelyn Waugh.

As a very beautiful debutante, E. M. D. came out in 1909, and led that strange chaperoned ritualistic life ordained by fashionable Edwardian society. Like Nancy Mitford, a fellow aristocrat and humorist, she endured rather than enjoyed the experience, and must have watched herself with a certain detachment as she politely went through her paces in ballroom and house party.

Then, with the war, she threw herself into VAD activity in Devon, and in slack periods in the summer sat on a bench in the park, mapping out her first novel, *Zella Sees Herself*; a savage, obsessive and alarming piece of writing attacking personal vanity and the defence mechanism of daydreaming. She took as her pen name de la Field, a joke on her own name de la Pasture, which her mother had used with such success.

Zella Sees Herself was well received, and three other novels followed before, in 1919, she married Francis Dashwood, second son of a sixth baronet. After two years in Malaya, she settled happily in Devonshire, had two children, a boy and a girl, and became a magistrate and a great worker for the WI.

The marriage was evidently a success. But alas, under the laws of primogeniture, younger sons do not inherit, though despite being notoriously impoverished, they are nevertheless used to a certain standard of living. To maintain this standard, and fill the family coffers, E. M. Delafield kept on writing – probably far too much. Her output included three plays, several comedy sketches, magazine pieces, and very nearly one book a year; among these was a novel called *Nothing is Safe*, drawn from watching the haphazard divorces of the interwar years, and the devastating effect they had on the children involved. She also studied criminology, and wrote a very good reconstruction of a famous murder called *Messalina of the Suburbs*.

Then she stumbled almost accidentally on the magic formula which was to turn her into a household name. The editor of *Time and Tide*, then a large-circulation weekly of which E. M. D. was a director, wanted something light and readable, preferably in serial form to fill the centre pages.

And so in her beautiful house in Devonshire, she began to note down the routine follies and storms in teacups of life in the provinces. From the moment they appeared, the diaries enchanted everyone. They were incredibly funny, and yet in a way as homely and reassuringly familiar as the rattle of pips in a Cox's apple. The demand grew. The *Provincial Lady* was gathered into a first, then a second volume, and two more followed taking her to America and then into wartime.

But wherein lies their universal appeal? Initially, I think, because they contain a marvellous portrait of a marriage, and it is hard to believe that the stuffy, monosyllabic, chauvinistic, but ultimately kindly Robert didn't have a great deal of E. M. D.'s own husband, Francis Dashwood, in him. But perhaps this is because he is so like all husbands – always turning the heating down to below zero in the house, yet grumbling if the bath water is cold; falling asleep over *The Times* every night, yet arriving at dinner parties even before the hostess has finished dressing; bored by the eternal female dickering over what to wear, yet resisting any change in his wife's appearance. Like every husband too, the right time has to be found to tell him that the new cat is not a tom and is about to have kittens. When the entire family except himself is prostrate with measles, he takes up the characteristically male attitude that 'We are All Making a Great Fuss about Very Little'. But he has only to return home and tread on a marble in the hall to complain that the place is a 'Perfect Shambles'.

Aggressively philistine like many upper-class men living in the country, when the heroine returns from a jaunt to London anxious to tell him about her literary and artistic activities, he is far more interested that she bumped into Barbara Blenkinsop, a local girl who'd be quite attractive if she didn't have 'those ankles'.

But although he is almost brutally undemonstrative (at a wedding when the heroine asks misty-eyed if it reminds him of *their* wedding, he replies 'No, not particularly, why should it?'), he never grumbles about her extravagance or her frequent jaunts. And once, when they visit a friend's stable, knowing she is terrified, he does rather touchingly stand between her and the horses.

Much of her life, however, is spent acting as a buffer state between Robert, who is a disciplinarian, and the children. There is the occasion which all mothers will recognize when, after repeated badgering, she agrees that Robin, the son at prep school, shall stay up for dinner in the holidays, but only for soup and pudding – a compromise which pleases no one, and is greeted with frosty disapproval by Robert, and bellowing rage by Vicky.

Vicky and Robin are brilliantly drawn. Like all children, they suffer from endless colds, play the same pop record incessantly, always ask for a banana in moments of high tragedy or drama, and insist on sleeping the night out in a tent, and waking up the entire household by coming in at two in the morning.

The heroine adores them, but tries to maintain the detached attitude of a modern mother. When Robin goes back to school, she cries her eyes out, but also drily notes his request not to touch anything in his room, 'which looks like [an] inferior pawnbroking establishment at stocktaking time'.

There is also a hilarious visit to the school, when the headmaster fends off all questions about Robin by talking about the New Buildings, or asking her if she's seen his letter to *The Times*. Later they take Robin's friend out, at the end of which Robin comments sotto voce: '"It's been nice for us, taking out Williams, hasn't it?"' To which the heroine adds: 'Hastily express appreciation of this privilege.'

It may seem strange to us today, battling with overdrafts and mortgage payments, that someone who employed a fleet of servants, went on trips to London and abroad, frequently bought new clothes, and entertained endlessly if unwillingly, should chronically worry themselves sick about money. But this was often the plight of upper- and middle-class wives (particularly, as we've said, those of younger sons) forced to keep up a certain standard of living. Throughout the diaries, therefore, great comic capital is made out of the heroine's constant juggling with her house-keeping accounts, pawning jewellery, selling clothes, and writing endless placating letters to bank managers and creditors ('far from overlooking it [her bill from a London shop], have actually been kept awake by it at night').

In the same way, because 'ladies' in those days tended to be undomesticated (my grandmother, for example, once went into the kitchen, saw a dishcloth, and fled, never to return), they were neurotically dependent on servants. Funnily enough, any career woman or working mother today who has to rely on a recalcitrant daily woman, or a capricious nanny in order to be able to go out to work, will understand this neurosis.

To the Provincial Lady every mealtime must have been an agony, as one disaster, burnt porridge, lumpy mashed potato, fortnight-old sponge-cake, too thick bread-and-butter, followed another. After enduring Robert's irritation and the disapproval of her guests, she would have to steel herself to go down to the kitchen and complain, whereupon the cook would either threaten to give notice, or retaliate by grumbling about the oven or demanding new teacups.

Reproving people was obviously an anguish: 'Must certainly make it crystal clear,' she writes about a new manservant, 'that acceptable formula, when receiving an order, is not "Right-oh!" Cannot, at the moment, think how to word this.'

On the other hand, her attitude to servants is very one-sided and egotistical: she does not see them as having lives of their own, but merely as elements to be battled with. Returning exhausted from a day at the local flower show, and meeting the maids going off happily to a village hop, all she feels is irritation that she will have to wash up, ruefully adding: 'Why are non-professional

women if married and with children, so frequently referred to as
"leisured"? Answer comes there none.'

But part of the charm of the diaries is that there is always
something happening: children's parties, literary soirées, disastrous rain-drenched picnics, hilarious parish meetings. Visitors
too flow through the house. Some come from London, and are
maddeningly patronising about life in the provinces and the
necessity of broadening one's outlook, but the majority are local.
There is Our Vicar's Wife, so incapable of leaving anyone's house
that even the phlegmatic Robert is reduced to turning out the
lights and barring the doors 'in case she comes back'.

And there is the already mentioned, impossibly high-handed
Lady Boxe, who, along with Mrs Elton and Lady Catherine de
Burgh, must be one of the great comic characters in literature.
'I've put you next to Sir William,' she whispers to the heroine as
they go into dinner. 'He's interested in *water supplies*.'

On another occasion she gives a dance, and puts the whole
neighbourhood in a tizzy by only putting Fancy Dress on half the
invitations. She then serves only her own house party with champagne, giving everyone else cup, and firmly plays the National
Anthem at midnight so people will know when to go.

Mention must also be made of Barbara Blenkinsop of the thick
ankles, whose secret on–off engagement to Crosbie in the face of
violent opposition from her mother and watched with fascination
by the entire parish, is one of the great set pieces of the book.

The women characters are more defined than the men. But the
best-drawn and most endearing of all is the heroine. For although
the whole diary is a gentle joke on her family and neighbours, first
and foremost E. M. Delafield was taking the mickey out of herself.
Time and again we see the heroine worsted outwardly by events
or by more forceful individuals, but triumphing inwardly because

she always sees the ridiculous side. Here she is after a particularly officious visit from Lady B.: 'Relieve my feelings by waving small red flag belonging to Vicky, which is lying on the hall-stand, and saying *À la lanterne!* as chauffeur drives off. Rather unfortunately, Ethel chooses this moment to walk through the hall. She says nothing, but looks astonished.'

Romance and beauty, said one reviewer, were outside her deliberately narrow range. And one feels her rather wistfully suppressing any such tendencies. This results in some splendid examples of bathos: 'Notice, and am gratified by, appearance of large clump of crocuses near the front gate. Should like to make whimsical and charming reference to these, and try to fancy myself as "Elizabeth of the German Garden", but am interrupted by Cook, saying that the Fish is here, but he's only bought cod and haddock, and the haddock doesn't smell any too fresh, so what about cod? Have often noticed that Life is like that.'

E. M. Delafield was born in Gemini, sign of the twins, which indicates a certain duality of nature. On the one hand, there was the successful, sophisticated writer, director of *Time and Tide*, the unblinking satirist whose field was the world, and who looked with reality at everything.

And on the other, as Kate O'Brien said in an excellent introduction to an earlier edition, 'there was the gentle, home-loving, Devon-loving dreamer, who loved to look back on childhood and old photographs, who prayed and meditated much on the hereafter and on her own wrongdoing, who loved her family, her house and her village and her WI committee, who was forever helping lame dogs over stiles, forever doing kindnesses, forever concerned with this or that one's happiness'.

The latter E. M. Delafield is the one guyed in the *Provincial Lady*, but it needed the satirical eye of her other self to do the guying and also chronicle so exactly the follies and idiosyncracies of an entire neighbourhood. The success of the books lies in the fact that both sides of her character were stretched to the full.

Alas she died in 1943, far too early. One imagines, from the way she was so devastated by measles and the constant references in the diary to shivering in draughty houses, that she was never very strong.

When she died she was at the height of her fame, and like many popular and readable writers – Kipling and Walpole being typical examples – soon afterwards sunk into the trough of neglect and reaction that often lasts fifty years or more until a new generation discovers them afresh. For although she has her devoted admirers today, she is not universally known.

ELIZABETH BOWEN
ON
ANTONIA WHITE

Frost in May (1933)

First Virago edition 1978

Antonia White was born in 1899 and educated in London at St Paul's and RADA. She worked as a journalist and in the Foreign Office. Over the course of her career she published four novels, a volume of short stories and a work of non-fiction, *The Hound and The Falcon*. She also translated more than thirty novels from French. She died in 1980.

Elizabeth Bowen was born in 1899 in Dublin. Her first book, a collection of short stories, *Encounters*, was published in 1923. Her novels include *The Heat of the Day*, *The Last September* and *The House in Paris*. She was appointed CBE in 1948, and was made a Companion of Literature by the Royal Society of Literature in 1965. She died in 1973.

Frost in May is a girls' school story. It is not the only school story to be a classic; but I can think of no other that is a work of art. What, it may be wondered, is the distinction? A major classic is necessarily also a work of art. But a book may come to be recognised as a minor classic by right of virtues making for durability – vigour, wideness, kindness, manifest truth to life. Such a book gathers something more, as the years go on, from the affection that has attached to it – no question of its aesthetic value need be raised. A work of art, on the other hand, may and sometimes does show deficiency in some of the qualities of the minor classic – most often kindness. As against this, it brings into being unprecedented moments; it sets up sensation of a unique and troubling kind.

School stories may be divided and subdivided. There is the school story proper, written for school-age children; and the school novel, written for the grown-up. There is the pro-school school story and the anti-school – recently almost all school novels have fallen into the latter class. *Tom Brown's Schooldays* has a host of dimmer descendants, all written to inculcate manliness and show that virtue pays. *Stalky and Co.* fits into no classification: one might call it an early gangster tale in a school setting. The Edwardian novelist's talent for glamorising any kind of society was turned by E. F. Benson and H. A. Vachell on two of the greater English public schools. The anti-school school novel emerged when, after the First World War, intellectuals captured, and continued to hold, key positions along the front of fiction. A few, too few, show a sublime disinfectedness that makes for comedy, or at least satire. In the main, though, the hero of the anti-school novel is the sombre dissentient and the sufferer. He is in the right: the school, and the system behind it, is wrong. From the point of view of art, which should be imperturbable, such novels are marred by a fractious or plangent note. Stephen Spender's *The Backward Son*, not thus marred, is a work of art; but I should not call it strictly a school novel – primarily it is a study of temperament.

To return to the school story proper (written for young people), those for boys are infinitely better than those for girls. The curl-tossing tomboys of the Fourth at St Dithering's are manifestly and insultingly unreal to any girl child who has left the nursery; as against this, almost all young schoolgirls devour boys' school books, and young boys, apparently, do not scorn them. For my own part, I can think of only one girls' school story I read with pleasure when young, and can reread now – Susan Coolidge's *What Katy Did at School*. As a girls' school novel (other than *Frost in May*) I can only think of Colette's *Claudine à l'École*.

I began by calling *Frost in May* a school story. By subsequent definition it is a school novel – that is to say, it is written for grown-ups. But – which is interesting – Antonia White has adopted the form and sublimated, without complicating, the language of the school story proper. *Frost in May* could be read with relish, interest and excitement by an intelligent child of twelve years old. The heroine, Nanda Grey, is nine when she goes to Lippington, thirteen when, catastrophically, she leaves. She is in no way the born 'victim' type – she is quick-witted, pleasing, resilient, normally rather than morbidly sensitive. Call her the high-average 'ordinary' little girl. She is not even, and is not intended to be, outstandingly sympathetic to the reader: the scales are not weighted on her behalf. We have Nanda's arrival at Lippington, first impressions, subsequent adaptations, apparent success and, finally, head-on crash. *Frost in May* deviates from the school-story formula only in not having a happy ending. We are shown the school only through Nanda's eyes – there is no scene from which she is off stage. At the same time there is no impressionistic blurring, none of the distortions of subjectivity: Lippington is presented with cool exactness. Antonia White's style as a story-teller is as precise, clear and unweighty as Jane Austen's. Without a lapse from this style Antonia White traverses passages of which the only analogy is to be found in Joyce's *Portrait of the Artist as a Young Man*.

The subject of this novel is in its title – *Frost in May*. Nanda shows, at the start, the prim, hardy pink-and-white of a young bud. What is to happen to her – and how, or why?

Of the two other girls' school books named, one is American and the other French. *Frost in May* is English – but English by right only of its author's birth and its geographic setting. Lippington is at the edge of London. But it is a convent school – of a Roman Catholic Order which Antonia White calls 'the Five Wounds'. Its climate is its own; its atmosphere is, in our parlance, international. Or, more properly, as one of the girls put it, 'Catholicism isn't a religion, it's a nationality.' A Lippington girl is a Child of the Five Wounds; she may by birth be French, German, Spanish or English, but that is secondary. Also the girls here show a sort of family likeness: they are the daughters of old, great Catholic families, the frontierless aristocracy of Europe; they have in common breeding as well as faith. From Spanish Rosario, Irish Hilary and French-German Léonie the rawness of English Protestant middle-class youth is missing. Initially, Nanda is at a twofold disadvantage, never quite overcome. Her father is a convert; she herself was received into the Catholic Church only a year before her arrival at Lippington. And, she is middle-class; her home is in Earl's Court. There is one Protestant here, but she is aristocratic; there are two other middle-class girls, but they come of Catholic stock.

Lippington is a world in itself – hermetic to a degree possible for no lay school. It contains, is contained in, and represents absolute, and absolutely conclusive, authority. Towards what aim is that authority exercised? On the eve of the holiday that is to celebrate the canonisation of the foundress of the Order, the Mistress of Discipline addresses the school. '"Some of that severity which to the world seems harshness is bound up in the school rule which you are privileged to follow ... We work today to turn out, not accomplished young women, nor agreeable wives, but soldiers of Christ, accustomed to hardship and ridicule and ingratitude."' What are the methods? 'As in the Jesuit Order, every child was under constant observation, and the results of this observation were made known by secret weekly reports to Mother Radcliffe and the Superior.' How did one child, Nanda, react to this? 'Nanda's rebelliousness, such as it was, was directed entirely against the Lippington methods. Her faith in the Catholic Church was not affected in the least. If anything, it became more robust.' None the less, when, at thirteen, Nanda is faced by her father with the suggestion that she should leave Lippington to receive a more workaday education elsewhere, her reaction is this: 'She was overwhelmed ... Even now, in the shock of the revelation of her dependence, she did not realise how thoroughly Lippington had done its work. But she felt blindly she could only live in that rare, intense element; the bluff, breezy air of that "really good High School" would kill her.' And, elsewhere: 'In its [Lippington's] cold, clear atmosphere everything had a sharper outline than in the comfortable, shapeless, scrambling life outside.'

That atmosphere and that outline, their nature, and the nature of their power over one being, Nanda, are at once the stuff and the study of *Frost in May*. They are shown and felt. The result has been something intense, sensuous, troubling, semi-miraculous – a work of art. In the biting crystal air of the book the children and the nuns stand out like early morning mountains. In this frigid, authoritarian, anti-romantic Catholic climate every romantic vibration from 'character' is, in effect, trebled. *Frost in May* could, for instance, go down to time on the strength, alone, of Léonie de Wesseldorf – introduced, in parenthesis almost, but living from the first phrase. Momentum gathers round each sequence of happenings and each event – the First Communion, the retreat, the canonisation holiday, Mother Frances's death, the play for the cardinal, the measles idyll ... Lyricism – pagan in the bonfire scene, sombre on the funeral morning – gains in its pure force from the very infrequency of its play ... Art, at any rate in a novel, must be indissolubly linked with craft: in *Frost in May* the author's handling of time is a technical triumph – but, too, a poetic one.

The *interest* of the book is strong, though secondary; it is so strong that that it should be secondary is amazing. If you care for controversy, the matter of *Frost in May* is controversial. There exists in the mind of a number of English readers an inherited dormant violence of anti-popery: to one type of mind *Frost in May* may seem a gift too good to be true – it is. Some passages are written with an effrontery that will make the Protestant blink – we are very naive. As a school Lippington does, of course, run counter to the whole trend of English liberal education: to the detached mind this is in itself fascinating. The child psychologist will be outraged by the Lippington attitude to sex and class. Nanda's fate – one might almost feel, Nanda's doom – raises questions that cannot be disposed of easily, or perhaps at all. This book is intimidating. Like all classics, it acquires further meaning with the passage of time. It was first published in 1933: between then and now our values, subconscious as well as conscious, have been profoundly changed. I think it not unlikely that *Frost in May* may be more comprehensible now than it was at first.

MARK BOSTRIDGE
ON
VERA BRITTAIN

Testament of Youth (1933)

First Virago edition 1978

Vera Brittain was born in 1893 and grew up in the north of England. At the end of the war she moved to Oxford where she met Winifred Holtby, author of *South Riding*. Brittain was a convinced pacifist, a prolific speaker, lecturer, journalist and writer. She devoted much of her energy to the causes of peace and feminism. She wrote twenty-nine books in all: novels, poetry, biography and autobiography, and other non-fiction, but it was *Testament of Youth* which established her reputation and made her one of the best loved writers of her time. She died in 1970.

Mark Bostridge's books include *Vera Brittain: A Life*, shortlisted for the Whitbread Biography Prize, the NCR Award for Non-Fiction and the Fawcett Prize, the bestselling *Letters from a Lost Generation*, *Florence Nightingale: The Woman and Her Legend*, awarded the Elizabeth Longford Prize for Historical Biography, and *The Fateful Year: England 1914*.

On 28 August 1933, *Testament of Youth*, Vera Brittain's classic memoir of the cataclysmic effect of the First World War on her generation, was published by Gollancz to a generally enthusiastic reception and brisk sales. 'Oh what a head-cracking week ...', Brittain recorded in her diary, after reading the early reviews. 'Never did I imagine that the *Testament* would inspire such praise at such length, or provoke – in smaller doses – so much abuse.'*
Lavish praise came from, among others, Rebecca West, Pamela Hinkson, Compton Mackenzie and John Brophy while, in the *Sunday Times*, Storm Jameson commented that 'Miss Brittain has written a book which stands alone among books written by women about the war'.† By the close of publication day, *Testament of Youth* had sold out its first printing of 3000 copies, and was

* Vera Brittain (VB), 28 August–3 September 1933, *Chronicle of Friendship. Vera Brittain's Diary of the Thirties 1932–1939*, edited by Alan Bishop, London: Gollancz, 1986, p. 148.
† The main British reviews of *Testament of Youth* in 1933 included: N. Mitchison, *Week-End Review*, 26 August; J. Brophy, *Sunday Referee*, 27 August; S. Jameson, *Yorkshire Post*, 28 August; E. Sharp, *Manchester Guardian*, 29 August; *Morning Post*, 29 August; *Queen*, 30 August; *Times Literary Supplement*, 31 August; J. Agate, *Daily Express*, 31 August; C. Mackenzie, *Daily Mail*, 31 August; R. Pippel, *Daily Herald*, 31 August; P. Hinkson, *Time and Tide*, 2 September; S. Jameson, *Sunday Times*, 3 September; *Punch*, 6 September; *The Listener*, 6 September; *Church Times*, 8 September; R. West, *Daily Telegraph*, 15 September; *New Statesman & Nation*, 16 September; M. R. Shaw, *The New English Weekly*, 12 October.

well on its way to becoming a bestseller. In Britain, up to the outbreak of the Second World War, it would sell 120,000 copies in twelve impressions. In the United States, where Macmillan published the book in October, and where Brittain was fêted on a triumphant lecture-tour in the autumn of 1934, it enjoyed similar success.

Several of the original reviewers, though, were unnerved by the autobiography's frankness. James Agate struck a blow for misogyny when he wrote that it reminded him of a woman crying in the street. However, in her diary, Virginia Woolf expressed the more widespread response. Although she mocked Brittain's story – 'how she lost lover and brother, and dabbled hands in entrails, and was forever seeing the dead, and eating scraps, and sitting five on one WC'* – she admitted that the book kept her out of bed until she had finished reading it, and later wrote to Brittain about how much *Testament of Youth* had interested her.† Woolf 's interest in the connections that Brittain had 'lit up' for her between feminism and pacifism would leave its mark on the novel she was then writing that would eventually become *The Years*, and even more decisively on the radical analysis of *Three Guineas*.‡

For Vera Brittain, the publication of *Testament of Youth* represented the crossing of a personal Rubicon. Approaching forty, she had at last passed from relative obscurity to the literary fame she had dreamed about since childhood, when as a girl she had

* Virginia Woolf, 2 September 1933, *The Diary of Virginia Woolf*, vol. 4, edited by Anne Olivier Bell, London: The Hogarth Press, 1982, p. 177.
† Virginia Woolf to VB, 15 June 1934. VB Archive, McMaster University, Hamilton, Ontario.
‡ Marion Shaw, 'Alien Experiences: Virginia Woolf, Winifred Holtby and Vera Brittain in the Thirties' in *Rewriting the Thirties: Modernism and After*, edited by Keith Williams and Steven Matthews, London: Longman, 1997.

written five 'novels' on waste-cuts from her father's paper-mill. In the process she had exorcised her 'brutal, poignant, insistent memories'* of the war, releasing her deeply felt obligations to her war dead: her fiancé Roland Leighton, shot and fatally wounded at Christmas 1915; her brother Edward, killed in action on the Italian front just months before the Armistice; and her two closest male friends, Victor Richardson, shot through the head and blinded at Arras, who survived for a matter of weeks until June 1917, and Geoffrey Thurlow, killed in an attack on the Scarpe earlier that spring.

Brittain had been attempting to write about her experiences of the war, during which she had served as a Voluntary Aid Detachment (VAD) nurse in military hospitals in London, Malta, and close to the front line in France, for more than a decade. In 1922 she had selected and typed sections of the diary she had kept from 1913–1917, and submitted it for a prize offered by a firm of publishers for a personal diary or autobiography.† It was not chosen, and in the course of the next few years she struggled with several unsuccessful attempts to write her war book as fiction. Having finally settled on the autobiographical form, with the intention of making her story 'as truthful as history, but as readable as fiction',‡ she subsequently found her progress on the book impeded by all manner of domestic interruptions and tensions. Within weeks of beginning *Testament of Youth*, in November

* VB to Elizabeth Nicholas, 16 October 1961. VB Collection, Somerville College, Oxford.
† The published version of the diary, *Chronicle of Youth. Vera Brittain's War Diary 1913–1917*, edited by Alan Bishop with Terry Smart, London: Gollancz, 1981, reduces the diary's length by about a half. The original manuscript is in the VB Archive at McMaster University, while a typed transcript of the complete diary is available in the VB Collection at Somerville College, Oxford.
‡ VB, *Testament of Experience*, London: Gollancz, 1957, p. 77.

1929, Brittain had unexpectedly discovered that she was pregnant with her second child, her daughter Shirley, born the following summer. In 1931, a year after Shirley's birth, she wrote to her friend Winifred Holtby: 'My "Testament of Youth", if only I get the time ... to do it properly, might be a great book. It is boiling in my mind and I shall become hysterical if I am prevented from getting down to it very much longer ... If I am to continue sane I must have ... a) rest from the children & house and b) freedom and suitable circumstances to continue my book'.*

By the middle of February 1933, she had completed her manuscript, but other problems soon became apparent. In the final stages leading to publication, she was confronted by the strong objections of her husband, the political scientist George Catlin, to his own appearance in the book's last chapter. Catlin scrawled his comments in the margins of the typescript: 'intolerable', 'horrible', 'pretty terrible'.† Believing that his wife's book would hold him up to ridicule among his academic colleagues – not least, one suspects, because of the account of the continuing importance to her of her intimate friendship with Winifred Holtby – he begged Brittain to make changes to certain passages, and prayed that 'this spotlight' would pass swiftly.‡ She complied by reducing him to a more shadowy figure in the final draft, though she bitterly regretted that the theme of her post-war resurrection, symbolised by her marriage, had been irretrievably weakened.

Testament of Youth underwent its own remarkable resurgence in

---

* VB to Winifred Holtby, 24 August 1931. Winifred Holtby Archive, Hull Central Library.
† For the circumstances surrounding the writing and publication of *Testament of Youth*, see Paul Berry and Mark Bostridge, *Vera Brittain: A Life*, London: Chatto & Windus, 1995; Virago, 2001, especially pp. 236–68.
‡ George Catlin to VB, 21 February 1933. VB Archive, McMaster University.

the late seventies, almost a decade after Brittain's death. Brittain had been heartened by the assessment of Oliver Edwards (*nom de plume* of Sir William Haley) in *The Times* in 1964, the year of the fiftieth anniversary of the outbreak of the First World War, that *Testament of Youth* was 'the real war book of the women of England'.* However, she had believed in her final years that as a writer she was largely forgotten, and that any future interest in *Testament of Youth* would be of only a minor kind. She would certainly have been surprised by the extent of the book's renewed success after it was reissued in 1978 by a feminist publishing house and adapted as a landmark BBC TV drama. Carmen Callil, head of the nascent Virago Press, found herself weeping while reading it on holiday in her native Australia, and back home propelled the book once more to the top of the bestseller lists; while the five-part television adaptation in 1979, with a luminous performance by Cheryl Campbell in the central role, and an intelligent script by Elaine Morgan, introduced Brittain's story to a wider audience than ever before. It has never been out of print since.

Today, *Testament of Youth* is firmly enshrined in the canon of the literature of the First World War. It remains the most eloquent and moving expression of the suffering and bereavement inflicted by the 1914–18 conflict, as well as offering generally reliable testimony of a VAD serving with the British army overseas,† together with a host of other aspects of the social conditions of the war as experienced by the English middle classes. Furthermore, in

* Oliver Edwards, 'The Writer's War', *The Times*, 19 November 1964.
† See Joyce Ann Wood, 'Vera Brittain and the VAD Experience. Testing the Popular Image of the Volunteer Nurse', Ph.D thesis, Department of History, University of South Carolina, 2000. UMI no. 9981306. For a more critical view of VB's portrayal of the VAD experience see Sharon Ouditt, *Fighting Forces, Writing Women. Identity and Ideology in the First World War*, London: Routledge, 1994, pp. 3–4.

writing her autobiography – or 'autobiographical study' as she preferred to call it – Vera Brittain was also contributing a chapter to the wider history of women's emancipation in England. It has sometimes been overlooked that a little more than a third of *Testament of Youth* is concerned with Brittain's account of her wartime experiences. Two chapters of almost a hundred pages precede the beginning of her narrative of the war, which describe Brittain's attempts to escape from her provincial young-ladyhood as well as her personal struggles for education. Rebecca West saw this as 'an interesting piece of social history, in its picture of the peculiarly unsatisfying position of women in England before the war'.* And in the book's final section, after the declaration of the Armistice in November 1918, and following the granting of the vote to women over thirty in February of that year (an event that passed unnoticed by Brittain at the time because of her absorption in her work as a nurse in France), *Testament of Youth* returns to feminist themes: to Brittain's post-war involvement in equal-rights feminism, to her working partnership with her great friend Winifred Holtby and, finally, to her engagement to a survivor of the war generation, and the promise of a marriage that will be defined in feminist terms.

More insidiously, though, Brittain's autobiography dramatises a conflict between a pre-war world of 'rich materialism and tranquil comfort' and the more liberated society that developed partly as a consequence of the war. Its avoidance of modernist idioms seems to underline this, while the autobiographical figure of Brittain herself embodies a central paradox: that though she proposes a form of egalitarian marriage and other radical

* Rebecca West, 'The Agony of the Human Soul in War', *Daily Telegraph*, 15 September 1933.

reforms, and despite the fact that she envisages herself as a modern woman, she remains at heart a product of her Victorian bourgeois background.

For an understanding of *Testament of Youth* in a broader context, the book needs to be viewed as one of the large number of women's autobiographies and biographical histories published in the twenties and thirties, which attempted to reconstruct and assess the pre-war period and the years between 1914 and 1918. Works like Beatrice Webb's *My Apprenticeship* (1926), Ray Strachey's *The Cause* (1928), Sylvia Pankhurst's *The Suffragette Movement* (1931) and Helena Swanwick's *I Have Been Young* (1935), adopted what had hitherto been a predominantly masculine form of writing in order to celebrate the achievements of women's public lives. Vera Brittain, too, was concerned to place on record the unsung contribution of women to the war effort, though, ironically, much of the confidence and assurance of her autobiographical voice emanates from her passionate identification with her young male contemporaries and her experience of living vicariously through them. But in keeping with her fundamental belief in 'the influence of world-wide events and movements upon the personal destinies of men and women',* she was also anxious to write history in terms of personal life, and to illustrate what she had come to regard as the inextricable connection between the personal and the political.†

The germ of the idea behind *Testament of Youth* can be traced back to March 1916, when Vera Brittain wrote to her brother

* VB, *Testament of Youth*, p. 12.
† Deborah Gorham, *Vera Brittain: A Feminist Life*, Oxford: Blackwell, 1996, pp. 234–5.

Edward that '... if the War spares me, it will be my one aim to immortalise in a book the story of us four ...'* (her close friendship with Geoffrey Thurlow, the fifth member of her war-time circle, still lay in the future). The seventeen years between this statement and the appearance of her autobiography saw Brittain produce a bewildering number of fictional versions of her war experiences, some of which are preserved in the vast Brittain archive at McMaster University in Ontario.† As early as the summer of 1918 – at the time when Brittain's earliest published utterances about the war, her *Verses of a V.A.D.*,‡ were just appearing – she was close to completing her first war novel. Variously entitled 'The Pawn of Fate' or 'Folly's Vineyard', and drawn from her spell as a VAD at Étaples in northern France, it centred on a melodramatic plot involving a senior nursing sister, based on Faith Moulson, the sister in charge of the German ward where Brittain had nursed in 1917.

Fear of potential libel action led Brittain to put this manuscript aside, and when she returned to plans for a war novel in the early twenties, after the publication of two other works of fiction, *The Dark Tide* (1923) and *Not Without Honour* (1924), it was to a more broadly conceived book. The survival of a variety of incomplete novel drafts, together with references in Brittain's correspondence to several similar projects that appear never to have materialised,

---

* VB to Edward Brittain, 8 March 1916, *Letters From a Lost Generation: First World War Letters of Vera Brittain and Four Friends*, edited by Alan Bishop and Mark Bostridge, London: Little, Brown, 1998, p. 242.
† For finding aids to the VB Archive at McMaster, including details of unpublished works, see *McMaster Library Research News*, vol. 4, nos. 3, 4 and 5 (1977–79), and the website http://library.mcmaster.ca/archives/findaids/findaids/b/brittain.htm.
‡ VB, *Verses of a V.A.D.*, London: Erskine MacDonald, 1918; reprinted in VB, *Because You Died: Poetry and Prose of the First World War and After*, edited with an introduction by Mark Bostridge, London: Virago, 2008.

indicates the extent of her confusion as to how best to commit her experiences to paper. 'The Two Islands' contrasts the 'sombreness of the Grey Island' (Britain) with 'the brightness of the Gold' (Malta, where Brittain had served 1916–17), but portrays the deepening of the shadow that war cast over both of them. The Roland Leighton character, Lawrence Sinclair, killed at Loos, is little more than a cipher. This is probably because Brittain was still wary of how his family, especially his dominating mother Marie, would react to his appearance in a book by her. However, one of Roland's characteristics, as a poet, has been transposed to the brother figure, Gabriel, whose loudly proclaimed hatred of women, depicted in his preference for being nursed by male orderlies rather than pretty young VADs, is an extreme version of Brittain's view of her own brother Edward.* In 'The Stranger Son', another novel from the late twenties, Brittain makes a determined effort to write away from her direct experience through the character of Vincent Harlow who dramatises 'the clash between the desire to serve one's country, & the desire to be true to one's belief that War is wrong'. But with 'Youth's Calvary', she is entrenched in firmly autobiographical territory. Nominally it is still fiction, but surviving chapters show it to be a very close progenitor of *Testament of Youth*. Yet, without a first-hand narrative, and especially without the first-hand testimony provided by letters and diaries, 'Youth's Calvary' altogether lacks the vivid immediacy of its famous successor.

Testament of Youth's eventual appearance came at the tail-end of the boom in the war literature of disillusionment that began a decade after the Armistice with the publication in 1928 of Edmund Blunden's autobiography, *Undertones of War*, and of

* For the question of Edward Brittain's sexuality, see Berry and Bostridge, *Vera Brittain: A Life*, pp. 129–35.

Siegfried Sassoon's skilfully fictionalised *Memoirs of a Fox-Hunting Man*. In 1929 the spate of war books had reached its numerical peak: twenty-nine were published that year, including the English translation of Erich Maria Remarque's *In Westen nichts Neues* as *All Quiet on the Western Front*, which sold 250,000 copies in its first year, Robert Graves's *Goodbye to All That*, and Richard Aldington's *Death of a Hero*.*

Vera Brittain made a close study of the war books of Blunden, Sassoon, and Graves, and they revived her own hopes of contributing to the genre. 'I am reading "Undertones of War",' she wrote at Christmas 1928; 'grave, dignified, but perfectly simple and straightforward; why shouldn't I write one like that?'† Early in 1929 she went with Winifred Holtby to see R. C. Sherriff 's trench drama, *Journey's End*, the theatrical hit of the season; and towards the end of that year, she reviewed Aldington's *Death of a Hero* in *Time and Tide*, finding it to be 'a devastating indictment of pre-war civilization, with its ignorance, its idiocies and its values even falser than those of today'.‡

In none of these works, however, did Brittain find adequate acknowledgment of the role of women in the war; indeed, she attacked Aldington's novel for its misogyny and for the way in which it poured a 'cynical fury of scorn' on the wartime suffering of women. It was obvious to her that no man, however sympathetic, would be able to speak for women.

---

* A recent account of the publication of 'disillusioned' novels and memoirs, which observes that disenchantment with the First World War was mainly literary in character and limited in its impact on other war veterans and the public in general, is Gary Sheffield, *Forgotten Victory. The First World War: Myths and Realities*, London: Headline, 2001, pp. 5–12.
† VB to Winifred Holtby, 26 December 1928. Winifred Holtby Archive, Hull Central Library.
‡ VB, *Time and Tide*, 4 October 1929.

The war was a phase of life in which women's experience did differ vastly from men's and I make no puerile claim to equality of suffering and service when I maintain that any picture of the war years is incomplete which omits those aspects that mainly concerned women ... The woman is still silent who, by presenting the war in its true perspective in her own life, will illuminate its meaning afresh for its own generation.*

By the time she wrote those words, at the beginning of 1931, she had already embarked on her own book, and clearly intended to be that woman.

Of course, *Testament of Youth* was very far from being the only account by a woman of her wartime experience, though it remains the best known.† A large number had been published both during the war and in the years since, and for some of these, like Mary Lee's 1929 novel, *It's a Great War*, written from an American standpoint, Brittain had expressed warm words of commendation. She would also later read, 'with deep interest and sympathy', Irene Rathbone's novel, *We That Were Young* (1932), based on Rathbone's own experiences as a VAD, like Brittain, at the 1st London General Hospital in Camberwell. It conveyed, as no other book had done to date, the full horror of nursing the mutilated and wounded.‡ In the later stages of writing *Testament of Youth* in the summer of 1932, Brittain was concerned that Ruth Holland's recently published novel, *The Lost Generation*,

* VB, *Nation and Athenaeum*, 24 January 1931.
† See the extensive bibliography of war books by women in Claire Tylee, *The Great War and Women's Consciousness. Images of Militarism and Womanhood in Women's Writings, 1914–64*, London: Macmillan, 1990, pp. 263–71, and *Women and World War 1. The Written Response*, edited by Dorothy Goldman, London: Macmillan, 1993.
‡ Quoted in Berry and Bostridge, *Vera Brittain: A Life*, p. 240.

anticipated her own theme. Overall it is difficult to avoid the impression that Brittain wanted to perpetuate the idea that hers was the one work about the war by a woman that mattered.* On the other hand, none of these other books are of comparable stature to *Testament of Youth*, lacking its range and narrative power. As Winifred Holtby wrote on one occasion when Brittain needed particular reassurance, 'Personally, I'm not in the least afraid of other people's books being like yours. What other woman writing has *both* your experience *and* your political training?'†

However, it is the men in Vera Brittain's story who typify the central founding myth on which *Testament of Youth* is based. Although in the early stages of the book's evolution she claimed to be writing for her generation of women, she was subsequently to expand her claim to include her generation of both sexes.‡ Certainly, nothing else in the literature of the First World War charts so clearly the path leading from the erosion of innocence, with the destruction of the public schoolboys' heroic illusions, to the survivors' final disillusionment that the sacrifice of the dead had been in vain. *Testament of Youth* is the *locus classicus* of the myth of the lost generation, and it is important to understand why this should be so. Brittain's male friends were representative of the subalterns who went straight from their public schools or Oxbridge, in the early period of the war, to the killing fields of Flanders and France. As a demographic class these junior

---

* A point made by Maroula Joannou in 'Vera Brittain's *Testament of Youth* revisited', *Literature and History*, 2, 1993, p. 67.

† Winifred Holtby to VB, 27 August 1932. Winifred Holtby Archive, Hull Central Library.

‡ Thus in the foreword to the '1st version, Holograph manuscript' of *Testament of Youth*, at McMaster, VB writes of showing 'what the whole war and post-war period . . . meant to the women of my generation'. In the published edition, this is amended to 'the men and women of my generation'.

officers show mortality rates significantly higher than those of other officers or of the army as a whole. Uppingham School, where three of Brittain's circle were educated, lost about one in five of every old boy that served. The Bishop of Malvern, dedicating the war memorial at another public school, Malvern College, said that the loss of former pupils in the war 'can only be described as the wiping out of a generation'.* The existence of a lost generation is not literally true, and is entirely unsupported by the statistical evidence;† but, given the disproportionate death rate among junior officers, it is perhaps no wonder that Brittain believed that 'the finest flowers of English manhood had been plucked from a whole generation'. Robert Wohl has shown how this cult of a missing generation provided 'an important self-image for the survivors from within the educated elite and a psychologically satisfying and perhaps even necessary explanation of what happened to them after the war'.‡

Vera Brittain had another aim in writing her book: to warn the next generation of the danger of succumbing out of naive idealism to the false glamour of war. This gives *Testament of Youth* a significant difference of tone that sets it apart from the work of the war's male memoirists. Whereas a writer like Edmund Blunden tries to evoke the senselessness and confusion of trench warfare by revealing the depth of the war's ironic cruelty, Brittain, contrastingly, tries to provide a reasoned exposition of why the war had occurred and how war in the future might be averted.

* C. F. Kernot, *British Public Schools' War Memorials*, London: Roberts & Newton, 1927, p. 136.
† J. M. Winter, *The Great War and the British People*, London: Macmillan, 1986, pp. 65–99, provides a detailed study of war losses relating to 'The Lost Generation' myth.
‡ Robert Wohl, *The Generation of 1914*, London: Weidenfeld & Nicolson, 1980, p. 115.

The publication of *Testament of Youth* at the end of August 1933 exactly matched the mood of international foreboding. It was the year in which Hitler had become chancellor of Germany, the Japanese had renewed their attack on Manchuria, and there had been difficulties over negotiations for disarmament at the League of Nations in Geneva. As a result, parallels between the tense world situation and the weeks leading up to the outbreak of war in 1914 were endemic in the press. Yet while Brittain often referred to *Testament of Youth* as her 'vehement protest against war', she was, at the time of writing it, still several years away from declaring herself a pacifist. In 1933, as the final chapters of her autobiography show, she clung to the fading promise of an internationalist solution as represented by the League of Nations. However, the process of writing her book undoubtedly hastened her transition to pacifism in 1937, for looking back at the tumultuous events of her youth, she could for the first time separate her respect for the heroism and endurance of her male friends from the issue of what they had actually been fighting for.

Testament of Youth has been so often adduced as an historical source in studies of the First World War that it might be easy to forget that it is not history but autobiography and, moreover, autobiography that at a number of points uses novelistic devices of suspense and romance to heighten reality. This is particularly true of Brittain's treatment of her relationship with Roland Leighton, where rather than dealing with the complex web of emotions that existed on both sides she creates a conventional love story. She had carefully researched the background to the war in historical records, like the *Annual Register* and in the collections of the British Red Cross Society and the Imperial War Museum, and also employed a patchwork of letters and diaries to bring the characters of her major protagonists alive, which provide the backbone of the finished book. But she was fearful of 'numerous inaccuracies through queer tricks of memory',* and inevitably some mistakes slipped through the net. Her narrative of the period she had spent as a VAD at the 24 General at Étaples, from August 1917 to April 1918, does not possess the reliability of precise chronology and detail of earlier parts of *Testament of Youth*. She had ceased to keep a diary after returning from Malta in May 1917, and had only some letters to her mother, a few rushed notes to Edward, and a sometimes hazy recollection of events some fifteen years or so after they had taken place. For her – highly inaccurate – description of the Étaples mutiny, which had occurred in September 1917 while she was at the camp, she had been forced to rely on little more than the memory of Harry Pearson, an ex-soldier and friend of Winifred Holtby, who had had no direct involvement in the events either.†

The publication of Vera Brittain's wartime diaries and correspondence has revealed the extent of the complexity and ambivalence underlying her contemporary responses to the war. The evidence of these private records demonstrates that while at times she could rail against the war with anger and distress, at others she took refuge in a consolatory rhetoric rooted in traditional values of patriotism, sacrifice and idealism of the kind espoused by the wartime propaganda of both Church and State, or the sonnets of Rupert Brooke. In her letters written after Roland's death, for instance, her need to continue believing that

* VB, 23 August 1933, *Chronicle of Friendship*, p. 147.
† The discrepancies between the records kept by the base administrative staff at Étaples and VB's account in *Testament of Youth* of nursing German prisoners are discussed by Douglas Gill in 'No Compromise with Truth. Vera Brittain in 1917', *Krieg und Literatur*, v, 1999, pp. 67–93. However, his conclusion, that Brittain exaggerated the plight of the wounded Germans, ignores the testimony of her wartime correspondence.

the war was being fought for some worthwhile end – manifest in such gung-ho sentiments as, 'It is a great thing to live in these tremendous times',* or her conviction that war is an immense purgation† – is perhaps entirely understandable. But equally, in *Testament of Youth*, it is not surprising to find that this kind of ambivalence is largely absent, and that Brittain is reluctant to confront her own susceptibility as a younger woman to the glamour of war, and unwilling to probe too deeply the roots of her own idealism in 1914.‡ For by the time she had completed her autobiography, Vera Brittain was ready to reject anything that identified war 'with grey crosses, and supreme sacrifices, and red poppies blowing against a serene blue sky'.§

In 1989, while writing Vera Brittain's biography, I travelled to the Somme to pay a visit to Roland Leighton's grave at Louvencourt. Our party of four, including two of Vera Brittain's grandchildren, spent the night in Albert, at the Hôtel de la Paix, where Brittain herself had lunched in July 1933 during the second of her two visits to the cemetery where Roland was buried; and the next morning, which happened to be Remembrance Sunday, we made the hilly drive to Louvencourt. On the south-east side of the village, a large stone cross dominates the skyline, surrounded by acres of tranquil farmland. It is a small cemetery, of

* VB to Edward Brittain, 27 April 1917, *Letters from a Lost Generation*, p. 344.
† VB to Edward Brittain, 31 May 1916, *Letters from a Lost Generation*, p. 259.
‡ For examples of this unwillingness, see Berry and Bostridge, *Vera Brittain: A Life*, pp. 60–2.
§ VB, 'A Woman Speaks for Her Generation', *Sunday Chronicle*, 23 October 1933. For an interesting examination of the ways in which the Battle of the Somme solidified into myth in VB's writing, from her diary account to *Testament of Youth*, see Alan Bishop, 'The Battle of the Somme and Vera Brittain', *English Literature of the Great War Revisited*, edited by Michel Roucoux, Amiens: University of Picardy, 1986, pp. 125–42.

151 Commonwealth and 76 French graves, beautifully cared for, as are all the military cemeteries of the First World War, by the Commonwealth Graves Commission. Roland's grave is in the middle, not far from the memorial cross and cenotaph, and its inscription includes the closing line from W. E. Henley's 'Echoes: XLII', 'Never Goodbye'.

I found the visitors' book in a little cupboard in the wall. Among its messages, I counted no fewer than ten people from around the world who, in the period of just two months, had come to this relatively out of the way area of the Somme in order to pay tribute to Roland Leighton – and to pay tribute to him because they had read about his brief life and early death in *Testament of Youth*. As Shirley Williams, Vera Brittain's daughter, says in her preface, it is a precious sort of immortality.

More than seventy years after its first publication, *Testament of Youth*'s power to disturb and to move remains undiminished.* Vera Brittain's 'passionate plea for peace', which attempts to show 'without any polite disguise, the agony of war to the individual and its destructiveness to the human race',† is one that, tragically, still resonates in our world today.

---

* Terry Castle reconsiders *Testament of Youth* in the light of 9/11, in *Courage, mon amie*, London: London Review of Books, 2003, pp. 41–54.
† VB, manuscript material for *Testament of Youth*. VB Archive, McMaster University.

ALEXANDER McCALL SMITH
ON
ANGELA THIRKELL

Wild Strawberries (1933) and *High Rising* (1934)

First Virago editions 2012

Angela Thirkell was born in 1890. She was educated in London and Paris, and began publishing articles and stories in the 1920s. In 1931 she published her first book, a memoir, *Three Houses*, and in 1933 her comic novel *High Rising* met with great success. She went on to write nearly thirty novels set in the fictional county of Barsetshire, as well as several further works of fiction and non-fiction. She died in 1961.

Alexander McCall Smith is the author of over eighty books on a wide array of subjects, including the award-winning The No.1 Ladies' Detective Agency series. He is also the author of the Isabel Dalhousie novels and the world's longest-running serial novel, 44 Scotland Street. His books have been translated into forty-six languages. Alexander McCall Smith is Professor Emeritus of Medical Law at the University of Edinburgh and holds honorary doctorates from thirteen universities.

Angela Thirkell is today relatively unknown, by no means as familiar to readers as Benson or Trollope, or even Nancy Mitford, writers with whom she is sometimes compared. Unlike Barbara Pym, she has not enjoyed a significant moment of rediscovery; unlike Rose Macaulay, she did not write anything of quite the same status as *The Towers of Trebizond*. Yet her work has its adherents, and the republication of these two works, *High Rising* and *Wild Strawberries*, will be welcomed by those who feel that these unusual, charming English comedies deserve a wider audience.

She led her life in much the same milieu as that in which she set her novels. She came from a moderately distinguished family: her father became Professor of Poetry at Oxford, and her mother was the daughter of Edward Burne-Jones, the pre-Raphaelite painter. She was related to both Rudyard Kipling and Stanley Baldwin; she was the goddaughter of J. M. Barrie. Her life, though, was not always easy: there was an unhappy spell living in Australia, and two unsuccessful marriages. Financial exigency meant that she had to make her own way, first as a journalist, and then as the author of a series of novels produced to pay the bills.

Books flowed fast from her pen, and their quality was perhaps uneven. Many of them are now largely forgotten, but amid this enthusiastic somewhat breathless literary output there are some highly enjoyable and amusing novels. *High Rising* and *Wild Strawberries* are two such. These books are very funny indeed.

The world she depicts is that of rural England in that halcyon period after the First World War when light began to dispel the stuffiness and earnestness of the Victorian and Edwardian ages. It was a good time for the upper middle classes: they still lived in largish houses and they still had servants, even if not as many as they used to. They drove cars – made of enamel! Angela Thirkell informs us – and they entertained one another with stylish throw-away comments in which exaggeration played a major role. They were in turn delighted or enraged – all in a rather arch way – by very small things.

The social life depicted in these books is fascinating. We are by no means in Wodehouse territory – Thirkell's characters do have jobs, and they do not spend their time in an endless whirl of silliness. Occasionally, though, they express views or use language that surprises or even offends the modern ear – there is an instance of this in the wording of one of the songs in *Wild Strawberries*. But this, of course, merely reflects the attitudes of the time: it is a society in which nobody is in any doubt about his or her place. Servants observe and may comment, for example, but they must not get above themselves. Miss Grey, who takes up the position of secretary to Mr Knox in *High Rising*, is not exactly a servant, but she is an employee and should remember not to throw her weight around with her employer's friends. Of course she does not remember this, which is a major provocation to the novel's heroine, Laura Morland. One cannot help but feel sympathy for Miss Grey, who is described as having no relations to whom she can be expected to go. That was a real difficulty for women: unless you found a husband or were able to take one of the relatively few jobs that were available to you (and somebody like Miss Grey could not go into service), you were dependent on relatives. Finding a husband was therefore a deadly earnest task – almost as important as it was in the time of Jane Austen.

The children in this world were innocent and exuberant. In *High Rising* we see a lot of Laura's son, Tony, whom she brings home from his boarding school at the beginning of the book. Like most of those whom we encounter in Thirkell's novels, Tony is overstated to the point of being something of a caricature. He is as bouncy and excitable as a puppy dog, full of enthusiasm for trains, a subject by which he is obsessed. He knows all the technical details of trains – their maximum speed, and so on – and spends the 'tips' he receives from adults on the purchase of model carriages and engines. These tips are interesting. It was customary for adult visitors to give presents to the children of the house, and a boy might reasonably expect such a gift simply because he was there at the time of the visit. As a child I remember getting these tips – not earning them in any way, just getting them as of right. Today, children would be surprised if anybody gave them money and would probably immediately reject it, it having been drilled into them that such gifts are always to be refused.

Tony also has a degree of freedom unimaginable today. Not only is he interested in model trains; his passion for railways extends to the real thing, and he is allowed to go off to the local railway station by himself. There the stationmaster permits him to sit in the signal box and also to travel in the cab on shunting engines. Whatever else is unlikely in the novels, this sounds entirely realistic. Childhood was different then.

Engaging though these period details may be, this is in itself insufficient reason to read Thirkell. What makes her novels so delightful is their humour. The affairs that occupy the minds of her characters are classic village concerns. In that respect, we could as easily be in Benson's Tilling as we are in the Risings.

There are dislikes and feuds; there are romantic ambitions; there are social encounters in which people engage in highly amusing exchanges. These come thick and fast, just as they do in Tilling, and are every bit as delicious. Affection for the social comedy is not something we should have to apologise for, even if that sort of thing is eschewed in the contemporary novel. Such matters may seem unimportant, but they say a lot about human nature. Above all, though, we do not read Angela Thirkell for profundity of emotional experience; we read her for the pleasure of escape – and there is a perfectly defensible niche for escapist fiction in a balanced literary diet.

Another attraction is the coruscating wit of the dialogue and, to an extent, of the authorial observations. Angela Thirkell is perhaps the most Pym-like of any twentieth-century author, after Barbara Pym herself, of course. The essence of this quality is wry observation of the posturing of others, coupled with something that comes close to self-mockery. The various members of the Leslie family in *Wild Strawberries* are extremely funny. Lady Leslie, like Mrs Morland in *High Rising*, is a galleon in full sail, and we can only marvel at and delight in the wit of both.

The exchanges that take place between the characters in these books would look distinctly out of place in a modern novel – but therein, I believe, lies their charm. These people talk, and behave, as if they are in a Noël Coward play. In real life, a succession of insouciant sparkling observations would become tedious, but it is impossible to read these books without stopping every page or two to smile or to laugh at the sheer audacity of the characters and their ebullient enthusiasms. We are caught up by precisely those questions that illuminate the novels of Jane Austen: who will marry whom? Who will neatly be put in her place? Which men will escape and which will be caught? These are not the great questions of literature, but they are diverting, which is one of the roles of fiction. Angela Thirkell creates and peoples a world whose note can be heard today only in the tiniest of echoes, but in her books it comes through loud and clear, reminding us that the good comic novel can easily, and with grace, transcend the years that stand between us and the time of its creation.

SARAH DUNANT
ON
DAPHNE DU MAURIER

Jamaica Inn (1936)

First Virago edition 2003

Daphne du Maurier was born in 1907 in London. In 1931 her first novel, *The Loving Spirit*, was published. A biography of her father and three other novels followed, but it was the novel *Rebecca* that secured her position as one of the most celebrated writers of the twentieth century. Many of du Maurier's bestselling novels and short stories were adapted into award-winning films, including Alfred Hitchcock's *The Birds* and Nicolas Roeg's *Don't Look Now*.

In 1969 du Maurier was appointed DBE. She died in 1989.

Sarah Dunant is famous for her Italian historical novels: *The Birth of Venus, In the Company of the Courtesan, Sacred Hearts, Blood and Beauty* and *In the Name of the Family*, which have been translated into more than thirty languages. She has worked widely in television, radio and print, written eleven novels and edited two collections of essays. She lives in London and Florence.

Jamaica Inn opens with echoes of *Dracula*: a carriage rattling through a desolate landscape and wild weather to a place where even the locals won't go, so ferocious is its reputation. Inside rides Mary Yellan, newly orphaned and en route from the tame farmland of the Helford area to the rainswept moors of nineteenth-century Cornwall and the married home of her aunt, a woman once known for her rich curls and girlish laughter. We are in the territory of the Gothic novel, but one with an undercurrent of modern sensibility.

Mary's destination, Jamaica Inn, stands dark and forbidding at the top of the moor. It is the house from hell. At night the sign outside twists in the wind like a human body on a gibbet. Inside, the place reeks of neglect, drink and male violence. The lovely giggling Aunt Patience is now a gaunt, shaky wreck, her spirit destroyed by abuse, and her husband, Joss Merlyn, is a monster: physically overwhelming, lumbering, violent and drunk. By the end of the first day, as the light bleeds away and Mary barricades herself in her miserable little room, a pact has been made with the reader. This is going to be a journey into darkness, and it's going to deliver both violence and sensation.

It doesn't take long to find out why the Inn and its landlord are so feared. Early on, most readers will have guessed the reason. Cornwall, with its bleak, treacherous coastline and wild weather was for much of its history a law unto itself. Jamaica Inn may now be a tourist trap reduced to kitsch by the publicity of minor literary fame, but when du Maurier would have first seen it, in the 1920s, it would no doubt have been a more desolate place which, with the right imagination, could easily be transformed into Robert Louis Stevenson territory and the heart of a smuggling ring that not only hides the booty but runs a gang of wreckers who lure the ships onto the rocks to drown their crew and steal their cargo.

There's no doubt that many of the ingredients of Jamaica Inn – wild men, wild land, dark secrets and violent ends – are close to Gothic cliché and would have been even in 1936 when Daphne du Maurier wrote the book. But what makes the novel still vibrant is to see how in the hands of a master storyteller – because that is exactly what du Maurier is – the form can be revitalised and even to some measure reinvented.

The way she does it is twofold: first by sheer force of plotting. Mary, alarmed and demoralised, may have found herself in hell, but she has no option but to stay, held by her loyalty to her aunt and the need to protect her. In the eyes of the community that makes her virtually an outlaw herself. All good thrillers have to isolate their hero if the threat is really going to bite, and even when Mary manages to get herself out of the house, the desolation of the moors only mocks her helplessness, the landscape and the weather as much a force in this book as any of the characters. The only other people she meets are in their own way as bizarre as the inn's inhabitants. There is her uncle's younger brother Jem, a horse thief and an adventurer whose attraction keeps her on the wrong side of the law, and the strangely tender mercies of one Francis Davey, the Vicar of Altarnun, a fabulously unnerving character whose soft speech clashes with his bleached albino looks and his heavy whip on the horse's back.

But for most of the book it is Mary's battle with Joss Merlyn that keeps you turning the page. As a character he isn't to everybody's taste. Du Maurier's own biographer, Margaret Forster, finds him near to caricature, and it's true that he is larger than life. But there is also a terrible fascination to him. His brooding figure, craggy looks and wild temper are in their own way all attributes of the romantic hero inverted into violence and self-loathing – a Mr Rochester without a Jane to redeem him. Before guilt and drink disabled Joss he would have been a charismatic figure. (Du Maurier had lived too long with a glamorous, powerful father – the actor Gerald du Maurier – not to have understood that there is a price to be paid for charisma.) There is something in Joss Merlyn's torment that smells of damage done as well as inflicted. And it's here that *Jamaica Inn* pushes at the boundaries of the romantic genre to suggest how passion between men and women can lead to abuse. Joss's wife may now be a quivering victim, but at one point she was madly in love with this powerful man, believing she could somehow save him from himself. There is a hint of collusion here, and despite her fear Patience still makes excuses for Joss, trying to deflect his anger in a way that only provokes it further. Du Maurier herself doesn't excuse him. Admittedly, she gives him a childhood with its own history of violence, and an abused, helpless mother, but she never lets him off the hook. For all his physical strength he is a weak character, and though Mary may be morally and physically repelled by him she is also up for the battle. And a battle it is, from the moment he latches on to her both as his prey, the next woman after his wife that he must break and destroy – and also in some desperate hope that Mary will match him and somehow bring him to redemption.

There is an extraordinary scene halfway through the book – in its way much more frightening than the real thing, which comes later – when Joss emerges from a drinking bout to accost Mary in the kitchen. Crazed by waking nightmares, he offers up a lacerating confession about the ships he has lured onto the rocks and the survivors he has bludgeoned to death in the roaring surf, their faces coming back to haunt him. His terror at that moment is much greater than Mary's, but it is her sentence to be the helpless listener. It is worth knowing as you read this scene that du Maurier's own husband, the affable, charming, good-looking Frederick Browning, had been a war hero; one of the things that marked the early years of their marriage was the way he would wake at night screaming, and she would have to try and comfort him. Some of du Maurier's own helpless horror is in Mary as she watches, repelled and overwhelmed by her uncle's raving confessions.

This painful realism of the relationship between men and women also underpins Mary's growing attraction to her uncle's brother, Jem. There is a quiet cynicism to du Maurier's description of their courtship. Mary knows that Jem will probably bring her as much pain as happiness, but she accepts it as part of how the world works. She has watched it unfold too many times around her to be fooled: seen how a teasing courtship down sun-drenched lanes will be replaced by the mundanity and exhaustion of married life, the man 'calling sharply that his supper was burnt, not fit for a dog, while the girl snapped back at him from the bedroom over-head, her figure sagging and her curls gone, pacing backward and forward with a bundle in her arms that mewed like a cat and would not sleep'. Du Maurier had had her first child just a few years before she wrote this novel and while the nanny had done more caring than she ever did (the one time she was left with the baby it screamed its head off), there is a taste of experience to the vision. For a book which at one level is a romantic adventure story, *Jamaica Inn* is full of decidedly unromantic thoughts.

The novel doesn't dwell on them though. It's too busy winching the story ever tighter. Once you get past the second chapter it's almost impossible to read *Jamaica Inn* slowly. It is the burden of thriller writers to have the reader tell them admiringly how fast they read your books. 'I couldn't put it down' is both the greatest compliment and the cruellest cut of all, since it almost certainly means that a reader's greed to get to the end of the book will have made them careless with some of the best writing on the way. It's a trade-off thriller writers have to accept. But du Maurier never set out to write literary fiction. Her style is intelligent and fluid, sufficient unto the cause of telling the story. But then it wasn't her style that made her famous. That's not why she is still being reprinted when a hundred other writers of her age are footnotes in fiction. And while she has dated in certain respects – her dialogue can sometimes feel a little stilted and there are perhaps one too many dark nights and haunted moors for modern taste – almost seventy years have in no way dimmed her capacity to hook the reader like a fish and angle them in through the rising waters of the plot. There is virtually no spare action here. It would be invidious to give away the last twist, and while there will be those who see it coming, foresight doesn't rob it of its elegant baroque menace, with more than a touch of the Hannibal Lecter/Clarice Starling relationship thrown into the dark mix. Mary Yellan sups with many devils in this book and by the end there is not even a long spoon between them.

In the end – well, in the end the book resolves itself as any good Gothic adventure should, by bringing the reader out of darkness into at least a semblance of light. Mary Yellan survives. But even though the writer doesn't say it directly, you can be sure

Mary will not sleep well at night. That is the price you pay for winning such battles. The good triumph but, like du Maurier's husband, they remain damaged by the fight. For all of her privileged middle-class upbringing, by the time Daphne du Maurier wrote *Jamaica Inn* at the comparatively young age of twenty-nine, she too, already had something of darkness about her. She was, in fact, well on her way to *Rebecca*.

RACHEL COOKE
ON
STEVIE SMITH

Novel on Yellow Paper (1936),
Over the Frontier (1938),
The Holiday (1949)

First Virago editions 1980

Stevie Smith was born Florence Margaret Smith in 1902. She lived in Palmers Green, London, and for much of her life worked, until retirement, as a secretary for the magazine publishers Sir George Newnes and Sir Neville Pearson. When she tried to publish a volume of poems, she was told to 'go away and write a novel'. *Novel on Yellow Paper* was the result, and it turned her into an instant celebrity. Two further novels, (*Over the Frontier* and *The Holiday*) followed, but it is her poetry that has secured her legacy. In 1966 she received a Cholmondeley Award and in 1969 was awarded the Queen's Gold Medal for Poetry. She died in 1971.

Rachel Cooke was born in Sheffield. An award-winning journalist, she writes for the *Observer*, and is the television critic of the *New Statesman*. Her first book, *Her Brilliant Career*, is published by Virago.

Stevie Smith was the first poet I read. I can't remember how I discovered her; all I know is that I asked for her *Collected Poems* one Christmas. If the elaborately careful signature on the inside jacket is anything to judge by, I must have been about fifteen at the time. I liked the fact that she was a swift read, her poems so wondrously succinct I sometimes wondered if they really counted as Literature. Far too many writers were, in my youthful opinion, far too prolix. But it was her tone that really delighted me. Her irony, her wit, that slight edge of malice: these things spoke to a moody teenager. Her voice was irresistible, bending the world into a shape that was disorientatingly odd, even as it was instantly recognisable.

Wanting more, I bought her first book, *Novel on Yellow Paper*, and one grey Sunday – exactly the kind of dreary, slow-ticking afternoon she must often have endured in her Victorian villa, marooned in the outer reaches of suburban London – I sat down to read it. The shock was considerable. What's this? I thought, a question that's tricky to answer even now, for Stevie's novels (she wrote three, after which she abandoned fiction for ever) are nothing if not singular. Her debts – to Laurence Sterne's *Tristram Shandy*, to the Dorothys Parker and Richardson, and, above all, to Virginia Woolf* – might well be obvious, especially to those

---

* One literary figure of the time believed Virginia Woolf had written *Novel on Yellow Paper* under a pseudonym.

well-schooled in Modernism. Nevertheless, she remains her own writer, *sui generis*. A poem, she once told a friend, was a relatively light thing; it could be carried around 'while you're doing the housework'. A novel, though, was an altogether darker beast. She likened her fiction to the sea: on the surface bright and sunny, but seven miles down 'black and cold'. Her stories had for an engine some 'ghastly human confusion and chill'.

Pompey Casmilus, the narrator of both *Novel on Yellow Paper* (1936) and its sequel *Over the Frontier* (1938), is Stevie's alter ego: a more antic version of herself. The private secretary of Sir Phoebus Ullwater, Bt, a magazine publisher, she weaves back and forth through her life, offering as she goes her opinions on such important matters as love, marriage, death and Racine versus Shakespeare – 'For this book is the talking voice that runs on, and the thoughts come, the way I said, and the people come too, and come and go, to illustrate the thoughts, to point the moral, to adorn the tale.' These people include 'sweet boy Freddy', her fiancé; Karl, a student whom she visits in Germany just as Nazism is beginning to rise; and the Lion Aunt, with whom Pompey lives. Pompey is prone to apologise for her loquaciousness – 'And you Reader, whom I have held by the wrist and forced to listen, I am full of regret for you …' – but this is something of an act. For all that she wanders and digresses and seems sometimes to lose her thread, there is a certainty about Pompey; like her creator, she has the courage of her (somewhat weird) convictions. And she is never anything less than touchingly stoical, even when her tale grows 'richly compostly loamishly sad'. Far from feeling weary on finishing the book, the reader closes *Novel on Yellow Paper* – and its more slippery sequel, in which Pompey becomes embroiled in foreign espionage – feeling that everyday speech, in all its repetitive clumsiness, has been brought magically close to poetry. Thanks to this, something has been crystallised. The thirties, certainly, for it's all here: anti-Semitism, political self-delusion, 'the nervous irritability that has in it the pulse of our time'. But also the moods of a young woman, alone in the world at a moment when to be such a thing felt daring, insecure, perilous, *freakish*. They shift, these moods, like clouds in a strong wind, and find their ultimate expression in Smith's third and final novel, *The Holiday* (1949), in which another office-working, aunt-loving narrator, Celia Phoze, suffers from a 'black-split heart', experiences a nervous breakdown and contemplates suicide.

Stevie Smith was born Florence Margaret Smith in 1902, in Hull, Yorkshire, the second daughter of Charles Smith, a failed shipping agent, and his wife, Ethel. Her parents were, in her words, 'ill-assorted', and when she was only three, her father ran away to sea – an abandonment Stevie would feel for the rest of her life. His absence had a powerful effect on her character. While other girls of her class were brought up to bring Father his paper, and then to disappear into silence, Smith was a 'wicked, selfish creature' who mostly got to please herself, her eccentricity and determination (useful qualities in a poet) growing exponentially as a result. It was thanks to his sudden departure, too, that she grew up in a 'house of female habitation' in Palmers Green, north London. Stevie's maternal aunt Madge Spear, aka 'the Lion of Hull', came to live with the family, and soon afterwards Ethel, Madge, Stevie and her sister, Molly, moved south, probably – as her biographer Frances Spalding has speculated – to escape gossip. Stevie and Aunt would live in the red-brick house in Avondale Road until 1968, when Aunt died at the age of ninety-six, and this was the single most important relationship of her life. As Celia says in *The Holiday*: 'To have a darling Aunt to come home to, that one admires, that is strong, happy, simple, shrewd, staunch, loving, upright and bossy . . . ' If her father's sporadic postcards left her with a 'powerful sense of transiency', Aunt was an emotional standing stone, solid and immovable. She never loved anyone more.

Ethel died in 1919, an event Stevie would later evoke in *Novel on Yellow Paper* ('But all the time you are remembering that she did suffer. Because if you cannot breathe you must suffer. And the last minute when you are dying, that may be a very long time indeed.') In 1920, she and her sister left their school, North London Collegiate; Molly to take up a place at Birmingham University, Stevie to sign on at Mrs Hoster's Secretarial Academy in Hyde Park (money being thin on the ground by now, she hoped for a career that would provide a regular income). Her first post on completing her training was at an engineering firm; her second was at the magazine publishers C. Arthur Pearson, where she was appointed secretary to Sir Neville Pearson, the son of the firm's founder. She would hold down this unremarkable job for the next thirty years, her employer a 'lodestar in a disordered existence'. Pearson appears, a little idealised, as Sir Phoebus in her first two novels.

Life settled down. Her work was dull, but it did not capture her mind – 'I did not want a job where I had to use up my whole energy' – leaving her free to read, something she did omnivorously. She liked returning to Palmers Green in the evening, to its quietness and stillness. The house was old fashioned and overfurnished, crammed with fat armchairs and heavy sideboards, its garden made gloomy by a huge privet hedge. But its rhythms comforted her, and she was able to begin the process of becoming Stevie Smith (her nickname was acquired when, riding a hired horse on a London common, some boys yelled at her: 'Come on,

Steve!', a reference to a popular jockey, Steve Donoghue). Those who knew her in this period were already struck by her zest, originality, quick-wittedness and disparate crowd of friends (she vastly preferred the idea of friendship to that of marriage and turned away from the latter forever in the mid-thirties, having broken off her brief engagement to an insurance broker called Eric Armitage). A colleague described her as 'a busy little person'.

Little. This isn't the right word, however affectionately used. It's true that Stevie was birdlike, her mannerisms dainty and her looks gamine, and this was certainly something she chose to emphasise in later life when she began to wear self-consciously girlish clothes: shifts, pinafores, pretty brooches, Peter Pan collars. But in every other respect, she was far from little. Aunt wasn't the only lion in Avondale Road. Behind the lively, darting façade, behind the nervousness, caprice and periodic depressions, there was steel. She was not a person to be put off. Nor, in creative terms, was she a person to compromise. In 1934, she submitted a collection of poems to the literary agent Curtis Brown. They did not go down well, the company's bewildered reader finding them neurotic. Stevie, however, was not discouraged, and a further bundle was soon dispatched to an editor at Chatto & Windus, who told her: 'Go away and write a novel and we will then think about the poems.' This she did, and in just ten weeks – one evening, she claimed, she wrote six thousand words at a stroke – only for Chatto to turn it down, too. Undaunted, Stevie now turned to Hamish Miles, a reader at Jonathan Cape whose eye had been caught by the poems she'd recently had published in the *New Statesman*. Bingo! *Novel on Yellow Paper* had found its publisher. Acclaimed by some critics and abhorred by others, it turned her overnight into the kind of writer who received fan letters. It also prepared the ground for the poetry. It wasn't just that it was a throat-clearing kind of novel, one in which she could let off steam, the better that she might pare down future work. She now had an audience, one that relished her voice. Its publication was followed swiftly by that of her first collection of poetry, *A Good Time Was Had By All*. Starting as she meant to go on, she illustrated it with her own drawings, angular and spindly, just like her.

The career that followed had highs and lows. *A Good Time Was Had By All*, and her second novel, *Over the Frontier*, were well-received. But further volumes of poetry didn't do so well, and the publication of *The Frontier* was delayed for several years. In the forties and fifties, she was unfashionable. Some of this must have been connected to her gender. The post-war literary world was irredeemably masculine; she wasn't the only woman writer to be shut out. But it was also easy to underestimate Stevie's work. Her outward simplicities could be taken at face value, the pain beneath ignored. It's possible, too, that some men were wilfully deaf to the sound of themselves. Stevie was dissatisfied with their world, and she parodied it mercilessly, her ear wonderfully attuned to its absurdities, to what Seamus Heaney called 'the longueurs and acerbities, the nuanced understatements and tactical intonations of educated middle-class English speech'. She hit her targets smart on the nose, and perhaps this irritated them.

Though bolstered by her friendships – her circle now included Olivia Manning, Rosamond Lehmann and George Orwell – she grew increasingly fragile: spiky on the outside, easily bruised within. The title poem of *Harold's Leap*, her fourth collection of poetry, describes a suicide ('Harold, I remember your leap,/ It may have killed you/But it was a brave thing to do.') and thus foreshadows the events of 1953, when she cut one of her wrists in the office. It was decided after this that she would not return to her job. It wasn't until 1957, and the publication of what is now her most famous collection of poetry, *Not Waving but Drowning*, that she re-emerged as a writer. The sixties came to her rescue. Poetry readings were popular, and Stevie unselfconsciously took her place alongside the Liverpool poets, her neat dresses and sensible shoes in polite contrast to their leather and denim. She had a gift for performance, her stylised recitations, half spoken and half sung, half cheerful and half desperate, unnerving her audiences with their sense of something – madness? rage? – kept only just at bay.

Stevie died in 1971 of a brain tumour (during her final illness, she wrapped her head in a pink turban; friends were amazed by how beautiful she looked). At the end, she was again lion-like. Frances Spalding has described how, in hospital awaiting a biopsy, she performed her last poem 'Come Death' ('Come Death. Do not be slow.') from her bed, astonishing visitors and patients alike. Perhaps she was content, knowing there were books to live on after her – and sure enough, in the years that followed, her critical reputation bloomed. Her *Collected Poems*, published in 1975, felt reassuringly solid in the hand, its six-hundred-page bulk physically underlining the substance concealed in her short, uncluttered lines. In 1977 Hugh Whitemore's play, *Stevie*, was staged, starring Glenda Jackson, and while it bought wholesale into some terrible clichés – wasn't she innocent? wasn't she *odd*? – it greatly added to her legend. In 1980 Virago Modern Classics republished her three novels, and they were acclaimed all over again.

Stevie will always stand alone, at an angle to everyone else. She belongs to no group; she cannot easily be appropriated by any cause. Her verses are unlikely to appear in those carefully marketed volumes that hope to console us in certain states of mind (love, grief, melancholy). Her poems are too sly for that; their sophistication, extreme once you notice it, is elusive at first. The same is true of the novels. What confounding, idiosyncratic books they are, garrulous to a fault and yet somehow so keenly observant, so cold-eyed, so full of pity for all that is most melancholy. 'We carry our own wilderness with us,' says Pompey, in *Over the Frontier* – and isn't this precisely it? As Stevie knew all too well, even the suburbs come with desolate expanses. Their avenues, parks and crescents have their fair share of exiles, restless and forever in search of home.

ZADIE SMITH
ON
ZORA NEALE HURSTON

Their Eyes Were Watching God (1937)

First Virago edition 1986

Zora Neale Hurston was born in 1891. In the Harlem Renaissance of the 1930s, she was the preeminent black woman writer in the United States. She died in 1960 in a welfare home, was buried in an unmarked grave, and quickly faded from literary consciousness until 1975 when Alice Walker almost single-handedly revived interest in her work. Maya Angelou, Toni Morrison and Alice Walker have all acknowledged Zora Neale Hurston as their literary foremother.

Zadie Smith was born in north-west London in 1975. She is the author of the novels *White Teeth*, *The Autograph Man*, *On Beauty*, *NW* and *Swing Time*, as well as *The Embassy of Cambodia* and an essay collection, *Changing My Mind*. She is also the editor of *The Book of Other People*, a fellow of the Royal Society of Literature and has twice been listed as one of Granta's 20 Best Young British Novelists. She has won the Orange Prize for Fiction, the Whitbread First Novel Award and the Guardian First Book Award among many others, and been shortlisted for the Man Booker Prize and the Baileys Women's Prize for Fiction.

When I was fourteen I was given *Their Eyes Were Watching God* by my mother. I was reluctant to read it. I knew what she meant by giving it to me and I resented the inference. In the same spirit she had introduced me to *Wide Sargasso Sea* and *The Bluest Eye*, and I had not liked either of them (better to say, I had not *allowed* myself to like either of them). I preferred my own freely chosen, heterogeneous reading list. I flattered myself I ranged widely in my reading, never choosing books for genetic or socio-cultural reasons. Spotting *Their Eyes Were Watching God* unopened on my bedside table, my mother persisted:

'But you'll like it.'

'Why, because she's *black*?'

'No – because it's really good writing.'

I had my own ideas of 'good writing'. It was a category that did not include aphoristic or overtly 'lyrical' language, mythic imagery, accurately rendered 'folk speech' or the love tribulations of women. My literary defences were up in preparation for *Their Eyes Were Watching God*. Then I read the first page:

Ships at a distance have every man's wish on board. For some they come in with the tide. For others they sail forever on the horizon, never out of sight, never landing until the Watcher turns his eyes away in resignation, his dreams mocked to death by Time. That is the life of men.

Now, women forget all those things they don't want to remember, and remember everything they don't want to forget. The dream is the truth. Then they act and do things accordingly.

It was an aphorism, yet it had me pinned to the ground, unable to deny its strength. It capitalised Time (I was against the capitalisation of abstract nouns), but still I found myself melancholy for these nameless men and their inevitable losses. The second part, about women, struck home. It remains as accurate a description of my mother and me as I have ever read: *Then they act and do things accordingly.* Well, all right then. I relaxed in my chair a little and lay down my pencil. I inhaled that book. Three hours later I was finished and crying a lot, for reasons that both were, and were not, to do with the tragic finale.

I lost many literary battles the day I read *Their Eyes Were Watching God.* I had to concede that occasionally aphorisms have their power. I had to give up the idea that Keats had a monopoly on the lyrical:

She was stretched on her back beneath the pear tree soaking in the alto chant of the visiting bees, the gold of the sun and the panting breath of the breeze when the inaudible voice of it all came to her. She saw a dust-bearing bee sink into the sanctum of a bloom; the thousand sister-calyxes arch to meet the love embrace and the ecstatic shiver of the tree from root to tiniest branch creaming in every blossom and frothing with delight. So this was a marriage! She had been summoned to behold a revelation. Then Janie felt a pain remorseless sweet that left her limp and languid.*

* But I still resist 'limp and languid'.

I had to admit that mythic language is startling when it's good:

> Death, that strange being with the huge square toes who lived way in the West. The great one who lived in the straight house like a platform without sides to it, and without a roof. What need has Death for a cover, and what winds can blow against him?

My resistance to dialogue (encouraged by Nabokov, whom I idolised) struggled and then tumbled before Hurston's ear for black colloquial speech. In the mouths of unlettered people she finds the bliss of quotidian metaphor:

> 'If God don't think no mo' 'bout 'em than Ah do, they's a lost ball in de high grass.'

Of wisdom lightly worn:

> 'To my thinkin' mourning oughtn't tuh last no longer'n grief.'

Her conversations reveal individual personalities, accurately, swiftly, as if they had no author at all:

> 'Where y'all come from in sich uh big haste?' Lee Coker asked.
> 'Middle Georgy,' Starks answered briskly. 'Joe Starks is mah name, from in and through Georgy.'
> 'You and yo' daughter goin' tuh join wid us in fellowship?' the other reclining figure asked. 'Mighty glad to have yuh. Hicks is the name. Guv'nor Amos Hicks from Buford, South Carolina. Free, single, disengaged.'

'I god, Ah ain't nowhere near old enough to have no grown daughter. This here is mah wife.'

Hicks sank back and lost interest at once.

'Where is de Mayor?' Starks persisted. 'Ah wants tuh talk wid *him*.'

'Youse uh mite too previous for dat,' Coker told him. 'Us ain't got none yit.'

Above all, I had to let go of my objection to the love tribulations of women. The story of Janie's progress through three marriages confronts the reader with the significant idea that the choice one makes between partners, between one man and another (or one woman and another) stretches far beyond romance. It is, in the end, the choice between values, possibilities, futures, hopes, arguments (shared concepts that fit the world as you experience it), languages (shared words that fit the world as you believe it to be) and lives. A world you share with Logan Killicks is evidently not the same world you will share with Vergible 'Tea Cake' Woods. In these two discrete worlds, you will not even think the same way; a mind trapped with Logan is freed with Tea Cake. But how can we talk of freedoms? In practical terms, a black woman in turn-of-the-century America, a woman like Janie, or like Hurston herself, had approximately the same civil liberties as a farm animal: 'De nigger woman is de mule uh de world.' So goes Janie's grandmother's famous line – it hurt my pride to read it. It hurts Janie, too; she rejects the realpolitik of her grandmother, embarking on an existential revenge which is of the imagination and impossible to restrict:

She knew that God tore down the old world every evening and built a new one by sun-up. It was wonderful to see it take form with the sun and emerge from the gray dust of its making. The familiar people and things had failed her so she hung over the gate and looked up the road towards way off.

That part of Janie that is looking for someone (or something) that 'spoke for far horizon' has its proud ancestors in Elizabeth Bennet, in Dorothea Brooke, in Jane Eyre, even – in a very debased form – in Emma Bovary. Since the beginning of fiction concerning the love tribulations of women (which is to say, since the beginning of fiction) the 'romantic quest' aspect of these fictions has been too often casually ridiculed: not long ago I sat down to dinner with an American woman who told me how disappointed she had been to finally read *Middlemarch* and find that it was 'Just this long, whiny, trawling search for a man!' Those who read *Middlemarch* in that way will find little in *Their Eyes Were Watching God* to please them. It's about a girl who takes some time to find the man she really loves. It is about the discovery of self in and through another. It suggests that even the dark and terrible banality of racism can recede to a vanishing point when you understand, and are understood by, another human being. Goddamnit if it doesn't claim that love sets you free. These days 'self-actualisation' is the aim, and if you can't do it alone you are admitting a weakness. The potential rapture of human relationships to which Hurston gives unabashed expression, the profound 'self-crushing love' that Janie feels for Tea Cake, may, I suppose, look like the dull finale of a 'long, whiny, trawling search for a man'. For Tea Cake and Janie, though, the choice of each other is experienced not as desperation, but as discovery, and the need felt on both sides causes them joy, not shame. That Tea Cake would not be *our* choice, that we disapprove of him often, and despair of him occasionally, only lends power to the portrait. He seems to act with freedom, and Janie chooses him freely. We have no power; we only watch. Despite the novel's fairy-tale structure (as far as husbands go, third time's the charm), it is not a novel of wish-fulfilment, least of all the fulfilment of *our* wishes.* It is odd to diagnose weakness where lovers themselves do not feel it.

After that first reading of the novel, I wept, and not only for Tea Cake, and not simply for the perfection of the writing, nor even the real loss I felt upon leaving the world contained in its pages. It meant something more than all that to me, something I could not, or would not, articulate. Later, I took it to the dinner table, still holding on to it, as we do sometimes with books we are not quite ready to relinquish.

'So?' my mother asked.

I told her it was basically sound.

At fourteen, I did Zora Neale Hurston a serious critical disservice. I feared my 'extra-literary' feelings for her. I wanted to be an objective aesthete and not a sentimental fool. I disliked the idea of 'identifying' with the fiction I read: I wanted to like Hurston because she represented 'good writing', not because she represented me. In the seventeen years since, Zora Neale Hurston has gone from being a well-kept, well-loved secret amongst black women of my mother's generation, to an entire literary industry – biographies† and films and Oprah and African-American literature departments all pay homage to her life‡ and work as

---

* Again, *Middlemarch* is an interesting comparison. Readers often prefer Lydgate and are disappointed at Dorothea's choice of Ladislaw.
† The (very good) biography is *Wrapped in Rainbows: The Life of Zora Neale Hurston* by Valerie Boyd. Also very good is *Zora Neale Hurston: A Life in Letters*, collected and edited by Carla Kaplan.
‡ *Dust Tracks on a Road* is Hurston's autobiography.

avatars of black woman-ness. In the process, a different kind of critical disservice is being done to her; an overcompensation in the opposite direction. In *Their Eyes Were Watching God*, Janie is depressed by Joe Starks's determination to idolise her: he intends to put her on a lonely pedestal before the whole town and establish a symbol (The Mayor's Wife) in place of the woman she is. Something similar has been done to Hurston herself. She is like Janie, sat on her porch-pedestal ('Ah done nearly languished tuh death up dere'), far from the people and things she really cared about, representing only the ideas and beliefs of her admirers, distorted by their gaze. In the space of one volume of collected essays, we find a critic arguing that the negative criticism of Hurston's work represents an 'intellectual lynching' by black men, white men and white women; a critic dismissing Hurston's final work with the sentence, '*Seraph on the Suwanee* is not even about black people, which is no crime, but *is* about white people who are bores, which is'; and another explaining the 'one great flaw' in *Their Eyes Were Watching God*: Hurston's 'curious insistence' on having her main character's tale told in the omniscient third person instead of allowing Janie her 'voice outright'. We are in a critical world of some banality here, one in which most of our nineteenth-century heroines would be judged oppressed creatures, cruelly deprived of the therapeutic first-person voice. It is also a world in which what is called the 'Black Female Literary Tradition' is beyond reproach:

> Black women writers have consistently rejected the falsification of their Black female experience, thereby avoiding the negative stereotypes such falsification has often created in the white American female and Black male literary traditions. Unlike many of their Black male and white female peers, Black

women writers have usually refused to dispense with whatever
was clearly Black and/or female in their sensibilities in an effort
to achieve the mythical 'neutral' voice of universal art.*

Gratifying as it would be to agree that black women writers
'have consistently rejected the falsification' of their experience,
the honest reader knows that this is simply not the case. In place
of negative falsification, we have nurtured, in the past thirty years,
a new fetishisation. Black female protagonists are now too often
unerringly strong and soulful; they are sexually voracious and
unafraid; they take the unreal forms of earth mothers, African
queens, divas, spirits of history; they process grandly through
novels thick with a breed of greeting-card lyricism. They have
little of the complexity, the flaws and uncertainties, depth and
beauty of Janie Crawford and the novel she springs from. They
are pressed into service as role models to patch over our psychic
wounds; they are perfect;† they overcompensate.The truth is,
black women writers, while writing many wonderful things,‡
have been no more or less successful at avoiding the falsification
of human experience than any other group of writers. It is not
the Black Female Literary Tradition that makes Hurston great.
It is Hurston herself. Zora Neale Hurston – capable of expressing human vulnerability as well as its strength, lyrical without
sentiment, romantic and yet rigorous, and one of the few truly

* All the critical voices quoted above can be found in *Zora Neale Hurston's
Their Eyes Were Watching God: Modern Critical Interpretations*, edited by
Harold Bloom.
† Hurston, by contrast, wanted her writing to demonstrate the fact that
'Negroes are no better nor no worse, and at times as boring as everybody else'.
‡ Not least of which is Alice Walker's original introduction to *Their Eyes Were
Watching God*. By championing the book she rescued Hurston from forty years
of obscurity.

eloquent writers of sex – is as exceptional amongst black women writers as Tolstoy is amongst white male writers.*

It is, however, true that Hurston rejected the 'neutral universal' for her novels – she wrote unapologetically in the black-inflected dialect in which she was raised. It took bravery to do that: the result was hostility and disinterest. In 1937, black readers were embarrassed by the unlettered nature of the dialogue and white readers preferred the exoticism of her anthropological writings. Who wanted to read about the poor Negroes one saw on the corner every day? Hurston's biographers make clear that no matter what positive spin she put on it, her life was horribly difficult: she finished life working as a cleaner, and died in obscurity. It is understandable that her reclaiming should be an emotive and personal journey for black readers and black critics. But still, one wants to make a neutral and solid case for her greatness, to say something more substantial than: 'She is my sister and I love her.' As a reader, I want to claim fellowship with 'good writing' without limits; to be able to say that Hurston is my sister and Baldwin is my brother, and so is Kafka my brother, and Nabokov, and Woolf my sister, and Eliot and Ozick. Like all readers, I want my limits to be drawn by my own sensibilities, not by my melanin count. These forms of criticism that make black women the privileged readers of a black woman writer go against Hurston's own grain. She saw things otherwise: 'When I set my hat at a certain angle and saunter down Seventh Avenue . . . the cosmic Zora emerges . . . How *can* anybody deny themselves the pleasure of my company? It's beyond me!'

This is exactly right. No one should deny themselves the

---

* A footnote for the writers in the audience: *Their Eyes Were Watching God* was written in seven weeks.

pleasure of Zora – of whatever colour or background or gender. She's too delightful not be shared. We all deserve to savour her neologisms ('sankled', 'monstropolous', 'rawbony') or to read of the effects of a bad marriage, sketched with tragic accuracy:

> The years took all the fight out of Janie's face. For a while she thought it was gone from her soul. No matter what Jody did, she said nothing. She had learned how to talk some and leave some. She was a rut in the road. Plenty of life beneath the surface but it was kept beaten down by the wheels. Sometimes she stuck out into the future, imagining her life different from what it was. But mostly she lived between her hat and her heels, with her emotional disturbances like shade patterns in the woods – come and gone with the sun. She got nothing from Jody except what money could buy, and she was giving away what she didn't value.

The visual imagination on display in *Their Eyes Were Watching God* shares its clarity and iconicity with Christian story-telling – many scenes in the novel put one in mind of the bold-stroke illustrations in a children's Bible: young Janie staring at a photograph, not understanding that the black girl in the crowd is her; Joe Starks atop a dead mule's distended belly, giving a speech; Tea Cake bitten high on his cheekbone by that rabid dog. I watched the TV footage of Hurricane Katrina with a strong sense of déjà vu, thinking of Hurston's flood rather than Noah's: 'Not the dead of sick and ailing with friends at the pillow and the feet ... [but] the sodden and the bloated; the sudden dead, their eyes flung wide open in judgment.'

Above all, Hurston is essential universal reading because she is neither self-conscious nor restricted. Raised in the real

Eatonville, Florida, an all-black town, this unique experience went some way to making Hurston the writer she was. She grew up a fully human being, unaware that she was meant to consider herself a minority, an other, an exotic, or something depleted in rights, talents, desires and expectations. As an adult, away from Eatonville, she found the world was determined to do its best to remind her of her supposed inferiority, but Hurston was already made, and the metaphysical confidence she claimed for her life ('I am not tragically colored') is present, with equal, refreshing force, in her fiction. She liked to yell 'Culllaaaah Struck!'* when she entered a fancy party – almost everybody was. But it is of fundamental significance to her writing that Hurston herself was not. 'Blackness', as she understood it and wrote about it, is as natural and inevitable and complete to her as, say, 'Frenchness' is to Flaubert. It is also as complicated, as full of blessings and curses. One can be no more removed from it than from one's arm, but it is no more the total measure of one's being than an arm is. It begins a million of your songs – it ends none of them.

But still after all that there is something else to say – and the 'neutral universal' of literary criticism pens me in and makes it difficult. To write critically in English, even to write a little introduction, is to aspire to neutrality, to the high style of, say, Lionel Trilling or Edmund Wilson. In the high style, one's loves never seem partial or personal, or even like 'loves', because white novelists are not white novelists but simply 'novelists', and white characters are not white characters but simply 'human', and criticism of both is not partial or personal but a matter of aesthetics. Such critics will always sound like the neutral

* See Chapter 16 for a sad portrayal of a truly colour-struck lady, Mrs Turner.

universal, and the black women who have championed *Their Eyes Were Watching God* in the past, and the one doing so now, will seem like black women talking about a black book. When I began this introduction, it felt important to distance myself from that idea. By doing so, I misrepresent a vital aspect of my response to this book, one that is entirely personal, as any response to a novel shall be. Fact is, I *am* a black woman,* and a sliver of this book goes straight in to my soul, I suspect, for that reason. And though it is, to me, a vulgar absurdity to say, 'Unless you are a black woman, you will never fully comprehend this novel', it is also disingenuous to claim that many black women do not respond to this book in a particularly powerful manner that would seem 'extra-literary'. Those aspects of *Their Eyes Were Watching God* that plumb so profoundly the ancient build-up of cultural residue that is (for convenience's sake) called 'Blackness'† are the parts that my own 'Blackness', as far as it goes, cannot help but respond to personally. At fourteen I couldn't find words (or words I liked) for the marvellous feeling of recognition that came with these characters who had my hair, my eyes, my skin, even the ancestors of the rhythm of my speech.‡ These forms of identification are so natural to white readers – (Of course Rabbit Angstrom is like me! Of course Madame Bovary is like me!) – that they believe themselves above personal identification, or at least that they are identifying only at the highest, metaphysical levels (His soul is like my soul. He is human; I am human). White readers often believe

---

* I think this was the point my mother was trying to make.
† As Kafka's *The Trial* plumbs that ancient build-up of cultural residue that is called 'Jewishness'.
‡ Down in the muck, Janie and Tea Cake befriend the 'Saws', workers from the Caribbean.

they are colour-blind.* I always thought I was a colour-blind reader – until I read this novel, and that ultimate cliché of black life that is inscribed in the word 'soulful' took on new weight and sense for me. But what does *soulful* even mean? The dictionary has it this way: 'expressing or appearing to express deep and often sorrowful feeling'. The culturally black meaning adds several more shades of colour. First shade: *soulfulness* is sorrowful feeling transformed into something beautiful, creative and self-renewing, and – as it reaches a pitch – ecstatic. It is an alchemy of pain. In *Their Eyes Were Watching God*, when the townsfolk sing for the death of the mule, this is an example of *soulfulness*. Another shade: to be soulful is to follow and *fall in line* with a feeling, to go where it takes you and not to go against its grain.† When young Janie takes her lead from the blossoming tree and sits on her gate-post to kiss a passing boy, this is an example of *soulfulness*. A final shade: the word *soulful*, like its Jewish cousin, schmaltz,‡ has its roots in the digestive tract. 'Soul food' is simple, flavoursome, hearty, unfussy, with spice. When Janie puts on her overalls and joyfully goes to work in the muck with Tea Cake, this is an example of *soulfulness*.§

This is a beautiful novel about soulfulness. That it should be so is a tribute to Hurston's skill. She makes 'culture' – that slow and

---

* Until they read books featuring non-white characters. I once overheard a young white man at a book festival say to his friend, 'Have you read the new Kureishi? Same old thing – loads of Indian people.' To which you want to reply, 'Have you read the new Franzen? Same old thing – loads of white people.'
† At its most common and banal: catching a beat, following a rhythm.
‡ In the *Oxford English Dictionary*: '**Schmaltz n**. informal. excessive sentimentality, esp. in music or movies. ORIGIN 1930s: from Yiddish *schmaltz*, from German *Schmalz* "dripping, lard."'
§ Of course, there are few things less soulful than attempting to define soulfulness.

particular* and artificial accretion of habit and circumstance – seem as natural and organic and beautiful as the sunrise. She makes 'black woman-ness' appear a real, tangible quality, an essence I can almost believe I share, however improbably, with millions of complex individuals across centuries and continents and languages and religions ... Almost – but not quite. Better to say, when I'm reading this book, I believe it, with my whole soul. It allows me to say things I wouldn't normally. Things like: *She is my sister and I love her.*

* In literary terms, we know that there is a tipping point in which the cultural particular – while becoming no less culturally particular – is accepted by readers as the neutral universal. The previously 'Jewish fiction' of Philip Roth is now 'fiction'. We have moved from the particular complaints of Portnoy to the universal claims of Everyman.

An image that appears frequently in Rumer Godden's work, both fiction and autobiography – and the line between the two is a fine one – is that of a girl flying a paper kite, as she used to on the flat rooftop of her home in Bengal. In the memoir *Two Under the Indian Sun*, which she wrote with her sister Jon, she remembers:

> To hold a kite on the roller was to hold something alive ... something that kicked in your hand, that pulled up and sang as the string thrilled in the wind. The string went up and up until the kite seemed above the hawks circling in the sky; it linked us with another world, wider, far wider than ours.

The young heroine of *The River* declares, 'If it flies, I shall fly.' In both books the kite is used as a metaphor for childhood and the end of childhood. It might as well stand for her long and extraordinary life.

Rumer Godden was born in 1907 and died in 1998, so her life spanned almost the entire twentieth century. She lived through all its great upheavals – two world wars, the expansion of the British Empire, as well as its collapse – and through periods of personal joy and success, as well as struggle and betrayal. Throughout, she wrote with exemplary steadfastness. What gave a life, which had been volatile and dramatic, its core of stability, of serenity, even?

Two strands ran through it: one was her childhood in India at a time when the British ruled with a sense of security and the continuity of history; the other was her unwavering conviction of writing as her vocation. Towards the end, a third strand became apparent: a spiritual awareness that grew to a point where she felt able to commit to Catholicism. Throughout the twists and turns of a turbulent life, she retained the inner focus and belief of the child on the rooftop, holding the roller as her paper kite is lifted into the sky, allowing it the freedom of the winds, but maintaining her control.

Her father, Arthur Godden, in what Rumer Godden's biographer Anne Chisholm calls 'the high-Victorian heyday of the Empire', fought in the Boer War and then, bored at the prospect of settling down to life as a stockbroker in London, chose instead to work as an agent in one of the shipping companies based in Calcutta that ran steamers up and down the great rivers of the Gangetic delta. In *Two Under the Indian Sun* his life is described as one of adventure, excitement and a passionate attachment to the landscape of the riverine Bengal that Rumer was to inherit and cherish all her life. She described the childhood she and her three sisters shared at the house in Narayanganj, a small town beside a river, as 'halcyon', painting it in golden light, filling it with flowers and birds and imbuing it with all the comfort and security that could be provided by a large staff of servants – there were fifteen for a family of five. Education was certainly haphazard, provided by their maiden aunt Mary who lived with them, but Rumer grew up with a deep love of books and reading, which led quite naturally to an aptitude for writing. She first saw her writing in print at the age of twelve, in the Calcutta newspaper the *Statesman*, which confirmed her commitment to the writing life: always an imaginative child, she wrote under a pseudonym, assuming the role of a mother, and offered advice on how to keep children cool in the hot weather.

As the girls grew into adolescents, the Goddens decided to follow the British colonial tradition of taking their children back to England for a more conventional education. In 1920 the girls went with their mother to settle in Eastbourne where they learnt that the life of luxury and comfort they had taken for granted as members of the ruling class in India – the flag that was raised on their house at sunrise and lowered at sunset had them think of their home as Buckingham Palace – was over. Rumer found life in Eastbourne bleak and dreary, and suffered from the rigours of school life, going through as many as five in two years. It was in the last of them, Moira House, a progressive institution run by enlightened women, that the vice principal, Miss Swann, saw her literary talent and encouraged her writing. Swann was a writer herself and an exacting critic, but Rumer trusted her, and turned to her even as an adult for advice. One of the most beneficial exercises she gave Rumer was in précis: she had to reduce the leader of *The Times* to fourteen lines so that not a word was wasted. 'I owe her a tremendous debt,' said Rumer in later life.

No one in the family seems to have considered a university education as the next logical step. Instead, in 1925 their mother took them back to India with trunkfuls of new clothes to launch them in Calcutta society with its parties, dances, polo and riding. Rumer never felt comfortable in that social milieu and in 1927 she returned to London where, knowing she would have to support herself financially, she decided to train as a dancing teacher. She studied for two years and was offered a job on the staff, but instead went back to India to open her own dance school, first in Darjeeling and then in Calcutta. She rented premises in the best neighbourhood in the city and the school proved popular, particularly with the Eurasians of Calcutta. The British rather looked down on it for that very reason and there was gossip, hinting that Rumer must have Indian blood herself. She even received anonymous offensive letters and phone calls. Rumer was genuinely interested in the Eurasian community; her contact with the students and her assistant and pianist taught her much about it. She also did a great deal of research for her second novel, *The Lady and the Unicorn*, which she wrote while 'sitting on the verandah of the school building among the waiting pupils, mothers and ayahs'.

Of course, Rumer still belonged to the expatriate British society, and by this time she was married to Laurence Foster, a stockbroker, sportsman, and a popular figure in the exclusive Tollygunge Club circle. The couple honeymooned in Puri by the sea and nearly sixty years later she wrote a novel, *Coromandel Sea Change*, about an unhappy bride's realisation that she had made a mistake. It wasn't a marriage of minds or sensibilities, as was evident from her family's misgivings. In Calcutta she was expected to take part in Laurence's social life: 'for a while I tasted how beguiling it could be – as long as you stayed on the surface', but she remained critical of it: 'They were still in Britain, adapting their exile to as close a British pattern as they could, oblivious of everything Indian except for their servants.' *The Lady and the Unicorn* was born of this criticism of the common British disdain for Indians and Eurasians. She had already written a book called *Chinese Puzzle* about a Pekinese dog – she had a lifelong passion for the breed – which was published in 1935 when she was in England awaiting the birth of her daughter. It was not a commercial success but it gave her the opportunity to meet her publisher and agent in London. They had faith in her writing, which she took strength from when she returned to India.

Her third novel, *Black Narcissus*, published in 1939, was her first success – both commercial and critical. It was compared by Arthur Koestler to E. M. Forster's *A Passage to India* (which pleased Rumer, who said it was 'the book that changed my life') and turned into a movie. The film, which was enormously successful, disappointed Rumer but it did give her financial security and confidence.

Her marriage, on the other hand, went badly wrong. Her husband's career as a stockbroker failed and he joined the army, leaving Calcutta. Rumer, alone, took her two daughters to live in a small bungalow amidst the mountains and tea gardens of Darjeeling. This was a quiet, contemplative period of her life. She went for long walks and kept a diary that was later published as *Rungli-Rungliot* (subtitled 'Thus Far and No Further'). Next she went to live on a houseboat in Kashmir which was closer to where Laurence was posted, but his cantonment life and the company of soldiers' wives was no more attractive to her than expatriate society in Calcutta had been. Her marriage was effectively over. She moved to a small, basic cottage she called Dove House on a flowery hillside of streams and orchards.

Ultimately, this idyllic setting proved the scene of the most disturbing drama of her life: after the household fell ill and ground glass was found in the food, she became convinced they were being poisoned by the cook, Siddika. This could not be proved in court and he was acquitted but, ill and fearful, she left the place she had been happy and loved, and it would not be long before she would leave India for good. Many years later she wrote a fictionalised account in *Kingfishers Catch Fire*, which displayed her ability to write of the British in India with both intimate knowledge and a critical eye. The book was compared to Paul Scott's *The Jewel in the Crown* and, once again, to Forster's *Passage to India*.

It was much less overtly political than either and its scope was narrower but it was an imaginative reconstruction of the colonial situation. As is evident from her novels, which often feature narrow-minded British characters, Rumer had ambiguous feelings about imperialism, but when Prime Minister Jawaharlal Nehru was quoted as saying 'My quarrel with the British is that they left a land of poverty-stricken wrecks,' she rose up in its defence and in 1944/45 she worked on a non-fiction book of the Women's Voluntary Service in Bengal, touring the various organisations it ran, and wrote with admiration of the good work it did.

One of these tours took her back to Narayanganj and, on seeing her old home, was moved to write a short autobiographical novel called *The River*. On reading it, the French director Jean Renoir immediately bought film rights, describing it as 'exactly the type of novel which would give me the best inspiration for my work ... an unexpressed, subtle, heartbreaking innocent love story involving a little girl.' They began a correspondence and Rumer helped him plan a trip with his wife to the site. On their return, he invited Rumer to Hollywood so they could work on the script together. 'Working with Jean was the best and richest year I've spent,' she later said. So different in character and background, the two became very close and held each other in high regard. Staying with the Renoirs, she met their friends the Chaplins, the Stravinskys, James Mason, Charles Laughton, Elizabeth Taylor and Greta Garbo, and hugely enjoyed the social life. When the script was ready to be filmed, she accompanied the crew to Bengal, sharing many decisions with the director. The film was shown at the Venice Film Festival in 1951 and won the International Critics' Prize, then opened in France and the USA to good reviews and is now regarded as a classic. Although the Indian press was rather critical of it, it had a premiere at the New

Empire cinema in Calcutta that was attended by Prime Minister Nehru. Many of Godden's books were made into successful films in her lifetime, including Powell and Pressburger's famous adaptation of *Black Narcissus*; *Enchanted*, starring David Niven, which was based on *A Fugue in Time*; *The Battle of the Villa Fiorita*; *The Greengage Summer*; and *In this House of Brede*, but none of them brought her the satisfaction of *The River*.

Rumer divorced Laurence Foster, creating some turmoil for her daughters – which she later fictionalised in *The Battle of the Villa Fiorita* – and after filming *The River* she entered into a second, and very happy, marriage to James Haynes-Dixon, a civil servant who devoted himself to her and her career. Together they created a series of beautiful homes and gardens in London and in the countryside, including Lamb House in Rye, which was once the home of Henry James; her surroundings had always been very important to her.

In 1961 she made a new friend in Dame Felicitas Corrigan of Stanbrook Abbey in Worcestershire, and through her she established a link with the Benedictine order that led to her writing *In This House of Brede*, her longest, perhaps most complex novel, in which she strove to realistically depict convent life: many of the events were inspired by the nuns' own stories. In 1973 her husband died and a few years later she moved to a small house next to her daughter Jane's in Scotland, but she continued to write with her old regularity and determination. It was her habit to start a new book every New Year's Eve and in her lifetime she completed an astonishing twenty-three novels, twenty-six books for children, fourteen books of non-fiction and seven collections and anthologies of poetry. In 1993 she was awarded the OBE.

This was not to be retirement for her. In 1994 the BBC planned a documentary on her life for the *Bookmark* programme and she was persuaded to travel with them to India for the last time for the making of the film. She returned to Bengal and even to Kashmir where she had sworn never to go again. It was an exhausting undertaking but at a farewell dinner she toasted the crew and told them that if she were a sensible old lady she would not have agreed to the journey and that she was glad she 'had never been sensible in her life'. She died four years later at the age of ninety and was buried next to her husband James in the old cemetery in Rye.

Rumer Godden knew both success and popularity in her life. Perhaps for that very reason she was troubled that she might be considered not a very serious but an entertaining, lightweight writer. She was also conscious of her own attractions to the whimsical and the precious, and the need to be on her guard and reserve that aspect for her many charming books for children. She never lost the child's fascination with the miniature but if there is any criticism that this prevented her from addressing the large events and political movements of her time, it does not hold; the miniature in her books contained, by reflection, the vastness of the world. This is surely the reason why her work has given so much pleasure to generations in many lands, and continues to do so.

Perhaps no other book exemplifies Rumer Godden's strengths as well as this little book, barely over a hundred pages long. In her modest way, she herself seemed bemused by how well it was received when it was published, in 1946, and how it caught the eye of the French director Jean Renoir, who turned such unlikely material into an acclaimed film.

As in her other work, she does not directly refer to the Second World War, the time in which it is set. In fact, the young heroine, labouring over the Latin declension for war, thinks 'this war, the last war, any war, it does not matter which war.' Nor is there a reference to the struggle for freedom that cumulated a year later in India's independence and the end of the colonial empire. Yet it is imbued with a sense of time passing, of time being a river that never stands still, and the seasons that change inexorably from one to another.

These are profound intimations, all the more intense because they are perceived by a child. Harriet's world is a square grey-stucco house occupied by her family – parents, an older and a younger sister, a small brother – and the large domestic staff that serves them: the gatekeeper who makes time to play games with the children, the wise and practical Nan, and the many who bring the different religious beliefs and customs with them – Hindu, Muslim, Buddhist and Christian. Whatever the children learn of India and its diversity is through them. The outside world is the street beyond the walls with its bazaar life going on, and beyond that the river, with its steamers, sailing boats and ferries moving up and down it. A small area on a map, but Rumer Godden conveys an immense sense of space: the sky where birds wheel and paper kites fly; the river with its constantly moving kingfishers and porpoises; the garden with its teeming plant and insect life, minutely observed by the little boy Bogey, for whom it holds endless fascination.

In this seemingly safe and secure setting, the children live what might be thought an idyllic existence, but it is within its confines that Harriet finds herself thinking, in bewilderment, 'children don't have loves and wars. Or do they ... of their kind?' In a very real way, a serpent too inhabits this Garden of Eden, and the child who had been innocent learns of the existence of evil.

These events, or non-events, are written of with an artlessness, a spontaneity that make one think they must have flowed from her memory through her pen on to paper with the ease of running water. Actually, Rumer Godden wrote and rewrote these scenes but seemed unable to bring them together. Revisiting Narayanganj, where she had lived as a child, inspired her: 'As I walked through the bazaars and Jute works, along the river, past the Club, the bamboo-built church and school, the houses I had known, it was as if I had gone back ... seven, eight, nine, ten, eleven, twelve years ... again. Everything was the same.' She left by steamer and from its deck watched the town 'grow smaller but more and more clear until out of sight'. Out of this moment of clarity the final version of *The River* was born: she had discovered how to capture time, space and experience in exquisite miniature, no more than a dewdrop reflecting light.

SOPHIE DAHL
ON
STELLA GIBBONS

Nightingale Wood (1938)

First Virago edition 2009

Stella Gibbons was born in 1902 in London. She studied journalism at University College London, and worked for ten years on various papers, including the *Evening Standard*. Her first novel, *Cold Comfort Farm*, published in 1932, was (and is) hugely successful. Her other novels include *Linsey and Pa*, *Nightingale Wood*, *Westwood*, *Conference at Cold Comfort Farm* and *The Woods in Winter*. She married the actor and singer Allan Webb, who died in 1959. They had one daughter. Stella Gibbons died in 1989.

Sophie Dahl began her career as an international fashion model. In 2003 she wrote a bestselling illustrated novella, *The Man with the Dancing Eyes*. This was followed by a novel, *Playing with the Grown-ups*, in 2007. She has written for, amongst others, US *Vogue*, *Harper's Bazaar*, the *Observer* and the *Guardian*, and served on the judging panel for the Orange Prize. A devoted home cook, her food books include *Miss Dahl's Voluptuous Delights*, which led to her BBC series *The Delicious Miss Dahl*; and *From Season to Season*. She has also written and presented a BBC documentary about the Victorian domestic advisor Isabella Beeton and is a contributing editor at *Condé Nast Traveller*.

'She did not look quite a lady, which was natural; as she was not one.' So wrote Stella Gibbons, author of *Cold Comfort Farm*, as she introduced the heroine of her ninth book, the latterly forgotten treasure, *Nightingale Wood*. The not quite a lady is grey-eyed Viola Wither, née Thompson, a beguiling widow of twenty-one. Viola is a victim of circumstance, like so many of Gibbons's female protagonists; a shopgirl orphan, married briefly to a bumbling, bullying older man, to whom she felt unable to say no at precisely the wrong moment. In his death she is similarly muted, and when, with a sigh of middle-class duty, her in-laws, the aptly named Withers, summon her from London to live with them in their dour house in Essex, she hops on a train in her cheap black coat and pink satin blouse, meek as a sacrificial lamb.

Their house, The Eagles, runs thick with thwarted longing. Dwelling there are two daughters, spinsters (in 1930s parlance): the lumpen, unfortunate, thirty-nine-year-old Madge; and Tina, who at thirty-five, with an extreme penchant for dieting, is wasting away in every sense. Their mother, Mrs Wither, seemingly has no fight left in her after four decades with the petty, pedantic patriarch of the family, the hateful Mr Wither. Mr Wither delights in the casual put-down, stamping the most fragile hope in his pitiful daughters with a quick lash of the tongue, forbidding Marge her one desire of a puppy, and tormenting Tina at every opportunity:

'What time did you say Viola's train gets in?' Tina asked her mother; she sometimes found the Wither silences unendurable.

'Half-past twelve, dear.'

'Just in nice time for lunch.'

'Yes.'

'You know perfectly well that Viola's train gets in at half-past twelve,' intoned Mr Wither slowly, raising his eyelids to look at Tina, 'so why ask your mother? You talk for the sake of talking; it's a silly habit.'

It is in this bleak household, in which the clocks are constantly checked to see whether the day is ending, that poor Viola is deposited. And yet . . .

On the other side of the valley is an entirely different house, a house that sings with comfort and luxury, a house that has the feeling of 'moving a little faster than other places, as though it were always upon the brink of a party'. This is Grassmere, a polished nouveau paradise, home to the dashing Victor Spring. Victor lives with his mother, Mrs Spring, who only employs the comely because, quite simply, she 'hated plain maids; they depressed her', and bookish cousin Hetty, who despises the inertia of a moneyed life, believing The Eagles across the way to contain a life full of 'muted, melancholy beauty'. Oh, the grass is always greener.

Add to the cast, amongst others, a ravishing chauffeur living above the Withers' garage, his mother, a faded village beauty with slatternly ways, a Machiavellian millionaire, a fast fairy godmother named Shirley, and a voyeuristic chorus of sorts in the form of a tramp known as the Hermit, and you have a sense of the proceedings, because Nightingale Wood is, in essence, a sprawling, delightful, eccentric fairy tale.

Gibbons loved this medium, and wrote three books conjuring it in her lifetime: *My American* (1939) borrows from 'The Snow Queen'; *White Sand and Grey Sand* (1958) is influenced by 'Beauty and the Beast'; and *Nightingale Wood*, her first endeavour, makes a great curtsy to 'Cinderella'. Where she strays from the classic fairy tale in these books, and brilliantly so, is that there is no such thing as staid, straightforward good and evil. Prince Charming is charming, yes, but he's also a little dull, vulgar and complacent. Her Cinderella is beautiful and true, yet a tad apathetic. Each social stratum in *Nightingale Wood* is capable of its own brand of snobbery, which is a theme that permeates all of her books. A greying of characters that are otherwise empathetic stretches to their occasional bigotry, which is deeply jarring to the modern reader. Casual anti-Semitism and racism is insidious in much of the fiction from this period, and it serves as a stark commentary on the time. Virginia Woolf, T. S. Eliot, Agatha Christie and W. B. Yeats have all been accused of perpetuating this in their work. It is difficult to fathom whether Gibbons herself held such beliefs, or if she was casting judgement (and satirical scorn) upon her culture by making reference to them in her fiction. It is worth noting that these examples are used in conversation, perhaps as a narrative example of the characters' own narrow-mindedness. To edit them out would be a denial, and so, uncomfortable as it is to stumble upon them, they remain as a harrowing reminder of what went before.

It is staggering for a writer with an archive spanning twenty-five novels, four volumes of poetry and three volumes of short stories, to be best (and sometimes solely) known for one work. *Cold Comfort Farm* was Stella Gibbons's first novel, published in 1932, when she was thirty. She had grown up in a family similar to the ones she parodied so well: she was middle class, educated, and her father was a doctor. In their local community of Kentish Town he was publicly lauded for his humanity; in private, he was a domineering and violent man. Such roots must have had a profound impact on her, regardless of her career trajectory, but to my mind they also tattoo her writing: the men in her books are regarded somewhat warily, whatever their station, and she writes of a woman's plight with sensitivity, buckets of humour, and ceaseless compassion. The women of *Nightingale Wood* each suffer suffocating consequences of their sex. Perhaps the most succinct surmisal of the 1930s female lot comes from Viola's best friend, Shirley, who says wryly, '*Vote, Marie [Stopes], perms, and all, we can't do anything.*'

But with the shadows we have light, and, again, it is testament to the wily talent of Gibbons to dance between the two with her light touch. One realises that *Nightingale Wood* doesn't have just one heroine; it has many, and each is duly rewarded for her pains. There is romance galore: a transformative dress and a ball; much dizzy kissing in hedgerows and beyond; spying, retribution and runaways; fights and a fire; poetry and heartbreak; a few weddings and a funeral; and a fairy-tale ending with a twist.

What luxury to stumble upon this quirky book, and the fascinating modern woman who wrote it. It is a rare unadulterated pleasure, and high time for its encore.

Without further ado – I give you *Nightingale Wood*.

CLARE BOYLAN
ON
KATE O'BRIEN

The Land of Spices (1941)

First Virago edition 1988

Kate O'Brien was born in 1897 in Limerick, and worked as a journalist in London and Manchester, and for a year as a governess in Spain. Her first success was as a playwright, but the publication of *Without My Cloak* in 1931 won her rapid acclaim as a novelist. This was followed by eight further novels, two of which, *Mary Lavelle* and *The Land of Spices*, were condemned for their 'immorality' by the Irish Censorship Board. Kate O'Brien dramatised three of her novels and *That Lady* was made into a film. She also wrote travel books, an autobiography and a study of St Teresa of Avila. She died in 1974.

Clare Boylan was the author of seven novels and three volumes of short stories. Her novels include *Home Rule* and its acclaimed sequel *Holy Pictures*, *Beloved Stranger*, *Room for a Single Lady* and *Emma Brown*. Her non-fiction works include essays on the art and strategy of fiction writing, and *The Literary Companion to Cats*. She died in 2006.

Kate O'Brien has always been something of an enigma. A subtle and persuasive feminist, she could still dismiss any woman who fell short of her standards as 'a repetitious old bundle' or 'a vain tulip of a woman'. High-minded and serious, she once confessed to a liking for dance music, quoting Masefield: 'Don't despise dance music. It's the music hearts break to.'

It is the breaking of hearts, and the role of heartbreak in the moulding of character, that motivates *The Land of Spices*. Mère Marie-Hélène Archer, Reverend Mother to the Irish convent of a French order, is a formidable Englishwoman who has sealed up her heart to devote herself to the 'impersonal and active service of God'. Once a radiant and hopeful young girl, she turned her back on life to punish her beloved father for what she saw as an unforgivable act of treachery. Young Anna Murphy has her whole life before her, but before she begins to live it, she too must suffer a possibly fatal blow to her emotions.

Like many of her novels, *The Land of Spices* is set in O'Brien's native Limerick, disguised as the imaginary Mellick. It was, in the 1930s, a limited, self-satisfied place, prosperous, nationalistic and rigidly Catholic. It is interesting to think that the novel is set in the same county and covers much the same period as *Angela's Ashes*, but whereas Frank McCourt's memoir is a searing study of poverty and prejudice in the Limerick slums, the children in O'Brien's novel come from the newly emerged Catholic upper

middle classes, the prosperous business and professional groups.
O'Brien was one of the few Irish rural writers to write about the
middle classes and her preoccupations are of the Jane Austen
school, snobbery and property and the struggle for intelligent girls
to pursue their own destiny.

In *The Land of Spices* it is Anna Murphy who must overcome
the petty aspirations of her family. At six years of age she becomes
the youngest-ever boarder at the convent of *La Compagnie de
la Sainte Famille*. Timid and inquisitive, she is noticed by the
Reverend Mother, who responds to the spiritual and intellectual
hunger of the small, intelligent girl. Anna is ready to be shaped
by the sophisticated curriculum of the French order and Mère
Marie-Hélène, who has reached the limits of her patience with
the self-satisfied parochialism of her Irish nuns and clergy, now
finds a new purpose in her vocation.

The reissue of *The Land of Spices* is particularly timely in a
period when convent life has all but disappeared. This is no
routine Catholic schooldays lark but a serious study of the politics and power of an all-female hierarchy. O'Brien exquisitely
evokes the harem atmosphere of convent life, the beauty and
the silence, the bickering and the cruelties and their lasting
influence on the lives of young girls. The nuns are not figures
of fun but professional women, stubborn and ambitious (and
among the few of their sex in their time with authority and
autonomy). The girls are impressionable and irrepressible, but
along with the tug of life on their romantic sensibilities, there
are the assaults on the spirit of a life of stillness and commitment, vividly described in this passage where girls, soon to leave
school, hear the sounds of distant bathers and boaters as they
walk in the convent grounds.

... the trees of the convent spread their wide and tranquillising arms, and the great house stood deep-based in reproachful calm, secure in its rule, secure in Christ against the brief assaults of evening or of roses. Girls about to leave, awaiting life, felt this dismissal by the spirit of the house of the unanswered, lovely conflict implicit in the hour . . .

The author creates a beautiful balance between the relative worldliness of the governing nuns and the as yet untouched spirits of the girls. Beautifully balanced also is the contained emotional interplay of the characters. There is not a trace of sentimentality. There are to be no grand romantic resolutions. Anna never really develops any real affection for her mentor. In fact she lacks conventional childish appeal. At six, she is captivating in her solemnity but as she grows older her watchfulness and guardedness make her seem aloof and even charmless. O'Brien, who herself once said, 'I am entirely against the promotion of a sense of humour as a philosophy of life,' would almost certainly have shared Anna's disapproval of her adolescent companions' hysteria. Yet the emotions and vulnerabilities are revealed like a play of shadow and light: in the young girl who hardens with each hurt, in the older woman whose dulled emotions begin to show colour like an old painting restored. Merely by having her heart unlocked, Mère Marie-Hélène is able to forgive and progress. Anna's emotions never get unlocked, but a small epiphany at the book's ending makes a shaft of light that will guide her towards her true future. If novels can be music, then this is a novel with perfect pitch.

The Land of Spices is O'Brien's most autobiographical work. Her own mother died of cancer in 1903 when she was six and her father thought that life would be less lonely for her if she joined

her older sisters at Laurel Hill boarding school, a convent of a
French order, the Faithful Companions of Jesus. This convent
was the model for the order of the *Compagnie de la Sainte Famille*,
even down to the English Reverend Mother, who was considered
something of a cold fish, but who won Kate's immediate allegiance
by telling her that they had to order a special small chair for her
and had asked for three to be sent on approval so that she could
choose one for herself. The school was viewed with suspicion
locally because the children were taught languages other than
Irish and both nuns and pupils drank real coffee. Like Anna, Kate
O'Brien won a university scholarship and was pressured by her
family into taking a 'decent' job in a bank instead. She went to
college, got her degree, and was outraged when a waggish uncle
sent a letter of congratulation which ended: 'I wonder what the
next step will be – M.A. or Ma?'

Exposed to both religious and French influences at an impressionable age, she emerged both high-minded and broadminded.
The Land of Spices reflects O'Brien's own ideal of moral perfec-
tionism. Her books offer a cynical view of romance, almost as if
love were a childish resolution to life's more serious quest. When
Tom and Angèle fall in love in *The Last of Summer*, the serious-
minded Jo sees it as 'a trick of the senses and of their passing
needs' and reflected that 'she was inclined to see human love as
a mistake anyhow'.

But O'Brien was as contemptuous of prudery as of sentimentality. Long before other women writers tackled such subjects she
wrote about homosexuality and sexual disease and must have
enjoyed shocking the narrow sensibilities of her era when she had
the blunt Mrs Cusack in *The Last of Summer* declare of her moody
barmaid: ''Twill be an ease to me, I can tell you, when that one's
periods are concluded and done with.'

Even more shocking to her Irish public was her outspokenness in regard to the smug insularity of her own country. Mère Marie-Hélène, exasperated by complaints about the foreign cooking produced by the Normandy kitchen nun who is a superb chef, considers: 'How odd were these Irish, who believed themselves implacably at war in the spirit with England, yet hugged as their own her dreariest daily habits, and could only distrust the grace and good sense of Latin Catholic life!'

Later, after a failed conflict with a spiteful and petty-minded Irish nun, the Reverend Mother decides:

> The Irish liked themselves, and throve on their own psycho-logical chaos. It had been shown to be politically useless for an alien temperament to wrestle with them. Wrongheaded, vengeful, even by the long view stupid they might often seem, and apparently defeated – but on their own ground in some mystically arrogant wild way they were perpetual victors ... They were an ancient, martyred race, and of great importance to themselves ...

Kate O'Brien frequently employed an outsider's view to show up the less likeable facets of Irish life. French Angèle in *The Last of Summer* is dismayed by the 'cold fanaticism' of a display of Irish dancing. Old Miss Robertson, Anna's suffragette friend in *The Land of Spices*, disapproves when a bishop expounds the virtues of the nationalist youth movement 'Sinn Fein' by telling her, 'It means "ourselves".' To which the spirited Miss Robertson replies, 'It's an unattractive motto to give to young people.'

Kate O'Brien did not see these broadsides as an attack on her people but, like her feminism, as a crusade against those who would inhibit their development. The authorities understood this only too well and extracted vengeance by banning her work. Ostensibly, there was no bar on freedom of speech in Ireland, so *The Land of Spices* – one of her finest and most moral works – was banned for lewdness on the basis of a single line where an act of intimacy is described with such delicacy as to seem almost Victorian: 'She saw [them],' O'Brien wrote, 'in the embrace of love.'

It was not the first time the author had fallen victim to a censor. When her first novel, *Without My Cloak*, came out, it was a source of great pride to her Aunt Fan, who was a nun in the Presentation Convent. Fan begged Kate's sister Nance for a copy, but Nance said it was not suitable reading for nuns. But she continued to plead and Nance gave her a copy, with certain pages pinned together and the warning: 'if you don't remove the pins you should be all right'. The elderly nun left the pins in place and thoroughly enjoyed the novel.

The author was greatly amused by the latter incident, which she recounted with relish in her memoir *Presentation Parlour*, but she was distressed and wounded by the official censorship, which affected her sales and effectively made her an outsider in her own country.

And yet, in many ways, O'Brien *was* an outsider. 'To possess without being possessed,' she once wrote, 'is the gift an exile can take from a known place.'

'To possess without being possessed' might also have been a motif for her own life. A celebrated public figure, her private life remained extremely private. After a brief attempt at conventional marriage, she confronted her lesbianism, but so little is known of her relationships that survivors of her own family still debate as to whether Kate could really have been gay. Although she described herself as a Catholic-Agnostic, long years of convent life (and the fact that two of her favourite aunts were nuns) left her with a yearning for a life of perfection. She would probably have shared the rationalist Dr Curran's approval of religious practice in *The Ante-Room*: 'Religion exacts a soul of every man.' One of her acquaintances once said: 'What she really wanted most in life was to be a Reverend Mother.'

It may have been this private aspiration that thwarted her more public one. Kate O'Brien fell just short of being a great writer. Too polemical to let her books ever fully take flight, she was also too intellectually arrogant. She must have been an editor's nightmare. Large chunks of untranslated French and German punctuate *The Land of Spices*, yet this elegantly wrought novel is very close to a work of art. There is an enviable precision with ordinary emotions, as when little Anna is visited by her mother at boarding school: 'Anna stared contentedly up into a face which was, as it happened, pretty, but which was for her beyond qualification. It was Mother, and through it shone the images of fixity, the things that always were, and did not have to be mastered.' And the author accepted, as all great artists do, the role of the flawed in the scheme of perfection. Attempting to understand Pilar, a beautiful but frivolous South American student, Anna Murphy suddenly comes to a point of revelation, perceiving her as 'a motive in art'. By this understanding of how ordinary beauty is transformed by contemplation, Anna is herself saved from ordinariness. It is a wonderful moment in a book that is as delicate and as practical as a china cup.

PAULA MCLAIN
ON
MARY MCCARTHY

The Company She Keeps (1942)

First Virago edition 2011

Mary McCarthy was born in 1912 in Seattle. She was a short-story writer, bestselling novelist, essayist and a social and art critic. Her books include *The Company She Keeps*, *Memoirs of a Catholic Girlhood*, *The Stones of Florence* and *The Group*, which remained on the *New York Times* bestseller list for almost two years. She was a member of the National Institute of Arts and Letters and won the National Medal for Literature and the Edward MacDowell Medal. She died in 1989.

Paula McLain received an MFA in poetry from the University of Michigan and has been awarded fellowships from Yaddo, the MacDowell Colony, and the National Endowment for the Arts. She is the author of two collections of poetry, as well as a memoir, *Like Family*. Her novels include *The Paris Wife*, *Circling the Sun* and *Love and Ruin*. She lives in Cleveland with her family.

In her long and fruitful career in the world of letters, Mary McCarthy published seven novels, two collections of stories, three memoirs, two travel books, and nearly a dozen volumes of essays and criticism on art, culture and politics. Her best known work is undoubtedly *The Group*, with many millions of copies in print since its publication in 1963 – and yet I don't believe any of her efforts matched the audacity, aplomb and sheer literary merit of *The Company She Keeps*.

When the book was first released in May 1942, it contained a provocative author's foreword (dropped in subsequent editions), an intimate personal history which shared titbits about McCarthy (her favourite writer was Shakespeare; her favourite literary character was Byron), and a photograph on the dust jacket that made McCarthy look like a Hollywood starlet; dewy-eyed and ethereal enough to rival Ingrid Bergman or Greta Garbo. The book became an overnight sensation, due in no small part to the fact that it was *sensational* – deliciously bold in both form and content. It also only very thinly disguised the author's own exploits and indiscretions, which, at least in certain New York circles, McCarthy was already quite famous for.

The *Bildungsroman* is an obvious course for a young novelist, and so it may little surprise the reader to learn that the milieu Margaret Sargent inhabits was infinitely familiar to McCarthy's. Both the author and her heroine leave Vassar for New York City in the early 30s and marry too young; both launch an unsteady career trafficking in words; both hobnob with intellectuals and political radicals, align themselves with Trotsky, and regularly upend their personal lives by careening into and out of affairs. The novel crackles with the veracity of these autobiographical details, but the surprise and unalloyed brilliance of *The Company She Keeps* is the shocking accuracy with which McCarthy portrays women's inmost lives. She gets to that place because she doesn't flinch or falter when piercing through the details she and Sargent have in common to expose the fear, shame and confusion they also share when confronting their own existence and choices.

From the earliest, McCarthy didn't shy away from using her own life as material for her fiction – quite the contrary. Like Ernest Hemingway, who made his scandalously autobiographical debut in 1926 with *The Sun Also Rises*, she pillaged the ruins of her own experience with an astonishing degree of brazenness, disregarding the wagging tongues of friends and enemies alike. Like Hemingway, she had a rare appetite for truth-telling and didn't flinch when she turned the sharpness of her perception on her own missteps. 'Perhaps I delude myself,' she once told her good friend Elizabeth Hardwick, 'but I don't find it so hard to be honest about myself.'

McCarthy's personal frankness set off a ripple effect. *The Company She Keeps* mined territory that had scarcely, if ever, appeared in women's literary fiction. It became the kind of book that women excitedly pressed on one another, and urged men to read as well, so they might understand something essential about the female experience. But along with the book's symbolic and talismanic appeal was the very sure understanding that McCarthy was a writer of great calibre. In an interview with McCarthy's biographer, Frances Kiernan, Norman Mailer describes discovering *The Company She Keeps* while a sophomore at Harvard: 'It was a consummate piece of work. It seemed so finished. And at the same time she was taking this risk. She was revealing herself in ways she never did again. She was letting herself be found out.' John Updike reacted similarly, saying: '[McCarthy's] fiction never got better than *The Company She Keeps*. Maybe it was too hard to get better than that.'

Undoubtedly, some of the novel's power derives from its precocity. McCarthy was only twenty-eight when she began working on the book, her first real attempt at fiction. She'd had success in editing and publishing since graduating from Vassar in 1933, and also in writing reviews for the *Nation* and the *New Republic*, but she didn't try her hand at imaginative writing until 1938, when her second husband, the critic Edmund Wilson, insisted she had a gift for it. Pushing her into a small guest bedroom in their rented house in Connecticut, he vowed she could come out only when she'd completed a story. Apparently this cruel and barbarous treatment was precisely the right formula for McCarthy. She typed the story out whole in one sitting and titled the piece – as you've no doubt already guessed – 'Cruel and Barbarous Treatment'.

Over the next several years, Wilson continued to prod from his side of the door and McCarthy continued to pen and publish – in *Harper's Bazaar*, the *Partisan Review* and the *Southern Review* – other stories. Collected, they became 'a novel in six parts', which was a startlingly original way for McCarthy to present her heroine, Margaret Sargent, who is also startlingly original.

When the novel opens, we know very little about Meg, not even her name. She is simply a Woman with a Secret, embroiled in an affair that will end her first marriage, and obsessed by the harrowing politics of just whom she should tell and when and why: 'Three times a week or oftener, at lunch or tea, she would let herself tremble thus on the edge of exquisite self-betrayal, involving her companions in a momentous game whose rules and whose risks only she herself knew.' The story moves forward in a kind of emotional striptease. Each stage of the affair is probed and scrutinized, as is Meg herself. Her penchant for dramatics, her frivolousness, her ego, and her proneness to self-deception are all mercilessly exposed, and in a tone so cool and arch one can't help but be reminded of Sylvia Plath at the very height of her powers, in poems like 'Daddy' or 'Lady Lazarus'. The effect is altogether brilliant and unsettling.

In 'Rogue's Gallery', we see a warmer and more appealing facet of Meg as she recalls the decidedly precarious time in her life when she worked as a stenographer for an enigmatic gallery owner, Mr Sheer. Hers is the strangest of jobs and Mr Sheer, living entirely by his wits, is the strangest of men, and yet our heroine remains an affectionate, loyal and utterly reliable employee. Our understanding of Meg becomes infinitely more complicated just as the novel shifts into its third and most penetrating segment, 'The Man in the Brooks Brothers Shirt', which finds her in a Pullman car with a married businessman from Cleveland. Here, as Meg surrenders to a one-night stand that leaves her baffled and deeply chagrined, her character becomes clearer and clearer, and so does McCarthy's ingenious structure. This is a portrait of accumulated angles – with each segment offering a fragmented and often highly refracted view of our heroine. Margaret throws her gaze on the men who've functioned dramatically in her life, her liaisons and entanglements, reducing them to types as a way of trying to understand their role and her own: 'the Young Man', 'the Genial Host', and 'the Intellectual'.

Two things become increasingly clear as the novel progresses.

The first is that Margaret is often most visible to us when she's looking elsewhere, and the second is that she's on a perpetual and rather painful quest for identity. This journey swings her as wildly and as nauseatingly as any carnival ride, and often drops her right back where she started, looking to others to tell her the truth about herself. When the Man in the Brooks Brothers Shirt declares, 'Seems to me . . . you're still in love with that husband of yours,' our heroine snaps to attention. Leaning forward, she asks, 'Do you think so really?' and is driven to wonder:

> Perhaps at last she had found him, the one she kept looking for, the one who could tell her what she was really like. For this she had gone to palmists and graphologists, hoping not for a dark man or a boat trip, but for some quick blaze of gypsy insight that would show her her own lineaments. If she once knew, she had no doubt that she could behave perfectly; it was merely a question of finding out.

In a similar moment in the final segment, 'Ghostly Father, I Confess', Margaret hangs 'ardently' on the words of her psychoanalyst as he lays out her life and choices to her, as he interprets them, 'very much the magician'. She reports the moment, but also pierces it cleanly, exposing both her own need and the analyst's inadequacy to the task: 'Behind him you could see Mesmer and then Cagliostro, the whole train of illusionists, divine, disreputable charlatans, who breathe on the lead coin, and, lo, it is purest gold. In spite of herself, she felt a little excited. Her hands trembled, her breathing quickened. She was ready for the mystery.'

'Ghostly Father, I Confess' functions as a keystone in the collection. Only here do we learn Margaret's back story and begin to see her whole, the product of a traumatic beginning – orphaned at six in the wake of the Influenza Epidemic, beaten and emotionally abused by a close relative – a childhood that bears an undeniable resemblance to McCarthy's own. At the end of the novel, Meg surrenders to the thin offerings of an analysis she doesn't have faith in, prays to a God she doesn't remotely believe in, and vows to stay in a marriage she knows is doomed, and all because she seems to have reached the end of her emotional resources. She can't fool herself any longer. Each of her emotional missteps floats clear of the morass and offers the same lesson: 'some failure in self-love' has obliged her 'to snatch blindly at the love of others, hoping to love herself through them, borrowing their feelings, as the moon borrowed light'.

In the end, our comprehension of Meg is realer and more poignant for the novel's partiality. To represent a life, we have only six fragments, each intensely coloured, primitive and singularly misshapen. Thinking about McCarthy's accomplishment here, I'm reminded of Picasso's first real experiment in Cubism, *Les Demoiselles d'Avignon*, a painting that was as revolutionary and disconcerting in his world as McCarthy's novel was in hers. Both works reject traditional perspective in favour of a complex multiplicity, as if each plane of their subjects' many faces could be visible simultaneously. The result, in both cases, is richer and more representative of the world (and women) we recognize – more terribly beautiful, and terribly, beautifully true.

DIANA ATHILL
ON
ELIZABETH BISHOP
AND
SENHORA AUGUSTO MARIO
CALDEIRA BRANT

The Diary of Helena Morley (1942)

First Virago edition 1981

Elizabeth Bishop was born in 1911. She was the Poet Laureate of the United States from 1949 to 1950. She enjoyed critical acclaim in her lifetime, and is considered one of the finest poets of the twentieth century. She died in 1979.

Senhora Augusto Mario Caldeira Brant was born in 1880 in Diamantina, Minas Gerais, Brazil to a British father and a Brazilian mother. Her girlhood diaries were first published in 1942 under the pseudonym Helena Morley. She died in 1970.

Diana Athill was born in 1917. She helped André Deutsch establish the publishing company that bore his name and worked as an editor at Deutsch for four decades. Athill's distinguished career is the subject of her acclaimed memoir *Stet*. Her other books include six further volumes of memoirs, *Instead of a Letter, After a Funeral, Yesterday Morning, Make Believe, Somewhere Towards the End, Alive, Alive Oh!*, a novel, *Don't Look at Me Like That!*, and a collection of letters, *Instead of a Book*. In January 2009, she won the Costa Biography Award for *Somewhere Towards the End* and was presented with an OBE. She lives in Highgate, London.

It seems impertinent to contribute to this book when it already has a wonderfully informative and engaging Introduction by the American poet, the late Elizabeth Bishop, who chose to translate it from the Portuguese because she had been so strongly charmed by it. But it was partly her Introduction that seduced me into the self-indulgence of appearing here: I love the book as a whole, Introduction and all, and I want to talk about it.

In the first place, I am a keen but usually frustrated traveller who has rarely enjoyed anything more than setting foot in places far away from, and utterly unlike, home, but has often been prevented from doing so by lack of both money and nerve. This makes vivid descriptions of such places valuable and exciting, and Bishop's description of Diamantina, the little mining town where the diary was written, is irresistible. It is rare for a poet to write prose as fine as her poetry, but Bishop does, and by that I do not mean that she writes 'poetical' prose. No: it is unobtrusive, exact, the result of a consuming and sympathetic interest in its subject rather than of a desire to be beautiful, and therefore it leaves one with an astonishingly clear picture of the highest town in Brazil, tiny, remote, perched in a wild, extremely strange landscape: a town that even today would be so troublesome to reach that I would never choose to make the journey even if I could. And of course it is impossible for anyone to visit it as it was between 1893 and 1895, when a skinny, freckled girl in her early teens was scribbling away, usually by candlelight, at her diary.

Except that thanks to that girl and to Elizabeth Bishop, we can. Through the eyes of the latter we can see it as it was almost sixty years ago (it changes slowly so is probably much the same today), and in the person of that girl we can live in it as it was half a century or so before that – whereupon it suddenly becomes not remote at all, much bigger ('the city' she sometimes calls it), the familiar setting for an everyday life which teems with family dramas, with dreadful miseries (her nickname at school was 'Stormy'), with jokes, with raptures, and with two kinds of interest: Helena's, in everything she encountered, and the reader's, in the often surprising details of that distant life – smoothing one's hair with chicken-fat, for example, or no one's owning a watch. Though quite soon those details begin to seem as natural as they were to the writer.

Much of the diary's charm comes from the fact that 'Helena', who chose an English pen name because her father was half English, was warmly embraced by, and embraced, the love of an extensive and uninhibited family. Because her parents were the poorest members of it their life was very hard, materially speaking. Mother and daughters washed their few clothes and their linen in the river, there was no mirror in the house, hunger was not unknown. Their poverty, however, seems to have been remarkably unoppressive, perhaps because everyone in Diamantina was poor. Everyone either dug, or sieved the river, for diamonds, and Helena's beloved father had little luck, not that she often mentions anyone else having it, either: local diamond 'mining' had become by then a matter of obsession rather than reward. But the atmosphere within her family was not bitter. It was warm, and people took pleasure in each other in spite of pulling no punches about each other's shortcomings.

Piety contributed to this warmth. The maternal grandmother, a central figure in their lives, who lifted them far above a sense of inferiority however poor they were, made a regular distribution of alms and took it for granted that she would continue to support a kitchenful of freed and mostly idle slaves. Aunts were always taking on and bringing up orphaned infants, whether black or white. Looking after babies was Helena's greatest joy, though this was more because she had a passion for them than as a Christian duty. She greatly admired 'good and holy' people, particularly her very devout mother, but she took a realistic view of her own virtue because 'I can't possibly stop being the way I am'. From time to time she became quite sceptical: 'Mama says that one shouldn't be joyful in Holy Week because it's the week of Jesus' sufferings. I believe firmly in other religious things but I don't believe that anyone should feel sad about Jesus' sufferings after so many years, and since He's already in heaven, resurrected and happy.' And she dismissed a good many of the current superstitions equally briskly. On the other hand, there were times when she believed fervently in the efficacy of prayer. I particularly admire the boldness with which she summoned this faith to her aid when she happened badly to need a new dress. She prayed to Our Lady for it, where-upon the idea came to her of taking a brooch of her mother's and selling it – an idea that would have been wicked if it hadn't been sent by the Virgin in answer to her prayer, which it obviously had been because she would never have hit on it by herself. And what was more, the holy origin of this idea was proved when the dress turned out beautiful and her mother, when told how she had got it, forgave her at once.

The reader becomes very fond of Helena, sometimes amused by her absurdities, sometimes impressed by her vigorous pragmatism, often touched by the generosity of her heart. It would have been sadly frustrating if, when the diary cuts off, she had disappeared at the age of fourteen and we had been left wondering what became of her.

Luckily she was still alive when Elizabeth Bishop was in Brazil, and they met. Even more pleasing than Bishop's account of Diamantina is her portrait of Dona Alice, stately but spirited wife of Doctor Augusto Mario Caldeira Brant who was, at that time, President of the Bank of Brazil for the second time. For all her wealth and high standing in Rio society, this grand and contented old lady is still clearly the girl we have come to know so well.

How one wishes that Bishop had been able to persuade the Brants to allow her to translate *all* of Helena's – of Dona Alice's – diary! It is understandable that a couple of their distinction and their age would think it thoroughly unseemly to have the details of their courtship published, but when we learn of the five proposals of marriage she had received by the time she was seventeen, and that she married Doctor Brant when she was eighteen and still writing, the thought of what she, with her eye for character and her outspoken lack of hypocrisy, must have made of all those rejected lovers, and of how her touching emotional directness would have responded when she began to fall in love herself . . . well it is impossible not to regret that propriety prevailed.

'I never did make Dr Brant show me the original manuscript,' Bishop wrote to a friend. 'I worried about it at first, but if you ever met the Brants you'd realize that they are incapable of *faking* anything, and probably the reasons he gave, like bad spelling and handwriting, for not showing it, were real ones . . . The Brants haven't the slightest idea of why the book is good – it's like dealing with primitive painters.' (I am reminded of something said to the Irish novelist Molly Keane by an aristocratic old neighbour of hers: 'I read your book, Molly, and I absolutely hated it, but I must admit that it's very well written. I didn't find a single spelling mistake.')

This absence of literary sophistication sometimes became trying to Bishop once she had met the couple, much as she liked them. There was even a moment of exasperation when she told a correspondent that she would never again undertake a translation without being sure the writer was 'good and dead'.* It is, nevertheless, what makes the diary so fascinating. To quote Bishop (because I couldn't put it better), the writing 'comes off the pages of the diary and turns to life again'. As does her own writing. What works in writing, whether naive or sophisticated, is first the seeing eye, then concentration on the thing seen (or being experienced and thought about) so intense that it leaves no room for self-consciousness. A nervous ambition to be 'literary' can hinder the shedding of self-consciousness in an unpractised writer, but it didn't do so in Helena, whose state of literary innocence was so complete that she was blessedly free of any such ambition. Her writing therefore carries us away out of our own lives into hers, so different, so surprising, often so funny and always, because of her company, so enjoyable.

Bishop suspected that Dr Brant had smuggled in the trite conclusion to Helena's own Preface to the diary, about happiness not depending on 'worldly goods' and so on, which does indeed sound rather unlike her. But for all its triteness, it is true, and the rest of Helena's writing demonstrates as much, in a way wholly un-trite and refreshing. To me it seems that is why it is so winning, and why I love it so enduringly.

---

* These references to Bishop's relationship with the Brants come from *One Art*, her selected letters, edited by Robert Giroux, published by Chatto & Windus.

MARINA LEWYCKA
ON
MONICA DICKENS

One Pair of Feet (1942)

First Virago edition 2013

Monica Dickens was born in 1915 into a well-to-do London family and was the great-granddaughter of Charles Dickens. Chafing against her background and having been expelled from St Paul's Girls' School, she trained as a domestic servant and her experiences inspired her first memoir, *One Pair of Hands*, published in 1939. She then turned to nursing, and produced *One Pair of Feet* in 1942. In the 1950s she moved to the US, and remained there for much of her life, writing and doing humanitarian work – she founded the US branch of the Samaritans – before returning to the UK in 1985. She died in 1992.

Marina Lewycka's first novel, *A Short History of Tractors in Ukrainian*, sold more than a million copies in the UK alone and was shortlisted for the Orange Prize, longlisted for the Man Booker and won the Bollinger Everyman Prize for Comic Fiction and the Waverton Good Read Award. Her other novels are *Two Caravans*, *We Are All Made of Glue*, *Various Pets Alive and Dead* and *The Lubetkin Legacy*. She lives in Sheffield.

One Pair of Feet, first published in 1942, has retained such freshness and appeal that with this new edition another generation of readers will be given the chance to be informed, amused and occasionally maddened by it all over again. Monica Dickens was propelled to literary fame with the runaway success of her first book, *One Pair of Hands*, which came out in 1939 when she was just twenty-four years old. It describes her life as a cook-general at the bottom of the pecking order in English upper-class households in Knightsbridge and gets much of its bite from the fact that although she herself came from the upper class and had even been presented at court as a debutante, she chose to go into service, and her accounts of petty tyranny and malice straddle both the 'upstairs' and the 'downstairs' worlds. *One Pair of Feet* returns to the same genre but on a different terrain, that of a public hospital during wartime, where Monica Dickens trained to become a nurse. Inevitably, the book, while still humorous and irreverent in tone, has many sombre notes, and gives a fascinating view of a society on the cusp of great social change, and a health system on the eve of the foundation of the NHS.

Monica Dickens was the great-granddaughter of Charles Dickens. But although this fact is referred to in every description of her, she made little mention of it, except later in life in relation to her charity work. She was born in London in 1915 into a prosperous family. Her father, Henry Charles Dickens, was a barrister, and her mother Fanny (née Runge) came from a distinguished German family. Monica was expelled from St Paul's Girls' School for throwing her school uniform off Hammersmith Bridge, and it was her rebellious spirit that prompted her decision to go into service, which must have seemed rash to her family and friends but in literary terms was a very shrewd move.

One Pair of Hands was followed by a semi-autobiographical novel, *Mariana*, published in 1940, and *One Pair of Feet* in 1942, which was released as the film *The Lamp Still Burns* the following year. Between 1939 and 1992 she wrote some thirty books for adults and thirteen for children, including the famous *Follyfoot* series. She also wrote numerous magazine articles and a regular column for *Woman's Own* that ran for twenty years, so she was one of the most prolific and popular authors of her generation. Her wide readership and frank opinions, wittily expressed, made her an influential figure in public discourse in the 1950s.

In 1951 Dickens married a US naval officer, Roy O. Stratton. The couple moved to America and adopted two children, but she continued to write, and to set her books in England. Her growing support for humanitarian causes informed much of her subsequent writing. Work with the National Society for the Prevention of Cruelty to Children inspired her novel *Kate and Emma* (1964), and many of her books for children, especially those about horses, evidence her concern for animal welfare. She was involved with the Samaritans in London, which was the basis of her acclaimed novel *The Listeners* (1970) and she helped to found the first American branch of the organisation. After her husband's death in 1985 she returned to England, where she lived in a cottage in Berkshire and continued to write until she died, on Christmas Day, 1992.

One Pair of Feet is the third book in this long, creative career, written when Dickens was just twenty-seven and more interested in observing the personal habits, fashions, and love-lives of her colleagues than in discussing the big political issues of the day. This is a large part of its appeal. Even the war stays firmly in the background, though it is always present, and was indeed the motivation that prompted her to apply for a career in nursing: 'One had got to be something; that was obvious. But what? It seemed that women, having been surplus for twenty years, were suddenly wanted in a hundred different places at once ... Men's jobs were open to women and trousers were selling like hot cakes in Kensington High Street.' Should this seem rather serious and worthy, she quickly qualifies her intentions in a much more frivolous vein:

The Services? I didn't think my hips would stand the cut of the skirt and I wasn't too sure about my legs in wool stockings ... Nursing? The idea had always attracted me, even in peace-time, but I suppose every girl goes through that. It's one of those adolescent phases, like wanting to be a nun. It was reading *Farewell to Arms*, I think, that finally decided me, though what sort of hospital allowed such goings on, I can't imagine. However, that was the last war. Then I saw Madeleine Carroll in *Vigil in the Night*, and that settled it. I was going to be a nurse in a pure white halo cap, and glide swiftly about with oxygen cylinders and, if necessary, give my life for a patient ...

Needless to say, the practicalities of nursing as described in *One Pair of Feet* offer few opportunities for gliding 'swiftly about in a pure white halo cap'. The experiences that communicate themselves most forcefully in the book are the crashing fatigue and the senselessly rigid hierarchy within the hospital. Nor do many of the patients she describes prompt a desire to self-sacrifice.

The relationships with her colleagues and patients are inevitably constrained within this hierarchy. Dickens has retained her youthful rebelliousness and pulls no punches when describing, for example, the absurd system whereby a junior nurse may not directly address a doctor, but instead must convey information via her ward sister, or the almost sadistic obsession with uniforms, inventories and timetables that some sisters impose on the ward nurses. The contradiction between personal life and the demands of the job is an important strand running through the book, not least when she has to make the decision about whether to continue her nursing career.

The structure of the book is episodic, as Dickens moves from ward to ward, each with its own strong characters – ward sister, patients, fellow nurses – and new dramas unfold and are resolved within a couple of chapters. Although there is no strong overarching narrative, after a while the book acquires the compulsive quality of a soap opera as Dickens's friendships and enmities with the other nurses and patients take on a life of their own. The tone is of a confiding and funny older sister letting us into her secrets; the scenes of ward life, gruesome medical procedures, snatched cigarettes (all the nurses, including Dickens, seem to smoke) and ghastly food are horribly evocative.

One of her particular skills is sketching vivid recognisable characters who come to life with a few well-chosen words and observations: 'She looked like one of those potatoes that people photograph and send to the papers because it bears a curious resemblance to a human face.' Her gossipy, confessional commentary never leaves us in any doubt about her own feelings and judgements regarding the people in her narrative, but she is disarmingly self-deprecating and humorously candid about her own shortcomings as a nurse, for instance when she responds to a surgeon's command 'Fetch me the proctoscope!' by dashing away and returning with the coat of the bewildered night porter.

Just as fascinating as the accounts of hospital life are the descriptions of the nurses' off-duty activities. Because of the war, great numbers of young men and women, soldiers and nurses, were dislocated from their familiar environment and out and about searching for love and romance on rainy nights in dismal pubs and dance halls far from home. Her account of breaking out of the nurses' hostel late at night to cycle down muddy lanes to a dance miles away must seem quaintly innocent to young women today: 'Chaps have got to be very cracking indeed to be worth bicycling through the rain for, even downhill.' On the excruciating humiliation of sitting around the edge of the room waiting to be asked to dance she comments: 'I wished I were a man. I would then have had a drink and gone home.'

There are many examples like this where it is evident that she is keenly aware of gender inequalities but accepts them. This is, after all, a book from an era that preceded the feminist challenge to the status quo. For example, the rigid gender demarcation between doctors and nurses is not questioned (though there is one woman doctor in the hospital, who gets little sympathy from Dickens) nor is the fact that, unlike doctors, nurses could not get married without giving up their profession. Towards the end of the book is a harrowing account of a young woman who is admitted following a botched abortion:

Poor Irene had wanted that baby, but had allowed herself to be persuaded by her young man to visit someone that a pal of a fellow he knew swore by. Before I was a nurse, I was not in favour of legal abortion. Now I think that anything would be preferable to some of the ghastly things that are perpetrated outside the law. If women could see what some of their sex have to go through in consequence, nightmare old women in basement flats would lose their trade.

Irene would lie turning her peaky little face from side to side, watching the women with their babies. She wouldn't be able to have one now.

In her ambiguous attitude towards the predicament of women, she is very much of her time, aware of inequality, but accepting it as given. There are also several instances of what would now be called racism that strike a discordant note for a modern reader: she does not hesitate to call someone a 'nigger' or to describe a Jewish patient as keening 'like the lost tribes of Israel'. But within the context of the book, these usages seem not so much offensive as dated. Class distinctions that now seem obscure and old-fashioned also permeate the book, as when she describes 'people who have guaranteed subscriptions at libraries and get their groceries from Harrods and give tennis parties with one court and eight people'.

Monica Dickens described herself as a writer who set out to entertain rather than instruct, yet this makes the text all the more affecting and endearing. For a present-day reader there is something quite poignant in her unawareness of the radical transformation that would soon sweep through the nation's health provision with the founding of the NHS, and the huge social changes that would blow away much of the deference and social hierarchy that she chafed against but took for granted in her writing. *One Pair of Feet* is not just a spirited and entertaining account of the training of a hospital nurse in wartime but a fascinating glimpse into a time and a culture so recent and yet so utterly changed.

CLAIRE MESSUD
ON
PATRICIA HIGHSMITH

Strangers on a Train (1950)

First Virago edition 2016

Patricia Highsmith was born in 1921 in Texas, and moved to
New York when she was six. Her first novel, *Strangers on a Train*,
was made into a classic film by Alfred Hitchcock in 1951. *The
Talented Mr Ripley*, published in 1955, introduced the fascinating
antihero Tom Ripley, and was made into an Academy Award-
winning film in 1999 by Anthony Minghella. Graham Greene
called Patricia Highsmith 'the poet of apprehension' and *The
Times* named her no. 1 in their list of the greatest ever crime
writers. Patricia Highsmith died in 1995.

Claire Messud is a recipient of Guggenheim and Radcliffe
Fellowships and the Strauss Living Award from the American
Academy of Arts and Letters. Her novels include *The Burning
Girl*, *The Woman Upstairs* and *The Emperor's Children*, which
was a *New York Times* bestseller. She lives in Cambridge,
Massachusetts, with her husband and children.

Patricia Highsmith was born Mary Patricia Plangman, in Fort Worth, Texas, in 1921. *Strangers on a Train*, her first novel, was published in 1950 when she was just twenty-nine, inaugurating one of the twentieth century's most illustrious crime-writing careers. She was admired by, among others, Graham Greene, who called her 'a writer who has created a world of her own – a world claustrophobic and irrational which we enter each time with a sense of personal danger'. As Geoffrey Hodgson observed in his obituary for the *Guardian* newspaper (5 February 1995), 'her novels have more to do with the murky, airless worlds of Dostoevsky and Kafka than with the cops and gangsters of the American tradition or with clever ladies and gentlemen of the English "Golden Age" of detective fiction. They are, it has been well said, not "who-dunnits" so much as "why-dunnits".'

Famously adapted for film by Alfred Hitchcock in 1951, *Strangers on a Train* remains – along with *The Talented Mr Ripley* and *Carol*, which was originally published as *The Price of Salt* in 1952, under a pseudonym, and adapted for film in 2015 – one of the best known and most widely read of Highsmith's twenty-two novels. Its themes (including doubles, homoerotic obsession, the insep-arability of love and hate, and of good and evil) set the tenor for much of Highsmith's oeuvre; and the novel demonstrates, from the first, her uncanny ability to draw an apparently ordinary character into the realm of shadowy, even murderous, compulsion, achieved through eerily vivid quotidian detail ('His step had a moist elastic sound on the dirt road.') and a sophisticated psychological understanding of her characters.

If this novel's overarching premise can be easily summarized, its protagonists, Guy Haines and Charles Anthony Bruno, are less readily pinned down. Each inhabits his neuroses and inconsistencies, and wallows in his own existential drama. Guy and Bruno – as the narrative generally refers to them – don't know one another before their chance encounter on a train. Guy, a rising young architect, is headed from New York to his hometown of Metcalf, Texas, for a difficult meeting with his estranged wife Miriam, from whom he wants a divorce; while Bruno, the gadabout ne'er-do-well son of a moneyed family on Long Island, is going to Santa Fe to meet his mother. Bruno – depicted from the first as a heavy drinker – is as insistent as he is unappealing. Through Guy's eyes, we first see his 'pallid, undersized face' with 'a huge pimple in the exact centre of his forehead', his 'stubby lashes' and 'grey bloodshot eyes'. When Guy feels the evening air to be 'like a smothering pillow', we understand that Bruno is the true source of his oppression, Bruno who rants on about his 'theory a person ought to do everything it's possible to do before he dies, and maybe die trying to do something that's really impossible'.

Bruno's *idée fixe*, it transpires, is that each of them, with only the most fragile of connections, should murder the other's nemesis, thereby orchestrating the perfect, motiveless crime: Guy wants to be rid of Miriam in order to marry his new girlfriend, the aristocratic and lovely Anne Faulkner; petulant Bruno wants to eliminate his father, nicknamed the Captain, who limits Bruno's access both to his adored mother and to his funds. Bruno proposes that he do away with Miriam, and that Guy should then kill

Bruno's father. Guy, repelled by Bruno and his suggestion, looks back the next day at their brief meeting and reflects,

> He seemed only a voice and a spirit now, the spirit of evil. All he despised, Guy thought, Bruno represented. All the things he would not want to be, Bruno was, or would become.

Bruno, on the other hand, with a stalker's zeal, feels overwhelming admiration for Guy – 'He recreated every word he could of his and Guy's conversation on the train. It brought Guy close to him. Guy, he considered, was the most worthy fellow he had ever met.' In what will prove a characteristically Highsmithian spirit of perversity, Bruno unilaterally undertakes the mission he has proposed, surely in part in order to ensure that the two men's lives will be intertwined. He travels to Metcalf, seeks out Miriam, and strangles her on an island at an amusement park.

This scene is one of the most memorable in Hitchcock's film, and is justly acclaimed; in the novel, it's unforgettably rendered, but in effectiveness is ultimately, and rightly, superseded by Highsmith's depiction of her characters' interior lives. Bruno reflects later upon Miriam's death, in the typically unstable exclamatory style that Highsmith grants him:

> People talked about the mystery of birth, of beginning life, but how explainable that was! Out of two live germ cells! What about the mystery of stopping life? Why should life stop because he held a girl's throat too tightly? What was life anyway – What did Miriam feel after he took his hands away? Where was she? No, he didn't believe in a life after death. She was stopped, and that was just the miracle.

From this gratuitous act, the novel's plot must inevitably unfold. In Highsmith's hands, the story is not simple melodrama (although it's that, too), but an exploration, both literal and metaphorical, of the symbiotic tension between the creative force of desire and the destructive force of death, between Eros and Thanatos, light and darkness.

In Bruno, we find the oddly contemporary horror of a privileged sociopath who combines great entitlement with scant talent, a man who, on his path to self-destruction, seeks not to journey alone, and selects his antithesis – an architect (literally, a builder) of extraordinary talent – as his companion. Bruno, a clear antecedent of Highsmith's infamous Thomas Ripley, would ideally want to devour and replace the object of his attentions: 'Bruno knew he would never have the things Guy had no matter how much money he had or what he did with it.' Murder is the most meaningful act he will ever undertake: 'Everything was silly compared to the night in Metcalf. Every person he knew was silly compared to Guy.'

In spite of Highsmith's careful portrait of Charles Bruno's unstable and unformed psyche, at some level he remains a pawn in her narrative. The novel begins with, ends with, and belongs to, Guy Haines. Upright, gifted and ambitious, he has always felt himself to be destined:

It was a kind of arrogance, perhaps, to believe so in one's destiny. But, on the other hand, who could be more genuinely humble than one who felt compelled to obey the laws of his own fate?

His need to create enables him to 'feel in harmony with God'; he believes that 'the creation of a building was a spiritual act'; and his ultimate fantasy is to build a 'white bridge with a span like an angel's wing', an intimation of the divine. Anne Faulkner, of whom he says to Bruno, 'Anne is like light to me', is both a help-meet and an inspiration. She is also his vehicle for social mobility, lifting Guy from his modest Southern origins into the heart of the Northeast establishment. Their married home in rural Connecticut, which he designs, the symbol of their union, is an almost magical vision: 'The house was long, low, and flat-roofed, as if alchemy had created it from the rock itself, like a crystal.'

At the novel's outset, Guy's enviable future stretches before him: he has only to marry Anne, and to set to work on an impressive commission in Palm Beach, Florida, called 'the Palmyra', that he expects will make his name. Only Miriam – who announces a pregnancy (by someone else) and threatens not to divorce him – stands in his way. Bruno's murder of Miriam, then, will prove both Guy's liberation, the making of his fortune, and his destruction: like Rumpelstiltskin, he wishes to exact from Guy a price from which the latter will never recover. And yet Guy, relieved of the burden of Miriam and free to create without impediment, now designs and builds his first perfect structure:

> The hospital annexe in Chicago had been ruined, Guy thought, by the cornice that was of darker stone than he had intended. But ... the Palmyra was going to be as perfect as his original conception, and Guy had never created anything before that he felt would be perfect.

On a metaphorical level, then, Bruno functions in the novel as the externalized manifestation of Guy's dark ambition. Ultimately, Guy comes to see Bruno as a part of himself:

But love and hate, [Guy] thought now, good and evil, lived side by side in the human heart, and not merely in differing proportions in one man and the next, but all good and all evil . . .

And Bruno, he and Bruno. Each was what the other had not chosen to be, the cast-off self, what he thought he hated but perhaps in reality loved.

Or again:

[Guy] was not anxious at all lest the police find him, had never been. The anxiety had always been within himself, a battle of himself against himself, so torturous he might have welcomed the law's intervention. Society's law was lax compared to the law of conscience.

The young Highsmith seems to ask what price an artist must be willing to pay for artistic freedom. Guy's tortured subterranean relationship with Bruno, like any pact with the Devil, takes its toll on his spirit and, above all, on his relationship with Anne. Even their wedding becomes fraught:

He was standing beside Anne, and Bruno was here with them, not an event, not a moment, but a condition, something that had always been and would always be. Bruno, himself, Anne. And the moving on the tracks. And the lifetime of moving on the tracks until death do us part, for that was the punishment. What more punishment was he looking for?

Bruno looms invisibly between them: Guy's fate. Highsmith structures the novel in such a way that much more is at stake for Guy than for the alcoholic Bruno. *Strangers on a Train* is specifically the novel of Guy Haines's undoing. (Tellingly, the trajectory of *The Talented Mr Ripley* is the inverse: we understand early on that Dickie Greenleaf, the 'good' guy, is doomed, and are instead preoccupied chiefly with the fate of Tom Ripley, the remorseless sociopath.)

What Charles Bruno and Guy Haines do have in common is a fervent resistance to the norm. At one point, Bruno cites a Vachel Lindsay poem, 'The Leaden-Eyed': 'Not that they die, but that they die like sheep' – upon which Bruno's reflects, passionately: 'He and Guy were not leaden-eyed. He and Guy would not die like sheep now. He and Guy would reap.' At the end of the novel, Bruno drunkenly asserts, 'Guy and I are superman!' The two men are divergent versions of Nietzsche's *Übermensch*, willfully separate from the herd, indifferent to society's laws: Guy first because he is an artist; Bruno because he is a murderer. They are unlike, of course; but not entirely so. And should Guy submit to Bruno's plan, they will be fully kin.

Dostoevsky, another of Highsmith's early influences, is powerfully present in this novel: Guy's experience, in particular, owes much to Raskolnikov. From Dostoevsky, perhaps, she learned to follow with minute precision a guilty character's anxious meanderings. From him, she also gets much more: the motif of doubles that recurs throughout her work; the idea of the resentful underground man who simultaneously hates, envies and admires the stronger person; and finally, Rasknolnikov's particular weakness of thinking the impossible, 'dangerous' idea which, once lodged in the mind, is impossible to dislodge.

Highsmith was terrific at coming up with murder plots, and at following them through in their gruesome particulars, flaws and all. She owes a debt, too, to Edgar Allan Poe and Wilkie Collins, as the novel's dénouement relies on the deceptively sleepy Arthur Gerard, Bruno's father's personal detective (I'm still trying to figure out what sort of person has a personal detective, and why). Gerard is as repulsive to Bruno as Bruno initially is to Guy:

> He lighted another of the cigars that were shaped something like his fat fingers, and Bruno noticed once more, with disgust, the gravy stains on the lapels of his fuzzy, light-brown suit and the ghastly marble-patterned tie. Every single thing about Gerard annoyed Bruno.

Unlike Alvin MacCarron, the ineffectual detective in *The Talented Mr Ripley* (again, hired by a protagonist's father), Gerard sees much more than Bruno, or even Guy, allows. We aren't privy to his work – the narrative adheres, with only a few exceptions, to Guy's or Bruno's points of view – but are instead simply informed of his almost super-human results. His appearance in the novel's final scene therefore has something of the *deus ex machina* (indeed, literally so: Gerard's voice emanates, unexpectedly, from the telephone line); but we understand that for Guy, at the last, Gerard's noose isn't unwelcome.

Jeanette Winterson, celebrating Joan Schenkar's biography of Highsmith, described the writer as 'as secretive as an oyster'. A woman with many lovers, most of them women, she took pleasure in the clandestine homosexual social life of her generation, and kept details of her own life secret when it served her to do so. For years, she denied having written the overtly lesbian *The Price of Salt,* and according to Schenkar, even called it a 'stinking' book. Apparently she forged, fabricated and altered where necessary, just like her antihero Ripley. She lied all the time – to her lovers, to her friends, to the tax authorities, to publishers, agents, journalists, and to posterity. [Winterson, *New York Times*, 16 December 2009]

Her fictional creations are often similarly duplicitous, just as they echo, in complex ways, her understanding of her sexuality. The homoerotic tie between her male characters is intense ('The bond between Guy and him now was closer than brotherhood. How many brothers liked their brothers as much as he liked Guy?' Bruno muses; and Guy reflects, when Bruno gives him the gift of several neckties, 'He might have been Bruno's lover, he thought suddenly, to whom Bruno had brought a present, a peace offering.'), but its associations aren't positive. In accordance with the prevalent thinking of her generation, homosexual tendencies in much of Highsmith's fiction are linked to perversion and criminal behaviour. That said, they're also allied with freedom and exuberance. In both cases, think of Tom Ripley.

Highsmith moved permanently to Europe in 1963, settling ultimately in Switzerland, where she led a private, not to say misanthropically hermetic, life. In addition to her complicated views of homosexuality, she was avowedly anti-feminist and accused women of 'whining', and was known, alas, in later life, for her vocal anti-Semitism and her discomfort with black people.

In spite of – or perhaps because of – these unsavoury reactionary traits, Highsmith explored in her work obsessive friendships and the blurred lines between fantasy and reality with what now seems something like prescience. In *Strangers on a Train*, as in many of her subsequent novels, Highsmith traces the ways in which tenuous and apparently fleeting connections can alter, intractably, the course of ordinary lives. Twenty years after her death, in the age of the internet, we live more consciously with the potential consequences of our random interactions: today's Charles Bruno and Guy Haines can – and do – meet anywhere, at any time. We have to trust that very few of the strangers we brush up against share Patricia Highsmith's dark imagination.

PENELOPE FITZGERALD
ON
ROSE MACAULAY

The World My Wilderness (1950)

First Virago edition 1988

Rose Macaulay was born in 1881 in Rugby, and educated in Oxford. She wrote her first novel, *Abbots Verney*, in 1905. She moved to London and in 1914 published her first book of poetry, *The Two Blind Countries*. In 1918 she met the novelist and former Catholic priest Gerald O'Donovan, the married man with whom she was to have an affair lasting until his death. Her last novel, *The Towers of Trebizond*, was awarded the James Tait Black Memorial Prize. She was appointed DBE shortly before her death in 1958.

Penelope Fitzgerald was one of the most elegant and distinctive voices in British fiction. Three of her novels, *The Bookshop*, *The Beginning of Spring* and *The Gate of Angels* were shortlisted for the Booker Prize. She won the prize in 1979 for *Offshore*. Her last novel, *The Blue Flower*, won the National Book Critics' Circle Award. She died in 2000, at the age of eighty-three.

Rose Macaulay was born in 1881, and died in 1958. As a young woman she went bathing by moonlight with Rupert Brooke, and she lived long enough to protest, as a well-known author and critic, against the invasion of Korea. *The World My Wilderness* was published in 1950, when she was thought to have given up fiction, not having written a novel for nearly ten years.

The book disturbed her readers, because it was not what they expected. The most successful of her early novels had been social satires. They were delightful to read, and still are, brilliantly clear-sighted without being malicious (or at least more malicious than necessary) but they took a detached view; humanity was so misguided that one must either laugh or cry, and Rose had felt it best to laugh. *The World My Wilderness* showed that the power of ridicule, after all, was not the most important gift she had.

Rose Macaulay herself was most characteristically English, tall, angular, and given to wearing flat tweed caps, or hats like tea cosies – English, too, in her gaiety and wit which, at heart, was melancholic. But almost any conclusion you came to about her would be wrong. From the ages of six to thirteen she had grown up with her brothers and sisters in a small fishing town on the Genoese coast, and this interlude of scrambling about the Mediterranean hills and foreshore was as important to her as all her English education. Again, Rose was often thought to be sexless, or, as Rosamond Lehmann put it, 'sexless though not unfeminine'. But in fact she had, at the age of thirty-six, fallen irretrievably in love with a married man, Gerald O'Donovan, and in spite of much heart-searching she never broke with her lover till the day of his death. Both these episodes have a good deal to do with the writing of *The World My Wilderness*.

The book's seventeen-year-old heroine Rose herself described as 'rather lost and strayed and derelict'. Barbary Deniston has grown up in wartime Occupied France, only half attended to by her worldly, sensual charmer of an English mother. This mother, Helen, has been divorced from Deniston, and her second husband, 'a thriving and amiable French collaborator', is dead. Meanwhile Barbary and her stepbrother have lived in and out of the house as children of the maquis, trained by the Resistance in sabotage and petty thieving. Like Auden's boy with a stone, Barbary has never heard of any world where promises were kept. When she is sent from her fishing village to the respectable Deniston relatives in London, she is doubly lost. Like seeking like, she escapes from pallid WC2 to join the drifters and scroungers in the bombed area round St Paul's, where shrubs and green creeping things ran about a broken city. 'Here, its cliffs and chasms and caves seemed to say, is your home; here you belong; you cannot get away, you do not wish to get away, for this is the maquis that lies about the margins of the wrecked world.' Ironically enough she begins housekeeping at once, tidying and cleaning the gaping ruins of a church. She is not a wanderer by nature, it is only that she needs a home that she can trust.

In Rose Macaulay's earlier novels, notably *Crewe Train* (1926) and *They Were Defeated* (1932), there are young girls of Barbary's sort, precociously adult, and yet clinging for reassurance to childhood. Many have names which could be either masculine or feminine (Denham, Julian, Evelyn), as though rejecting all society's definitions. All of them are unwilling exiles from some lost paradise. They remember sunshine and freedom, as Rose remembered her Italy. But in this story of the nineteen forties, the world that Barbary longs for and looks back to is a black-marketing France. The paradise itself is corrupt. And the civilisation to which she is packed off is an equally shabby affair. Deniston, the honourable man, is an odd man out in post-war London. His son Richie describes himself as a 'gentle, civilised, swindling crook', who by bending the law a little – as all his friends do – hopes to make himself a comfortable life. Barbary is no doubt right, on the beach at Collioure, to examine the word *civilisation* 'and to reject it, as if it were mentioned too late'. In any society, she will remain a barbarian. The novel's painful question is: what have we done to our children?

The war years had brought deep personal trouble to Rose. In 1939 she was responsible for a serious car crash in which her lover was injured. In 1941 her flat was bombed and she lost nearly everything she possessed. In 1942 Gerald O'Donovan died, and Rose entered her own waste land of remorse. How much could be forgotten, and how much could she forgive herself? In spite of this, or more probably because of it, she is more compassionate in this novel than in any other. To be self-satisfied, to be stupid, to be cruel (Rose had always said) is undesirable, if we are to consider ourselves civilised, but at the same time she was not at all easily shocked. Asked on one occasion by a question-master whether she would prefer death or dishonour she replied: 'Dishonour, every time.' And *The World My Wilderness* is remarkable for the pleas in mitigation she makes for all her characters. Helen has no conscience, it seems to have been left out of her, but she creates pleasure for others. Deniston is stiff, bland and resentful, but his integrity must count for something. Richie is a young aesthete who prefers to withdraw rather than to be too much involved, but then he has been fighting through three years of 'messy, noisy and barbaric war'. Mrs Cox, the housekeeper, can't distinguish – which of us can? – between interference and what, to her, are good intentions. Even Pamela, Deniston's second wife, wholesome tweedy Pamela ('all Pamela's clothes were good, and of the kind known as cheaper in the end') – Pamela the young committee-woman, not at all Rose's favourite kind of person, redeems herself by suffering with dignity. If there is a responsibility to judge these people the author is asking us to share it.

In the same way, every turn of the story brings a different confrontation, genial against sceptical, honourable against amoral, will against emotion, rough against smooth, wild against tamed. And these encounters, too, are left unresolved. In the closing chapters, for instance, Helen comes back to London. At the Denistons' house she takes command, a supremely inconvenient guest. Her motives, as we have to admit, are generous. But poor Pamela has to hold her own against the sumptuous intruder. The contest of possessiveness, jealousy, and genuine love is so finely balanced that most readers would be hard put to it to say exactly where their sympathies lie. Rose has written the novel in terms of comedy, but all the satirist's air of knowing what's best for everybody has gone. Indeed there is, perhaps, no 'best' for any of them.

Rose Macaulay liked to insist that ideas for novels came to her as places – 'backgrounds' would hardly be a strong enough word for them. In *The World My Wilderness* (if we take the 'respectable, smoke-dark houses' of London as a kind of negation of place) we have three of them – Collioure in the South of France, Arshaig in the western Highlands, and the wilderness itself. Each corresponds to its own moral climate. Collioure is described in the most seductive terms. 'The cool evening wind rustled in the cork forest, crept about the thymey maquis; the sea, drained of light, was a wash of blue shadow, sparked by the lights of fishing boats putting out for the night's catch.' By day, the Villa Fraises offers serene warmth and relaxation for all comers, but always with a hint of excess. The garden is 'crowded', Helen 'inclined to lounge her days away', the most striking of her pictures is 'a large nude who was a French mayor, reclining on a green sofa with a blue plate of strawberries in his hand; his flesh tones were superb'. Arshaig is equally beautiful, but austere, with misty dawns and steel-pale water, and at the shooting lodge are a whole family of Barbary's relations, 'formidably efficient at catching and killing Highland animals'. But in saying this Rose reminds us that there has also been killing and hunting – of men as well as animals – in the forests of Collioure, 'savageries without number', from the days of the Saracens to the Gestapo and the Resistance. And on the beach there Barbary and Raoul had stood watching the fish in the nets as they struggled, leaped and died.

Barbary herself becomes a creature of the wilderness, the ruins of the city of London. In 1950 the rubble was still lying where it had fallen, carpeted with weeds and inhabited by rats and nesting birds. The whole area fascinated Rose – how much, can be felt in the lyrical opening to Chapter 18. To her they were the new catacombs. 'I spent much of today in the ruins round St Paul's, which I like ... part of my new novel is laid in this wrecked scene,' she wrote to Gilbert Murray.* Many people must still remember, as I do, the alarming experience of scrambling after her that summer (she made no distinction of age on her expeditions) and keeping her spare form just in view as she shinned undaunted down a crater, or leaned, waving, through the smashed glass of

* Quoted in Constance Babington Smith, *Rose Macaulay* (1972)

some perilous window. Foxgloves, golden charlock and loosestrife were flourishing everywhere they could take root in the stones, but Rose did not sentimentalise over the wild flowers. It was not man's business, in her view, to abandon what he has won from nature. She was studying obliteration.

Descended from historians, trained as a historian herself, she makes the ruins into something more than a metaphor for Barbary's desolate state; they give the novel a dimension in time. They are still alive with the indignation of all the generations who have lived and done business in the city, or worshipped in its fallen churches. 'The ghosts of churches burnt in an earlier fire, St Olave's and St John Zachary's ... the ghosts of taverns where merchants and clerks had drunk' all haunt their old precincts, even under the midday sun, so do the long-dead clerics and shopkeepers themselves. When Barbary is on the run, the phantoms of five centuries of London crowd together to watch, from their vanished buildings, the pitiful end of the chase. They are not sympathetic, they want her caught. History, as might be expected, is on the side of authority.

At the end of the book Richie is seen alone on the brink of the 'wrecked scene', and the squalor in front of him makes him feel sick. He reflects that 'we are in rats' alley, where the dead men lost their bones', quoting *The Waste Land*, from which Rose took one of the novel's epigraphs (she wrote the first one herself). But *The Waste Land* is also a fitful quest for spiritual healing, and Richie, in the end, takes the track from Moorgate Station 'across the wilderness towards St Paul's'. This is one of several hints in the book of a religious solution, or, at least, of curiosity about one, even though Barbary and Raoul perceive that 'if there is anything, there must be hell. But one supposes that there is nothing.'

The World My Wilderness is, in fact, not a pessimist's

book – heartfelt, yes, but pessimistic, no. However faulty the main characters may be, there is one striking fact about them; their mistakes are not the result of caring nothing about each other, but of caring too much. It is because he still loves Helen that Deniston fails to forgive her, and Helen herself learns in the end not only how much she loves her daughter, but a way to help her. 'She must have sunshine, geniality, laughter, love; and if she goes to the devil she shall at least go happily, my poor little savage.' This is probably the best that Helen can do. And if the inhabitants of this earth, in spite of the mess, the slaughter and the desolation they cause, can give up so much for each other, they must be redeemable. In the last resort, Rose Macaulay thought so. And she was, as her novel shows, too much interested in human beings to lose faith in them.

MICHÈLE ROBERTS
ON
JANET FRAME

The Daylight and the Dust (1952–79)

First Virago edition 2010

Janet Frame was born in 1924. She was one of New Zealand's most distinguished writers, best known for her autobiography, which inspired Jane Campion's internationally acclaimed film, *An Angel at My Table*. She was also the author of twelve novels, five collections of short stories, two volumes of poetry and a children's book. Throughout her long career Janet Frame received every literary prize for which she was eligible in New Zealand, honorary membership of the American Academy of Arts and Letters and the Commonwealth Writers' Prize. She was appointed CBE in 1983, to the Order of New Zealand in 1990, and awarded honorary doctorates and medals from three New Zealand universities. She died in 2004.

Michèle Roberts is the author of fourteen highly acclaimed novels, including *The Walworth Beauty*, *The Looking Glass* and *Daughters of the House*, which won the WHSmith Literary Award and was shortlisted for the Booker Prize. *Ignorance* was longlisted for the Women's Prize for Fiction in 2013 and her memoir *Paper Houses* was BBC Radio 4's Book of the Week. She has also published poetry and short stories. Half English and half French, Michèle Roberts lives in south-east London.

Janet Frame was one of the greatest writers in English of the twentieth century. Her work shines and burns unstoppably.

This volume offers a comprehensive selection of her short stories. What are these stories about? I could say: childhood, New Zealand, memory, sex, death, art, imagination, suffering and loss. Human life; its mysteries and tragi-comedies.

It feels impossible to describe these stories: they are so perfectly themselves; simply give a sense of perfect rightness. You can't separate the stories from their subjects; you can't separate their form from their content. They are made of word patterns, and of the meanings of those word patterns created between author and reader. The meanings can't be abstracted from the stories. You have to be in the stories' presence to know them. You have to read them. So you don't need to read this introduction: you could just go straight to the stories. They are not difficult and they do not need explaining. Their art seems effortless; does not flaunt itself.

Perhaps this introduction can act like a friend enthusing over her favourite book and urging you to read it. Why should you? Why is Frame's work so good? What does 'good' mean?

The Russian poet Marina Tsvetaeva said that she knew if a poem was any good because she got a shiver up and down her spine when she read it. Janet Frame's stories, like those good poems, similarly provoke an effect of physical joy in the reader (this reader), a delighted recognition, both earthy and mindful, of beauty. We know beauty through what it does to us: it cracks us open, pierces us, makes us both smile and cry, enters and changes us. Our edges loosen and dissolve and we take it in. A sensual, thoughtful process, sense and thought not held separate but reintegrated through the experience of witness.

Frame's stories embody and offer a sense of bounding lightness. Clarity. Simplicity. Acute honesty. Shocking re-visioning of daily life and daily grammar and daily punctuation. No fear of what's called ugly. Flashes of catching what it is to be human.

Frame creates her own world and draws us into it. Both processes happen at the same time, thanks to our act of reading. The stories come alive as we read them and we make them come alive by reading them. The stories exist in time, as narratives flowing from one page to the next and yet simultaneously they shimmer outside time, in a sort of eternal present, bubbles of hallucinatory brightness.

The opening works here come from Frame's first book, *The Lagoon and Other Stories* (1952). The eponymous lagoon holds all the themes of Frame's early writing in its depths; slowly reveals them. Initially it offers a reflection of the narrator's image, captures the 'under-water moon, dim and secret', and then turns the world upside down, reversing time and adult concepts, reaching through memory back beyond death. The narrator's grandmother creates the lagoon through her magical stories:

> When my grandmother died all the Maoris at the Pa came to her funeral, for she was a friend of the Maoris, and her mother had been a Maori princess . . .
>
> See the lagoon, my grandmother would say. The dirty lagoon, full of drifting wood and seaweed and crabs' claws. It is dirty and sandy and smelly in summer . . .

I used to say Grandma tell me a story. About the Maori Pa ... About the lagoon.

The adult narrator re-possessed by her childhood self finally discovers the 'real', 'proper' story that has been concealed from her. Her aunt tells it to her, as 'the sort of story they put in *Truth*': lurid journalism plus photos. The narrator repudiates her aunt's 'interesting' story, stakes her claim for fiction involving unclear depth: 'I prefer Dostoevsky to *Truth*.'

Subsequent stories continue playing with this idea of adults and children re-creating the world through their own art or denying its complexity through clichés. In 'Keel and Kool' a mother out on a family picnic reads the section called Over the Teacups in her *Woman's Weekly* as a way of trying to blot out the pain of her little daughter's death:

A sad blow, people said, to lose your first, just when she was growing up to be a help to you. But it's all for the best and you have Wonderful Faith Mrs Todd, she's happier in another sphere, you wouldn't have wished it otherwise, and you've got her photo, it's always nice to have their photos. Bear up Mrs Todd.

Against this claptrap, Frame balances the surviving small daughter's struggling quest for understanding, expressed in her questioning words, fantasy, play and need to make things. Even as she explores culture, Winnie remains part of nature, still able to translate the seagulls' cries of 'keel' and 'kool', still able to be honest. She hangs on to her desire for an inclusive vision of the world that can weave everything together. Frame expresses this through her repetition of 'and':

She could smell the pine and hear the hush-hush of its branches and beyond that the rainy sound of the river, and see the shrivelled-up cones like little brown claws, and the grey sky like a tent with the wind blowing under it and puffing it out.

Death rips open this universe woven round as a nest. At the end of the story Winnie's acceptance of death and human loneliness comes staccato: 'there was no one to answer her. Only up in the sky there was a seagull as white as chalk, circling and crying Keel Keel Come home Kool . . . And Kool would never come, ever.'

The child's freedom to dream stands opposed to adults' constricting need to wrestle nature into shape, as in 'My Cousins Who Could Eat Cooked Turnips': 'Now where we lived there were turnips in the garden, some for the cow and some for us. We used to go into the garden, pull up a turnip, wash it under the garden tap and then eat the turnip raw.' At Auntie Dot's, where everyone is 'Cultured', vegetables come cooked:

it didn't seem to have the good earthy taste raw turnip had, and we weren't eating it outside down the garden with the cow looking approval over the fence and the birds singing in the orchard and people hammering and dogs barking and everything being alive and natural uncooked.

In 'Dossy', a little girl, named only as Dossy's friend, cherishes her surreal artist's logic:

and the little girl thought I'll be a nun some day and wear black and white and have a black and white nightie . . . and I'll have a black and white bed.

The child's imagination is extraordinary enough, even before we discover something far more unnerving, and before the comments of adults pigeonhole and reduce Dossy's capacity for play.

The unconventional combining of images marks many of the stories, as in 'The Day of the Sheep', when Nancy's calm rhythm of housework is disrupted by her anger and daydreams and also by the irruption of animal life:

> Scared muddy and heavy the sheep lumbers from the wash-house and then bolts up the path, out the half-open gate on to the street and then round the corner out of sight, with the people stopping to stare and say well I declare for you never see sheep in the street, only people.

If you read this out loud you hear vowels irrupting too, in sparky clashes and echoes of each other. Frame's method of mixing internal stream of consciousness and over-the-shoulder free indirect narration, first person and third person, smuggles sly humour into the story. It also, exhilaratingly, confuses and distorts our sense of other opposing categories such as past and present:

> A long time ago there were sheep (she remembers, pulling out the plug so the dirty blue water can gurgle away, what slime I must wash more often why is everything always dirty) sheep, and I walked behind them with bare feet on a hot dusty road, with the warm steamy nobbles of sheep dirt getting crushed between my toes.

The sentence continues wonderfully over nine lines, speeding towards the future, Nancy's longing to leave. These techniques of compression, condensation, distortion and surreal mixing all turn up in Frame's later stories. She experiments with allegories and fables, prose-poems, short pieces full and dense as novels, and speculative thought-pieces courageously striving against conventional logic and received wisdom. The final stories combine a slower narrative pace with all the acuity of the earlier narratives.

Frame's art demonstrates the value of destructiveness and violence in creativity. She tears apart linguistic shapes then recombines them into collages that are also narratives. Lightly and tenderly her prose holds her characters' discovery of death and loss. The only consolation for growing up, necessarily abandoning the vision of paradise, falling into time and into language, is to make something with that brokenness, to pick up and order words into patterns. From the past, lost, imaginary perfection of childhood, smashing through adults' imposed opposed concepts (then/now, me/you, good/bad, inside/outside), Janet Frame creates present, real perfection.

Michèle Roberts, 2010

SIMON RUSSELL BEALE
ON
MARY RENAULT

The Charioteer (1953)

First Virago edition 2013

Mary Renault was born in 1905 in London and educated at St Hugh's College, Oxford. Her first novel, *Purposes of Love*, was published in 1937. In 1948, after *North Face* won a MGM prize worth $150,000, she and her lifelong partner Julie Mullard emigrated to South Africa. There, Renault was able to write forthrightly about homosexual relationships for the first time – in her masterpiece, *The Charioteer* (1953), and then in her first historical novel, *The Last of the Wine* (1956). Renault's vivid novels set in the Ancient world brought her worldwide fame. In 2010 *Fire From Heaven* was shortlisted for the Lost Booker of 1970. She died in 1983.

Simon Russell Beale was educated at St Paul's Cathedral Choir School and Clifton College in Bristol. After graduating with a first in English from Cambridge University he began training as an opera singer before he turned to acting. He started his theatrical career at the Royal Court, and went on to the Royal Shakespeare Company for eight years. Since then, he has spent twenty years at the National Theatre. Not only has Russell Beale performed all over the world, he has also appeared in award-winning TV and film. Russell Beale has presented many BBC programmes about classical music. In 2003 he was appointed CBE in the Queen's Birthday Honours for his services to the Arts.

As I write this, the House of Commons is about to debate gay marriage. The front page of every serious newspaper is carrying the story. The first thing I heard this morning was a heated argument about the issue on the radio. Tempers seem to be running high and the Tories are tearing themselves apart, apparently. Our country is catching up, at last, following where others have led. Gay marriage was legalised last week in France.

I am now a little over fifty years old. During that half century, life for gay men in Britain has changed in ways that I could never have foreseen as a young man. I grew up in a world where the idea of love between two men was, at best, merely tolerated. For most of the time the subject was ignored. Since then, despite predictable and poisonous outbreaks of homophobia, the courage of activists has ensured that the age of consent is now the same as that for heterosexuals, discrimination in the workplace is outlawed and civil partnerships – more popular than anticipated – are an unexceptional part of our lives. Gay men now stand very nearly equal with their heterosexual brothers before the law.

As you have picked up this book – a recognised 'gay classic' – then I guess you might know all this. I mention it because gay politics and the tortuous fight for dignity and equality are inextricably linked in my mind to my first reading of Mary Renault. This, I hope, would have pleased her; because, in her quiet way, she played an heroic part in that fight. I arrived to live in London a sheltered, possibly even privileged, young man and, to be frank, the first years were hard. I had little money, I was unsure what career I wanted to pursue and the city, which I have since grown to love and will never leave, seemed confusing and often intimidating. I had long known that I was gay, a fact that didn't seem to bother my family or my friends, something for which I will always be grateful. Although I knew that I was loved by those I cared about, I felt unsteady; and this unsteadiness was about to be exacerbated, because what I and so many others could never have anticipated was the arrival and devastating impact of AIDS. I remember clearly a friend running into the sitting room of my flat one evening and shakily asking whether I had heard about a new disease that was killing gay men. That is how AIDS became defined in the popular consciousness for too long a time, as a curse with some curious moral agenda: the 'gay plague'. Faced with the deaths of so many, in appalling circumstances, the only viable and bravest reaction available to the gay community was defiance, a reassertion of their pride.

It was during this time of insecurity, of fear even, when so much physical and psychological damage was done and when so much needed to change, that I picked up my first Mary Renault novel, *Fire From Heaven*. Despite reading English at university, I tended to avoid novels and I admit that I looked down my nose at historical fiction. But Renault's telling of the story of Alexander the Great bewitched me. I fell in love with the central character and within months had read all I could find about him. Alexander remained in my mind as Renault had drawn him, however; he was fabulously good-looking, golden-haired, bright-eyed, quite literally smelling of roses, fearsomely honourable and capable of deep, unwavering love.

Even as I fell under this spell, I knew Renault's portrait was, in large part, fabricated. The cruelties of Alexander's world, the megalomania of the man himself, were swept aside, as Renault intended they should be, by a vision of light, heat, and physical and spiritual beauty. But there was something of value, it seemed to me, in this attempt – part of a long and noble tradition – to extract what was pure and fine in classical culture. Anyway, at a simple, visceral level, the picture of handsome men falling in love without guilt or shame was the perfect antidote to life in a city traumatized by the arrival of a hideous disease. I shamelessly grasped at the offer of escape while appreciating too the historically accurate arguments the writer explored, about leadership, loyalty and the thirst for glory.

Renault wrote three novels about Alexander the Great and he appears as a shining hope in the final pages of a fourth, *The Mask of Apollo*. Recreating the Ancient world allows Renault the freedom to portray homosexual love as part of the unquestioned order of things, a possibility without judgemental baggage. In contrast, *The Charioteer*, a novel set during the Second World War, presents us with a more unsettling read. Renault cannot avoid confronting the prejudices that any gay man must have encountered during the war years, although she clings magnificently to her vision of a strong, ideal love. Compared to the lighter, racing style of the Alexander trilogy, the language of *The Charioteer* can seem convoluted as the writer negotiates her way through the psychological intricacies of the protagonist's development.

This intricacy, the care taken, is unsurprising if we take into account the world in which Renault was working – that sombre, twilit world of the early 1950s, when so much of homosexual life was thread through with fear of exposure and punishment. It is a small miracle that Renault, described by her biographer Michael Sweetman as a 'bookish, suburban girl', should write such an explosive and courageous book and this may be indicative that, perhaps as a result of a catastrophic world war, attitudes were beginning to change.

Not that this change was easy to spot. Renault's American publishers refused to bring out the novel for fear of prosecution and, in 1953, the year in which *The Charioteer* appeared in Britain, President Eisenhower's administration barred homosexuals from federal posts, the link between perceived sexual deviance and treason being an important focus for a new, paranoid orthodoxy. There were worries too about the reaction of Renault's loyal readership. She hadn't brought out anything for five years and this story – the last contemporary one she would write before her exploration of the remote magic of the classical world and her first to follow directly the fortunes of gay men – might take them by surprise. As it happened, these worries were groundless. Indeed, the sympathetic portrayal of homosexual men proved something of a winning formula and it was one which Renault would use again and again. There was even guarded support from the Church of England's official newspaper in its review of the novel.

As in other stories about a young man's sentimental education, the reader is asked to bear witness to the pursuit and definition of an individual, workable moral code. But here, this cannot be done without acknowledging, however delicately, the opinions of a wider world. There are plenty of sharply written portraits in the book – Laurie's pompous new stepfather, a proselytizing old lady – that give some indication as to how others may see and judge homosexuality. There is also a sad and uncomfortable scene where Laurie comforts a young boy and is suddenly acutely aware that his actions may be misinterpreted – a situation that rings true for many men today. Despite Renault's writing one particularly fine speech of passionate justification, there are moments when she allows Laurie to reveal himself to be, if not prejudiced, then at least censorious. It seems clear to me that, despite the fact that the legal implications of a homosexual life are barely mentioned, the careful writing and the opaque nature of some of the arguments are symptomatic of a degree of conflict.

The most memorable display of unease is when Laurie, our hero and a man whose side we never leave throughout the story, analyses his fellow guests, all gay men, at a clandestine party:

> They were specialists. They had not merely accepted their limitations, as Laurie was ready to accept his ... They had identified themselves with their limitations; they were making a career of them. They had turned from all other reality, and curled up in them snugly, as in a womb.

This may or may not refer specifically to homosexuality, but it is a passage that rings with the harsh certainty of youth. Like so many gay men before and since, Laurie dislikes the idea of being defined principally by his sexuality. For him, being classified as 'queer' is not liberating but restrictive. As he says, it's about 'shutting you away, somehow; roping you off with a lot of people you don't feel much in common with'. He needs to find his own way. This is fair enough and, indeed, sounds the bass note of the book. As Laurie puts it, he wants to be 'loyal to his humanity'.

In truth, many of the men whom Laurie meets at the party – one of the central set-pieces of the novel – are unattractive. This quality is exacerbated by their high theatrical mode of speech, including infantilising nicknames, and conversation that is necessarily coded and often arch. There is also an attempted suicide, a crude and manipulative grab for attention, by a man who has tried this trick before, which could be interpreted by an unsympathetic reader as a wearying reassertion that gay men are necessarily unhappy. What saves the party, for us and for Laurie is, of course, the arrival of Ralph Lanyon.

Ralph is, at first glance, another Alexander; or at least that is how Laurie sees him. He even has the same fair hair, piercing eyes and athletic physique. When we first meet them together, at school, classical associations are already a fundamental part of their emotional vocabulary – unsurprisingly, given their education. Talking to Ralph, Laurie becomes dizzy with the possibility of experiencing what he has only read about:

> He was lifted into a kind of exalted dream, part loyalty, part hero-worship, all romance. Half-remembered images moved in it, the tents of Troy, the columns of Athens, David waiting in an olive grove for the sound of Jonathan's bow.

It is a template that cannot survive intact. If Ralph is Alexander, then he is an Alexander darkened and hardened by the realities of war. Even at school, there is a hint of something less than ideal: in Renault's tart description, the nineteen-year-old Ralph has 'the bleak courage of the self-disciplined neurotic'. There seems little compensating glory in Ralph's life. It is no accident that Renault sets her story in the aftermath of the heroic scramble of Dunkirk or that we spend much of our time with Laurie in a hospital ward, a world Renault knew well from personal experience. She has been a nurse herself and had tended wounded soldiers evacuated from Dunkirk.

Here is the aftermath of war, dreary and painful. Despite the appearance of conscientious objectors as hospital orderlies and the potential for hurt and aggression that this implies, there is precious little talk of heroism or even moral justification. The ward is too wrapped up in the daily grind of convalescence and the conscientious objectors are quickly seen to be men with an acceptable code of behaviour. The time Laurie, tired and damaged, spends in hospital is time spent in acknowledging and accepting hurt. In one marvellous passage, Renault writes: 'With a poignancy he had never felt during the half-stupefying agony on the beach, he was beset by a terrible consciousness of the world's ever-renewed, ever-varied, never-dying pain.'

It is Ralph, now wounded, but still possessed of a steely, private self-discipline, who transforms Laurie's half-drugged, unfocused life. It takes some time, but he teaches Laurie about the response to pain and imperfection, the ever-shifting pattern of regret, compassion and forgiveness. He is a fearsome teacher too. It is through the force of his will that he not only opens Laurie's eyes to the muddied world around him but also to the inevitable progress of their mutual love. After all, Laurie spends most of the book in love with someone else and whether he and Andrew, a gentle soul, are a match for Ralph's single-mindedness is a question that provides the central thrust of the story. We can only hope, as at the end of a great play, that emotional upheaval will lead to a peaceful resolution.

Just before he leaves school, Ralph hands Laurie a book, Plato's *Phaedrus*. Laurie keeps it close during the war and the book, now battered and bloodied, is with him in hospital. It features a charioteer, a mythic figure who, among other things, provides Renault with the title of her novel. He drives an unstable team of two horses – one black and scruffy, the other fine and white – and the powerful music of this image of conflict and possible resolution beats in Laurie's mind throughout his story. At the time of his giving Phaedrus to Laurie, Ralph dismisses it as 'just a nice idea' and warns him that it might give him 'illusions'. This is disingenuous, or perhaps, since the emotional temperature is high at this point, Ralph is avoiding inappropriate intimacy. The fact is, of course, that the works of classical culture have always been more than 'a nice idea', and for gay men of a certain period, class and education, they had a particular significance. They provided some guidance and comfort in an essentially hostile world and this book is a testament to that. It is, in its way, an historical gay document. Writing within an intellectual and emotional landscape that was then familiar, but the details of which are now fading, Renault wrote a powerful memorial to those gay men for whom the study of classical literature was an essential means to an examined and happy life.

AMANDA CRAIG

ON

REBECCA WEST

The Fountain Overflows (1956)

First Virago edition 1984

Rebecca West was born in 1892 in London. She began to appear in print in London as early as 1911 in *The Freewoman*, and was soon deeply involved in the causes of feminism and social reform. Her first book, *Henry James*, was published in 1916; she went on to write novels, criticism, satire, biography, travel and history. Her works of fiction include *The Return of the Soldier*, *The Judge*, *Harriet Hume*, *The Harsh Voice*, *The Thinking Reed*, *The Fountain Overflows*, *The Birds Fall Down* and *Sunflower*. She was appointed DBE in 1959. She died in 1983.

Amanda Craig is a British novelist, short-story writer and critic for newspapers such as the *Sunday Times*, *Observer*, *Daily Telegraph* and *Independent*. For over a decade, she was the children's critic for *The Times*. She still reviews children's books for the *New Statesman*, and literary fiction for the *Observer*, but is mostly a full-time novelist. Her novels include *Hearts And Minds*, which was longlisted for the Baileys Prize for Women's Fiction; *A Vicious Circle* and, in 2017, *The Lie of the Land*.

Troubled families have been a source of fiction ever since Greek tragedy, but *The Fountain Overflows* is one of the most interesting and engaging novels about childhood and family ever written. Of Rebecca West's fiction, only her first novel, *The Return of the Soldier*, is as well-known, and though both offer piercing insights into a dysfunctional marriage, *The Fountain Overflows* is unusual in that it charts a progress towards an unexpected harmony and hope.

Published in 1957, fifty years after the events it describes, *The Fountain Overflows* is the first part of an unfinished trilogy (including *This Real Night* and *Cousin Rosamund*, both published posthumously), but stands on its own as West's highly autobiographical account of an extraordinary childhood. Its subject is, above all, the difficulty of leading an artist's life, but what makes this unusual is that this struggle is seen not from the traditional literary point of view, a young man's, but from that of a child. Only Carson McCullers, another novelist preoccupied with outsiders, described it so well in *The Heart is a Lonely Hunter* – also, interestingly, from the perspective of a child musician. Our narrator, Rose, is one of four children in an unusual intellectual family. Their Papa, Piers Aubrey, is a brilliant and charming man who cares for nobody but himself. His gifts are confined to editing a small suburban newspaper, and any money he earns is gambled away on the Stock Exchange.

Yet far from being angry or resentful, his wife and children adore him. He is their hero and champion in a world whose rules they do not understand and feel defenceless before. Uncomplainingly, they adapt themselves to each new home, bringing with them their miserable scraps of furniture, including the worthless copies of family portraits which the children love. 'I suppose if one accumulates a great fortune all sorts of rags and bones get mixed with the diamonds and the nuggets,' Papa says, and the reverse also proves to be true. Yet the internal progress of the novel is to get the family to realise that the man in their midst, the 'shabby Prospero' whom they all revere, is almost worthless and definitely bad for them.

Rebecca West was the pseudonym of Cicely Isabel Fairfield, and her parents were as cultured and intellectually advanced as the Aubreys of the novel. They were also as beleaguered by money troubles and social stigma. Like the Fairfields, the Aubrey parents came from widely different backgrounds and so existed in a social no man's land. 'We are not part of any world,' Rose observes and, unusually for the period, the three sisters of the novel are expected to earn their living as musicians instead of getting married. 'Feminism ... was in the air, even in the nursery air,' Rose says, and it's clear that marriage is what has not only ruined their mother's career but has brought both parents into spheres alien to those into which they were born. Each parent could not be more different from the other: Papa is from aristocratic Anglo-Irish stock; Mamma is from intellectual, middle-class Edinburgh circles. He is a handsome, magnetic, charming, irresponsible journalist; she is plain, awkward, intelligent, devoted and formerly a world-famous concert pianist. West's mother was a talented amateur pianist (and sister of the celebrated composer and conductor Sir Alexander Mackenzie), and her father was a mercurial charmer who abandoned the family when West was eight, dying penniless and alone five years later; the agonies of their lives ring fresh and true in these pages.

The novel begins abruptly with 'There was such a long pause that I wondered whether my Mamma and my Papa were ever going to speak to one another again,' and although this is ascribed to each having 'fallen into a dream' rather than a quarrel it's immediately clear that, like a piece of Baroque music, this novel is about discord. Tolstoy's famous observation, 'Happy families are all alike; every unhappy family is unhappy in its own way,' is dramatised for us, because this is an unusual family – a kind of nightmare version of the sort depicted in *Little Women* and other Victorian and Edwardian children's classics where the father, even if condemned as a criminal (as in *The Railway Children*), proves himself to be noble and right. Here, though Rose's Papa is capable of generosity (as in the murder case he takes an interest in), he is, to the adult reader, a cheat and an adulterer, reliable only in his unreliability.

Children are acutely aware of people's looks, and the Aubrey young know that although their Mamma is 'not good-looking', their Papa 'was far handsomer than anybody else's'. Nor is it just his own family that is under his spell, for Piers Aubrey also exploits the adoration of grown men who follow his writing, his talks and his sneers with humble patience. When they are uprooted at the start of the story to Lovegrove (the paradisiacal home based on West's own childhood memories of 21 Streatham Place in South London, where the Fairfields lived from 1894 to 1898) they are captivated as much by his own memories of it as by what they find.

For the reader, the enchantment of this novel lies both in West's extraordinary insights into the condition of childhood and the way that, despite living in genteel poverty, their lives are rich with love, ideas and *things*. The making of perfect pork pies, the arrangement of inherited furniture, the awkwardness of veiled hats and the imaginative possibilities offered by their new home's stable are gone into with the kind of gorgeous attentiveness normally reserved for a children's novel. Above all, this is about the way that the mundane, material world fails to notice the wealth of the spiritual and artistic life. All the Aubreys have gifts, of music, beauty or (strangest of all) clairvoyance; West herself believed in the paranormal, and the extraordinary scene in which Mrs Aubrey rids her friend's home of a poltergeist is convincingly matter-of-fact.

Yet though well received, Rebecca West's sixth novel was less understood then than now. Here is Orville Prescott in the *New York Times*:

> The odd thing about Rebecca West's new novel, *The Fountain Overflows*, is that it could just as well have been written by someone else. This is her first novel in twenty years and, although it is clever and moderately entertaining in a leisurely fashion, it lacks entirely the diamond brilliance, the fierce intelligence and the incisive vigor of an obviously superior mind that we have learned to expect in any book by Rebecca West. There is a high level of professional literary competence in this story about the alarms and excursions of life in an artistic family, but there is no particular distinction and that theme is threadbare and shiny with use.

One may only marvel at the obtuseness of critics, because this portrait of life in an artistic family has certainly struck a chord with generations of subsequent readers. To anybody who experienced what it was like to grow up in a family influenced by the counter-culture of the 1960s and 1970s it rings particularly true; these days, when deracination is the norm, the Aubrey parents' different backgrounds and attitudes to family responsibility seem strikingly contemporary. Then, it was very different. Decades later, when West was interviewed by Marina Warner for the *Paris Review*, she said that, though perceived as disliking the heterodox, 'I hate being disapproved of.' She suffered a good deal both as a woman writer (saying she saw 'no advantages whatsoever' in being one) and as the mother of an illegitimate child by the novelist H. G. Wells. Despite being acclaimed, and ultimately damed, as the foremost woman of letters of her time, the social isolation of the Aubrey family seems to reflect the truth of her feelings about the pains of being an artist and an outsider in a conventional society: 'It's awful, I think they're horrid and silly, but I wish they liked me,' Rose confesses to her cousin about her school. The sufferings imposed by convention on the unconventional are often a source of pointed comedy in the novel. West has a gift for summing up monstrous Philistines and snobs, such as Aunt Theodora: 'Most adults are rude to children, and many rich people are rude to the poor ... so we were victims of a double assault,' Rose tells us. 'On entering our sitting-room she would say to Mamma, "Well, you're still here, I see," as if it surprised her that we had not been swept away into some abyss, which, however, might yet receive us.'

The darkness to which their Papa repeatedly returns, leaving his family to face his debtors, is contrasted with the warmth, colour and love of the home that their mother creates. Only in the family can they find the sympathy and nurture they crave. In addition, the music which is their religion is threatened both from without and from within when pretty Cordelia, the one child who shows no musical talent whatsoever, has her pretensions fostered by an equally talentless teacher. The excruciating scenes in which the pretentious, stupid Miss Beevor rebukes Mrs Aubrey, the true musical genius, for her reluctance to let Cordelia perform are exquisitely judged.

However, the Aubrey family have more resources than they realise. They discover the power of friendship, especially when Rose and Rosamund meet. The children's love for each other, though cross-hatched with irritability for Cordelia, is incarnate in their captivating little brother Richard Quin. They have faith that their abilities will rescue them, and they have charity. When their schoolfellow Nancy, the tiresome daughter of a murderess, is offered a home with them as a result of their parents' eccentric generosity, all the Aubreys realise that 'her mind was so poorly furnished' that she is an exemplar of the 'new barbarism, from a world where life was reduced to nothingness'. The confidence that comes from intellectual and spiritual riches is something that any serious reader will recognise: part of the joy of this novel is the way it champions those who love art, and who love one another, *contra mundum*.

A trenchant and witty feminist, West once summed up the difference between male and female sensibility as that between 'idiots and lunatics'. It is the unkempt, despised mother who, though she behaves like an idiot to their father, is the true heroine of this tale. It is her devotion to her children and her exacting musical standard that strengthen the twins in their determination to become professional musicians. In the course of the story, the twins do eventually find themselves part of the 'friendly tribe' of true musicians who will give them the companionship they have longed for. Yet the 'emaciated and shabby and nerve-jerked' Mamma is the one who triumphs, and protects them all.

You might expect, given the fairy-tale structure of three sisters (and Cordelia's ominous Shakespearean name), that it would be otherwise. West's love for her own harassed, gifted mother shines through every sentence.

Although *The Fountain Overflows* can be read as a fascinating period piece – Rose's descriptions of the first fountain pen to arrive in England and her first ride in a motor car are, like the huge feathered hats of servants, the light of gas lamps and the glamour of steam trains, vividly evoked – it is also a novel for all time. As she wrote in her memoir 'A Visit to My Grandmother', 'My work expresses an infatuation with human beings. I don't believe that to understand is necessarily to pardon, but I feel that to understand makes one forget that one cannot pardon.' The 'fountains of rage and pain' that she describes at the end of the novel are still with us, as a part of the human condition she spent her life exploring in so many different ways. Yet a fountain, whose function depends on a perfect balance between volume and vacuum, overflows only if something extraneous to it is placed in its waters; once the children's father is removed, the 'strong flood' of life can continue. The novel is one of those rare books that leave the reader feeling happier and more hopeful than before. As such, it displays precisely that 'particular distinction' that her critics failed to find.

HILARY MANTEL
ON
ELIZABETH TAYLOR

Angel (1957)

First Virago edition 1984

Elizabeth Taylor was born in 1912. She is increasingly being recognised as one of the best writers of the twentieth century. She wrote her first book, *At Mrs Lippincote's*, during the war while her husband was in the Royal Air Force, and this was followed by eleven further novels and a children's book, *Mossy Trotter*. Her short stories appeared in publications including *Vogue*, the *New Yorker* and *Harper's Bazaar*. She died in 1975.

Hilary Mantel is the author of thirteen books, including *A Place of Greater Safety*, *Beyond Black* and the memoir *Giving up the Ghost*. Her novel *Wolf Hall* and its sequel *Bring Up the Bodies* both won the Man Booker Prize – an unprecedented achievement.

I must begin with a confession. Although Angelica Deverell is not a real author, I feel as if I have read her books; and indeed, as if I have come dangerously close to writing them.

When I was a schoolchild of seven or eight, half-dead with boredom and frustration, and required to write a 'composition' by Sister Marie, I decided to enliven my ink-spattered page by writing not 'it was a fine day' or 'the sky was blue' but rather, 'the sky was a perfect azure'. Sister Marie called me out to the front of the class, eyed me suspiciously, read out loud the startling phrase, and slapped me. It was for making blots, she said. But really, I believed, she slapped me because she thought I was getting above myself.

I now think 'the sky was blue' would have been better; or no doubt the sky could have been left out of it altogether. But I was right in one respect. Sister Marie was acting as a social commentator, not a literary critic. One day it's azure sky, the next it's red revolution. When, as a precocious schoolgirl, Angelica is begged by her mother and aunt to 'say something in French' she chooses a stanza of 'La Marseillaise'. A rebel from a back street – though in search of a revolution in self-esteem, not in society – she is raising the bloody standard against boredom; against the crushing low expectations of her milieu; against the threat of living an ordinary life.

When I try to work out where I had picked up such an affectation as 'azure', I can walk without hesitation up to the attic in my grandmother's house, where there was a little cache of books – in effect, the only books in the house – which I read at lunch-times when I came home from school. These were precisely the kind of books which made Angelica Deverell rich and famous, but I don't know who, in fact, their authors were. The covers were greasy and blackened, the stitching frayed, the edges of the pages were mustard in colour, but the content was, as Angelica would say, 'coruscating' and possibly 'iridescent'. They were about upper-class gals with soaring spirits and unorthodox beauty – red hair, or 'auburn locks' featured. They were pining after some lost or unsuitable man, and on a collision course with their families and convention. Their backdrop was the hunting field, where they were dauntless under an azure sky. At dusk the ballroom awaited; but this was not the ballroom of the whispering virginal debut. They were beyond first-night nerves, beyond condescending to the disapproving rustle of dowagers' fans. These heroines moved through the scene at midnight, through the melancholy ruins of the buffet, on to the dazzling expanse of moonlit terrace, and stood alone, listening to the cry of ancestral peafowl (if no nightingale was available), while the orchestra played a last poignant waltz. I expect the gals dwindled into matrimony, but I don't remember the end of these books; I only remember forever beginning them, senses filled with the frou-frou of silk petticoats and the perfume of gardenias. It was all a great change from Enid Blyton.

Angel is a book in which an accomplished, deft and somewhat underrated writer has a great deal of fun at the expense of a crass, graceless and wildly overpaid one. Taylor is a writer of impeccable taste, while Angelica Deverell is a high priestess of schlock. Taylor excelled at the short-story form, where Angel, with her almost demonic energy, seems made for the epic. Taylor is quietly and devastatingly amusing, while her creation never makes a joke, and is upset and suspicious if anyone makes one in her vicinity. Taylor is observant, while Angelica never notices the life that goes on about her; for her, the only true reality is inside her head.

Born in 1912, and producing her stylish books for three decades after the Second World War, Elizabeth Taylor was not the sort of writer who lives so as to excite prospective biographers. A clever, formal restraint is the hallmark of her fiction, and though the compass of her works is restricted she has a formidable technique. All the same, what Taylor knows – and it is the one odd fact that ties her to her creation, and drives her book – is that good writers and bad writers, when they are talking about their art, sound remarkably the same. Their early struggles are the same. Their inner triumphs feel the same. The only way in which they differ is that the bad writers, once they get the initial breakthrough, usually make more money.

The phenomenon of Angelica Deverell illustrates the axiom that nobody ever went broke underestimating public taste. Nobody told Angel of this fact; she just instinctively knew it. She writes the books she wants to read herself. Her mind is passionate and commonplace, quick and shallow, and so she fulfils a perennial demand that readers make, to be 'taken out of themselves', to be 'transported'. From book to book, Angel does not learn; nor could you learn from her books. She switches her settings when she is jaded, picking up her characters from an Edwardian house party and putting them down in a banqueting hall in Ancient Athens, but she doesn't change her formula. When at last she does – when the demands of her ego override her instinctive knowledge of her market – then her royalties begin to dwindle. For any writer, good, bad or – as we mostly are – an ever-changing mixture of both, *Angel* provides a series of sharp lessons in humility.

The book begins in the last year of Queen Victoria's reign, in the red-brick terraces of the drab brewery town of Norley, where Angelica, the shopkeeper's daughter, having sulked and idled through fifteen years of existence, reveals to those about her that she is writing a book. Anyone who comes from an unbookish family, and who has made the same announcement, will vouch for what comes next. Her widowed mother and her aunt, a lady's maid, approach her with 'looks of bright resolve, as if they were visiting some relations in a lunatic-asylum'. They feel amazed, exposed and betrayed: 'Story-writing!' her aunt exclaims. 'Where's she got that from?'

Angel feels herself the rightful heir of a world from which she is excluded. Her aunt works just outside Norley at Paradise House, and Angel is named after the daughter of the family who employs her. Angel has spent much of her life, in fantasy, strolling the lawns and warming herself before the marble hearths. Yet 'fantasy' seems too weak a word for her sense of entitlement, her driven desire to warp reality by visualising it as different. Angel has a tyrannical imagination that excludes experience, even excludes the spirit of enquiry; she has no idea in which direction from Norley the real Paradise House lies, and on the one occasion she is invited to visit she dismisses the idea in a way that seems pettish but which is actually protective of her inner vision. Angel believes she has the right to impose her imagination on others. She tells her teacher that she spends her leisure hours playing the harp: when the woman looks dubious, Angel is angry because her private world has been slighted. But she is grimly accepting of knock-backs because she knows she is only biding her time. Her triumph will be to turn her fantasies loose, in all their devouring power: and make them pay.

Angel spends only one evening scribbling in an exercise book before she decides – in fact, she knows – that she has found her vocation, the only thing that will make her happy, and the only possible route out of Norley. We admire her tenacity, her robust self-starter's confidence, and we know she has some ability, in her florid way – enough style to make her schoolmistress nervously scan Ruskin and Pater before reluctantly concluding that Angel's homework is not plagiarised. But we fear for her when she bundles up her first torrid effort – 'The Lady Irania' – and sends it to the only publisher she has heard of, the Oxford University Press. But Angel is not cowed by rejection, and a little later she strikes lucky. Her manuscript lands on the desk of Theo Gilbright of Gilbright & Brace. Fascinated and appalled, he asks to meet the author.

Angel, who has never been away from Norley, sets off alone to London, and off goes the reader with her, heart thumping, through the wretchedly hot and dirty streets, to an alien building where she is given a cup of tea in what she hopes is Dresden china. Despite the derision of his partner, Theo is inclined to take a risk on the manuscript. But there must be a few changes, he suggests. Perhaps they might tone down the more risqué passages – Angel, who is as ignorant of convention as she is scornful of it, has made Lady Irania's virtue the prize in a card game. Perhaps certain domestic details could be refined; for instance, one does not need a corkscrew to open champagne.

'"So will you take away your manuscript for a while and see what you can do for us?"

"No," said Angel.'

It is the book's central moment – perfectly judged, and almost too painful to be funny. Angel marches out into the hostile streets, and weeps in the ladies' lavatories at Paddington Station. She should have given in, she thinks, compromised, because now she has lost what she most wanted in life. 'Yet still she felt something obdurate in herself, even in her state of frailty and defeat. It was a hard, physical pain in her breast, which might have been indigestion, but was vanity.'

But even as she is making her way home to Norley, Theo Gilbright is thinking, 'So are we to risk "Irania" as it stands, card-scene and all?'

The critics are savage; the public is ecstatic. Angel thinks the public is right and the critics are jealous. One bestseller follows another, and Angel is able to take her bright brave little mother away from the corner grocery – which was her solace as well as her living – and transplant her to an opulent new house in the suburbs. The minor characters are beautifully observed. There is Theo, harassed but unfailingly kind. There is Aunt Lottie, who quarrels in the spitefully genteel language of a lady's maid, and Lord Norley, the local grandee, who comes calling one day; possessor of a brewery fortune, he has a hazy idea that by taking tea with Angel he is paying his debt to culture. With him is his niece Nora, a 'poetess', who is enraptured by Angel – not just by her fame, but by her dramatic *jolie-laide* looks, her bony elegant body, the frailty that Angel has managed to conceal from everyone else. Lord Norley also brings his nephew Esmé, the pretty, treacherous waster who will become Angel's husband.

Angel buys him; he agrees to be bought. Esmé is Angel's opposite. He is a painter, his style observant and restrained, his taste advanced and original. But he works only sporadically, lacks tenacity, lacks courage, and he is easily diverted into days out at the racecourse, and expensive sexual adventures. A less subtle writer would have solicited our sympathy for Esmé, as altogether more human than the increasingly demanding and eccentric Angel, but Taylor allows us to understand that Esmé is not likeable and has no friends. We understand that real life, real relationships, will always be second-best to Angel. She cannot engage; she gives too much to fiction and has nothing left over for life. We foresee that when she at last comes to own the ruin that is Paradise House, she will, in restoring it to its old grandeur, build a prison for herself.

The last chapters of the book are melancholy, as Angel's public deserts her and Paradise House crumbles again. A cussed old lady, she survives to see the Second World War. All her scenes of glory are vanished; the harps as silent as the peafowl, the ball dresses turned back to rags, the Lady Irania just a bunch of old bones. But we feel that Elizabeth Taylor has allowed us a glimpse inside a peculiar but by no means unique psyche. Angel is self-deluded, at times almost deranged. She overrides the meek and the timid, she is callous in pursuit of the preservation of her glorified image of herself, and she is no admirer of 'human nature'. One could argue that the author is showing us Angel as an awful warning; that she is telling us 'this is how bad art is made'. But I don't think the book is as simple as that. It seems to me that what Elizabeth Taylor does is to de-romanticise the process of writing and show it to us close up, so that we are aware that if ten per cent of the process is exhilaration, the rest is tedium, backache and the fear of failure; that, whatever the impulse to art, however little or great the gift, a cast-iron vanity and a will to power are needed to sustain it. Writers are monsters, she is telling us; how else would you be reading this book?

ELIZABETH TAYLOR
ON
SETTING A SCENE

Sometimes, it seems odd to me that a part of my writing – setting a scene – that I think very important, is not an ingredient of the novels I love most – Jane Austen's and I. Compton-Burnett's. Their worlds are true and whole without scenery, their rooms are unfurnished, unless it happens that a piece of furniture is needed as an aid to the plot or situation. But for my sort of writing, whatever that may be, the background is part of the characters, and I confess that once or twice this has come to me first. Seeing a curious house, or walking through a strange street, I have begun to wonder what sort of people could live there and seeds of conjecture are sown, which may later begin to form into a story.

I am a great walker about strange streets and love to be alone in a town I have never visited before. When I was writing my last novel – *The Soul of Kindness* – I made several visits to a little old-fashioned Thames Estuary town – Towersey, in my novel. Most of the day, I walked round and about that place, or sat by the river. I looked for a house for my characters to live in (but didn't find one. I had to build a whole out of bits), I drank in the pubs where they would drink, and had awful teas in the awful teashops where they would meet. And I walked in the public gardens, and planned *their* walks there – the shabby chrysanthemums, the asphalt paths. 'There was a drinking-fountain of polished pink granite and a statue of a frock-coated town's benefactor – white and lumpy, like a thawing snowman, with green stains running out of his eye-sockets, and down his cheeks and dewlaps.' But I can't any longer remember if that were true – so much embroidery goes on.

I seldom, though, draw from a real model. My explorations store up a kaleidoscope of impressions in my head. They shift about and form their own patterns.

Once when I was out in the country, somewhere in the West of England, I saw a signpost pointing down a cart-track and it had the words 'To Paradise House only'. This for some reason gave me the strangest sensation. I didn't go down the track – now, years later, when I might venture to, I cannot remember where it was. But it became the Paradise House in *Angel* – a symbol of envy, attainment, decay. Here, Angel herself comes upon the house, and I am coming upon it, too – or rather, what I chose to imagine lying at the end of that leafy path. 'As they descended the slope into the valley, branches shut out the light and the vegetation was more lush; great ferns edged the rutted, grassy lane and there were leaves of a size she had never seen before. They tunnelled through dark foliage and came at last to a gateway. There was no longer a gate, but two posts and deer carved in stone surmounting them. The drive was mossy and the pony stumbled on rough flints that had broken the surface like the fins of sharks. Fir trees creaked and clashed their branches in the wind: there was a resinous, heavy smell and a continual commotion of rooks overhead

'"I think it is all rather eerie," Esmé said and he hunched up his shoulders and shivered. Eerie, said his echo.

'Then the trees parted and they drove into a cobbled space before some stables. They had come by a back entrance and the real drive lay ahead of them, a short avenue of lime-trees whose pale leaves had begun to fall over the tussocky grass. The house stood on a slight rise: a grey, Italianate façade with a broken balustrade. The stone above two of the windows had been blackened as if from a fire, and some of the dusty panes had stars of broken glass.'

I came to know all the rooms of that house, and its grounds. When I move characters from place to place, I like to go with them. I am rather like a ghost, unobserved; and *they* are the real ones at that moment.

There are some backgrounds I find especially, disturbingly evocative, I love places out-of-season, winter seaside resorts with everything shut down, a Greek island settling in for the winter. I enjoyed so much building the background for A *View of the Harbour* – an old-fashioned quayside emptied of visitors by the growth of a newer town nearby. Although no good at drawing, I tried to draw it. I knew where everything was – the lighthouse, the pub, the church, the waxworks, the café, the lifeboat-house, who lived in which house, and how their paths kept crossing in an intricate pattern. Because it is more compact than any place would be in real life, it seems more vivid to me. I see it rather as a film, with constantly shifting camera angles – much more so than any other of my books, which are static in comparison. Sometimes the harbour is viewed from a bedroom window, or from the jetty, through the eyes of an amateur painter doing his sketch of it, from the top of the hill by the church, from the lighthouse, and at the end by a yacht coming in from sea.

'As the yacht came into harbour, the view unclenched itself, the houses sank down tier after tier, the church-tower lowered itself behind the roofs, the lettering on the shop-fronts grew clear.'

I should like to be able to paint but, as in the case of the painter in the novel – the retired naval man, Bertram – I have no talent.

'Bertram had made a little sketch in water-colour, but was

dissatisfied with it. The sky looked as heavy as lead behind the two-dimensional church, the plaster peeled from the Mimosa Café in improbable shapes, the sea lay in a hard line against the wall.' And my painting would be as bad, or worse, so I have to try to do better with words.

Exaggeration is usually necessary if one is taking a picture from real life. I know that the big house from whose style my novel, *Palladian*, gets its title, was based on a much smaller house in which I once stayed. Really, in the end, they were quite unlike one another. By the time I had finished with it, building on lyre-shaped steps in front, running a gallery round the hall, erecting statues (even if broken ones) along the terrace, adding a wing here, out-buildings there, nothing remained of the original, but the fact that its pediment was not quite central and the conservatory was dangerous.

Many of my stories are set in the Thames Valley. I know it well. I have a distant view of it from my windows. It has been a part of my life since my childhood; but it rarely enchants me. It simply has a banal reality, which disturbs me. In some lights and conditions I find it depressing, and sometimes the smooth affluence of river-bank life oppresses me; but the reality remains. One drifts along in a boat and gazes at the houses one passes, and wonders about life going on in them. They seem, from the river, so very exposed. One can stare across lawns and hear the voices of people gathered on verandahs. Two of these houses are the settings of stories in the collection called *A Dedicated Man*.

Once I saw all of that familiar landscape submerged; the smooth lawns and flower-beds and shrubberies had disappeared under the flood water, and the stillness and the silence of that world haunted me. Soon after, from it grew the idea for 'The Thames Spread Out'. Although the story is about spiritual isolation, it came into my mind because I had felt the strangeness of the physical isolation of being cut off by flood. The water is a crisis. When it recedes, the heart is liberated.

And weather – the heat I tried to convey in *In a Summer Season* – that long hot summer we had, the hottest, it was said, for two hundred years. It was a singled-out summer for these characters – and for two of them their last. And I hoped the unusual weather would heighten the atmosphere, as I also tried to make it at the beginning of *A Wreath of Roses*.

'Afternoons seem unending on branch-line stations in England in summer time. The spiked shelter prints an unmoving shadow on the platform, geraniums blaze, whitewashed stones assault the eye. Such trains as come only add to the air of fantasy, to the idea of the scene being symbolic, or encountered at one level while suggesting another even more alienating.' This – I hope – hypnotic effect is shattered. 'With a collapsing sound, the signal dropped.' And, suddenly, a man jumped from the bridge before the oncoming express train. The afternoon was broken in two; the spell was shattered.

One knows a little, from some writers' own explanations and from other writers' patient researches (and none may be very reliable, since there is the time-lag between conception and birth) of where the germ of a novel took hold. In the Preface to *The Spoils of Poynton*, Henry James describes how the germ of that novel came to him, in conversation at a dinner party one Christmas Eve. The lady beside him gave him 'a casual hint' for that novel – 'a mere floating particle in the stream of talk'. This was enough for him. 'If one,' he writes, 'is given a hint at all designedly one is sure to be given too much; one's subject is in the merest grain, the speck of truth, of beauty, of reality, scarce visible to the common eye.' This was all he needed. This germ was enough, and he could make everything from it. He had no use for the rest of the story ('clumsy Life again at her stupid work').

Round the corner, with the next sentence, in the most unexpected place, some unexpected hint may come. There may be a signpost, pointing to 'Paradise House only', and the old process will begin over again. There is excitement in it.

ALI SMITH

ON

MURIEL SPARK

The Comforters (1957)

First Virago edition 2009

Muriel Spark was born in 1918. She wrote poetry, novels, children's books, radio plays, a comedy and biographies of nineteenth-century literary figures. She became internationally famous and received the Italia Prize, the James Tait Black Memorial Prize, the FNAC Prix Etranger and the Saltire Prize, among many others. She was elected an honorary member of the American Academy of Arts and Letters in 1978 and to L'Ordre des Arts et des Lettres in France in 1988, and was appointed DBE in 1993. She died in 2006.

Ali Smith was born in Inverness in 1962 and lives in Cambridge. She is the author of nine novels and five short story collections, as well as a re-telling of the myth of Antigone for young children.

In 1957, the year of first publication of *The Comforters*, angry young men were all the rage in literary Britain. Writers like John Wain, Colin Wilson, John Braine and John Osborne honed a documentary-realist art that by its fusion of kitchen-sink realism, fury and mundanity proclaimed itself authentic. Imagine a novel like this one, then, turning up at the post-war utilitarian realer-than-thou party, announcing a third of the way through itself something even more fundamentally 'true' than any literary realism – that it was, in fact, a novel, that 'at this point in the narrative, it might be as well to state that the characters in this novel are all fictitious, and do not refer to any living persons whatsoever'.

The Comforters was the first of the twenty-two novels Muriel Spark would write over nearly fifty years (she died in 2006), the first of what would become her recognisable but inimitable oeuvre of slim, intelligent, irreverent, aesthetically sophisticated, sometimes Hitchcockianly grim, always philosophically powerful works of fiction. Each of these – with a paradoxical lightness, and a sense of mixed resolution and unresolvedness which stealthily leaves its readers both satisfied and disturbed – would take to task its own contemporaneity and ask profound questions about art, life and belief. This first one went right to the source of metafictive metaphor – to the source of the novel form itself. 'Before I could square it with my literary conscience to write a novel, I had to work out a novel-writing process peculiar to myself, and moreover, perform this act within the very novel I proposed to write', she recalled much later, in the only volume of autobiography she wrote, *Curriculum Vitae*. 'I felt, too, that the novel as an art form was essentially a variation of a poem. I was convinced that any good novel, or indeed any composition which called for a constructional sense, was essentially an extension of poetry.'*

In a poem called 'Authors' Ghosts', written three years before she died, she celebrated the unruliness, the mystery, the vibrance held between the covers of books, even books a reader believes he or she already knows well, by imagining that 'authors' ghosts' must 'creep back' into houses every night, go to the bookshelves, and alter these fixed texts:

> Those authors put final, semi-final touches,
> Sometimes whole paragraphs.
>
> Whole pages are added, re-written, revised . . .
>
> How otherwise
> Explain the fact that maybe after years
> Have passed, the reader
> Picks up the book – But was it like that?
> I don't remember this . . . Where
> Did this ending come from?†

Back at the beginning of the 1950s, Spark's writing career had

---

* Muriel Spark, *Curriculum Vitae*, (London, Constable, 1992), p. 206.
† Muriel Spark, 'Authors' Ghosts', *All the Poems*, (Manchester, Carcanet, 2004), p. 13.

been kick-started by winning an *Observer* short-story contest with 'The Seraph and the Zambesi', which is about what happens when natural and supernatural collide – about a 'real' angel, who takes a rich and strange, paradoxically fixed but living form, and who turns up at a school nativity play and argues with its petty organisers about whose show it actually is.

> This was a living body. The most noticeable thing was its constancy; it seemed not to conform to the law of perspective, but remained the same size when I approached as when I withdrew. And altogether unlike other forms of life, it had a completed look. No part was undergoing a process; the outline lacked the signs of confusion and ferment which are commonly the sign of living things, and this was also the principle of its beauty.*

'I've always tried to make the supernatural into part of natural history,' Spark said in a 1997 interview in *Artforum* magazine. From the very beginning of her fiction-writing career until the end of her life, she was fascinated by the related disciplines and anarchies which go to make the life of art and the conduits between art, spirituality and reality. *The Comforters* was her first full-length foray into what would become unique Sparkian territory.

'Fiction to me is a kind of parable,' Spark said in the early 1960s. 'You have got to make up your mind it's not true. Some kind of truth emerges from it.'† From its opening paragraphs *The Comforters* is about the act of making things, and people, up,

---

* Muriel Spark, 'The Seraph and the Zambesi', *The Stories of Muriel Spark*, (London, Bodley Head, 1985), p. 81.
† Muriel Spark, 'My Conversion', *Twentieth Century*, (Autumn 1961), p. 63.

about how and why we make narrative, and about the 'kind of truth' which emerges from fiction. It opens with Louisa Jepp, Spark's delightful 'perpetual surprise' of a grandmother character, telling the baker things about her grandson, Laurence, which he, overhearing her voice, doesn't consider to be true. 'He won't eat white bread, one of his fads.' The charming Laurence shouts back his bantering disagreement.

So far, so mundane realism. But no trivial fact goes astray in *The Comforters*. Everything has meaning, sometimes annoyingly so, as its heroine, Caroline, later complains when she takes its 'author' to task: 'It's exactly as if someone were watching me closely, able to read my thoughts; it's as if the person was waiting to pounce on some insignificant thought or action in order to make it signify.'

Caroline is converting to Roman Catholicism, feeling isolated in her belief and finding the other converts she meets either maddeningly sheeplike and unintelligent or, like the beastly Mrs Georgina Hogg, whose religious impulse is all material, repulsive. Meanwhile there are hidden riches, it seems, in the mundane everyday realist bread, and Laurence is piecing clues together to prove a most unlikely story, about his sweet grandmother running 'a *gang* . . . maybe Communist spies'. But when Laurence asks too many questions of his grandmother's rather banal-seeming gentlemen callers, they worry, rather suspiciously, about him asking 'who we are, what we're doing here'.

Who are we? What are we doing here? The novel's heroine rents a flat in Kensington where other tenants knock on the wall if she's too noisy; in other words, she lives a life not unlike that of lots of heroines in British realist literary fiction. But Caroline, who is working on a book about the twentieth-century novel, *Form in the Modern Novel* ('I'm having difficulty with the chapter on realism'), is about to be subjected directly to the mystery of reality, when she starts being plagued by regular visits from an invisible being she names the Typing Ghost. The Typing Ghost interrupts her with sounds only Caroline can hear, of tapping typewriter keys and a voice that's both singular and plural, 'like one person speaking in several tones at once'. The voice insists on her fictionality, and that of everyone she knows. 'They speak in the past tense. They mock me.' Caroline is, understandably, a bit hurt to be told that her present-tense life is already a foregone conclusion, and that she isn't real.

Is it real, the voice? Is it a literary version of the Holy Ghost? Or, as all her supposedly helpful friends insist, is she 'imagining it all', suffering from a 'mild nervous disorder'? The hearing of voices is an age-old manifestation of saintliness, or madness. Caroline is no stranger to madness; she is, as it happens, piecing herself together after a breakdown, 'forming ... words in her mind to keep other words, other thoughts, from crowding in ... She had devised the technique in the British Museum Reading Room almost a year ago, at a time when her brain was like Guy Fawkes night, ideas cracking off in all directions, dark idiot-figures jumping around a fiery junk-heap in the centre'. But we know, as readers – because we've picked up the evidence, and because the Typing Ghost, since this is a novel after all, is every bit as 'real' as Caroline herself, and has Brechtianly unsettled our usual acquiescence to the prerequisites of the form – that Caroline, as a character, is full of good sense. We know this particularly because of the way she challenges the frightful non-character, Mrs Hogg (the first of Spark's holy devils, whose name, whose selfish pride and whose foulness are surely glittering references to James Hogg's nineteenth-century Scottish fable of the Calvinist elect, *The Private Memoirs and Confessions of a Justified Sinner*). *The*

Comforters is, after all, a book about the (quite literal) formation of character, and it's typical of Caroline's own character that she balks against the 'attempt being made to organize our lives into a convenient slick plot', wholeheartedly arguing with the Typing Ghost. 'It's a matter of asserting free will.'

It is all held so lightly, so playfully. But this paralleling of cheap smuggling mystery and Roman Catholic Mystery, this mischievous, merry challenge to British literary realism, this blatant parody of contemporary cold-war surveillance plotting and paranoia, becomes a life-and-death struggle in the end.

Spark, the European and international novelist, was 'certainly a writer of Scottish formation', as she put it herself.* Her upbringing was part Jewish, part Edinburgh Presbyterian; her childhood was spent in the genteel tenements of the Scottish capital, which, it could be said, gifted her a necessary objectivity, a 'constitutional exile'. Edinburgh was where she 'imbibed, through no particular mentor, but just by breathing the informed air of the place, its haughty and remote anarchism'.†

It never really helps to consider Spark's work autobiographically, though sometimes it can unearth an interesting anecdote or two. The narrator's voice in *The Comforters*, she made clear, was not her own voice. 'It's a character.'‡ She said this in a piece entitled 'My Conversion', one of the first of her considerations of her conversion to Roman Catholicism in her late thirties alongside what might be called her conversion at the same time from poet and critic to novelist.

---

* Spark quoted in *Muriel Spark* by Alan Bold, (London, Methuen, 1986), p. 26
† Muriel Spark, 'What Images Return', *Memoirs of a Modern Scotland*, edited by Karl Miller, (London, Faber, 1970), p. 153.
‡ Muriel Spark, 'My Conversion', p. 62.

But it's interesting that she was critically objective from the start, thinking the novel a rather low form compared to the precision of poetry; interesting, too, that when she was in her mid-twenties, her time working for the Foreign Office in the last years of the Second World War was 'in the dark field of Black Propaganda or Psychological Warfare', where she was part of a team tailoring and delivering a mix of 'detailed truth with believable lies' to German listeners, and where, quite surreally, the team learned much of what they needed by the surveillance method of bugging the trees above the paths where German prisoners of war walked and chatted.*

According to Spark herself, the notion of the Typing Ghost came from hallucinations she involuntarily gave herself by taking Dexedrine as an appetite suppressant in the mid-fifties, a time when she was overworking, converting to Catholicism, very poor and severely undernourished. As she relates it in *Curriculum Vitae*, she was working on a book about T. S. Eliot, when one night the text before her eyes mixed its words up by itself: 'They formed anagrams and crosswords. In a way, as long as this sensation lasted, I knew they were hallucinations. But I didn't connect them with the Dexedrine.' She decided a code must be built into the literature she was reading; the hallucinations lasted for three or four months, then simply stopped when she stopped taking Dexedrine. 'It is difficult to convey how absolutely fascinating that involuntary word-game was.'†

This blend of strange, puzzle-solving self-absorption and later objectivity produced the core metaphor for *The Comforters*: 'I could see that to create a character who suffered from verbal

* Muriel Spark, *Curriculum Vitae*, pp. 147–9.
† Ibid., p. 204.

illusions on the printed page would be clumsy. So I made my main character "hear" a typewriter with voices composing the novel itself.'*

'Is the world a lunatic asylum then? Are we all courteous maniacs discreetly making allowances for everyone else's derangement?' Caroline asks her friend, the Baron, one of her 'comforters'. This novel takes its title from the useless friends who comfort Job in the long Bible poem that considers the questions of human suffering and patience, the Book of Job, a text which Spark studied and wrote about in the fifties, and one to which she returned in her later fiction (particularly in her novel about terrorism and morality, *The Only Problem*, in 1984). Caroline's comforters in her suffering, like Job's, are convinced only of their own righteousness: Laurence is obsessed with the cheap smuggling plot; the Baron sees devils in the same silly way as Georgina Hogg 'hears' the Virgin Mary telling her which job to take.

But the Book of Job's real formal characteristic is its dialogue, which allows human and God to address each other, and *The Comforters* is a dialogue, too, a raging, vibrant argument held in a perfectly disciplined matrix, and a near-impossible blend, in the process, of subjectivity and objectivity. Probably the most exciting formal subtlety of the novel, carried off with such wit on Spark's part, is the way in which Caroline and the Typing Ghost pass beyond their loggerhead positions in a dialogue between character and form itself to an admittance of something much more fluid – to what you might call a compromise, even an interplay.

The early and middle parts of the novel reveal Caroline's hurt feelings at the Typing Ghost writing off her reality – and also the Ghost's hurt feelings at Caroline's criticisms of its lack of writerly

* Ibid., pp. 206–7.

talent. When Caroline challenges the Ghost's power as author and decides to go her own way, regardless of the plot, the Typing Ghost's vanity is ruffled. 'It was all very well for Caroline to hold out for what she wanted and what she didn't want in the way of a plot. All very well for her to resolve upon holding up the action. Easy enough for her to criticize.' The Ghost, peeved, spins the car in which Caroline is travelling off the road and breaks Caroline's leg – which, as it happens, does hold up the plot, even splits the book in two. Only Spark could so slyly, so hilariously, bend her form so as to have, on one page, her main character criticize her author for being too unimaginative to describe a hospital, then to follow it a page later with a full and unnecessary description of a hospital. If Caroline is hearing voices, then the voice is also hearing Caroline. Their working together is the novel's creative triumph, as well as a revelation of its final benignity.

Above all, the narrator's power is the ability to highlight time, to reveal the triviality of events themselves when contextualised by the long view: 'It was a hundred and thirty years after this event that Louisa was sitting down to breakfast with Laurence.' Throughout, it also draws attention to its own artifice; it makes its reader conscious of its own banality, its repeated structures. 'His mother told him repeatedly, "I've told you repeatedly, you are not to enter the maids' rooms."' By the time we reach the Typing Ghost, which declares itself to Caroline by its literal repetitions, this style is already embedded; in many ways the narrator is a joke, the narration a mocking of bad literary style – and, as we know by the end of the book, it's been the narrator all along having the joke, and not on us, but with us.

The Comforters is very much a book about what books do, about language and how we use it. It takes issue with empty media and literary and society chatter, it critiques empty-voiced

English cliché ('jolly good!', 'absolutely perfect!'); it opens the moral ear to codified social responses and their underlying truths and shamefulnesses, the unsayable beneath what's said out loud. With objectivity, the context assumes morality. What critics have called Spark's 'aesthetic of detachment' is really a Brechtian mode of connection.

In her address to the American Academy of Arts and Letters in the early seventies, Muriel Spark spoke about the importance of what she called 'the desegregation of art': 'The art and literature of sentiment and emotion, however beautiful in itself, however striking in its depiction of actuality, has to go. It cheats us into a sense of involvement with life and society, but in reality it is a segregated activity. In its place I advocate the arts of satire and ridicule.'* 'The art of ridicule,' she says, 'can penetrate to the marrow,' where 'pathetic depiction' only separates those who experience it from any real understanding. She imagines first a play which delivers its notions of suffering and violence via pathos, then its audience members, their 'moral responsibilities . . . sufficiently fulfilled by the emotions they have been induced to feel. A man may go to bed feeling less guilty after seeing such a play. He has undergone the experience of pity . . . Salt tears have gone bowling down his cheeks. He has had a good dinner. He is absolved, he sleeps well.'

Spark wants her readers to think rather than feel. A self-conscious work of aesthetic surface-tension, *The Comforters* involves its readers by revealing the mechanics of our involvement. It treats madness and evil with a disciplined, liberating lightness, in much the same way that Spark, throughout her

* Muriel Spark, *The Desegregation of Art*, (American Academy of Arts and Letters, New York, 1971), p. 24.

career, would liberate her readers from the vicissitudes of history and reality simply by redefining, each time, the terms of this 'reality'.

It's worth remembering the influence on her work of the Scottish Border Ballad form, a form where terrible things are reported with a dispassion that's almost merry; Sparkian dispassion, like Sparkian humour, is always a liberating device, and practically all of Spark's subsequent fiction has something of this novel's 'curious rejoicing' in it.

That this light, clever, mirthful *tour de force* was a first novel is astounding. But it was just the beginning of Spark's studies of authorship and authority, and of her dialogic explorations of the relationship between art, faith and life. It ends with its own genesis, neatly, like a good joke. It disrupts and charms its readers with its combination of wit, precision, intelligence and hilarity. As vibrant as ever, more than fifty years after its first appearance, it still knocks the stuffing out of the realist tradition, and probably always will.

LINDA GRANT
ON
BERYL BAINBRIDGE

Harriet Said (1958) and *A Weekend with Claude* (1967)

First Virago editions 2012

Beryl Bainbridge wrote eighteen novels, two travel books and five plays for stage and television. Shortlisted for the Booker Prize five times, she won literary awards including the Whitbread Prize and Author of the Year at the British Book Awards. Her novels *A Quiet Life* and *Sweet William* are also published by Virago. She died in July 2010. In 2011 the Booker Prize Foundation created a special prize, the Man Booker Best of Beryl, which was won by *Master Georgie*.

Linda Grant was born in Liverpool and now lives in London. She has published non-fiction and novels to great acclaim: *When I Lived in Modern Times* won the Orange Prize for Fiction; *Still Here* was longlisted for the Man Booker Prize; *The Clothes on Their Backs* won the South Bank Show Literature Award and was shortlisted for the Man Booker Prize; and *The Dark Circle* was shortlisted for the Baileys Prize. She is also the author of *We Had It So Good, Upstairs at the Party, Sexing the Millennium, Remind Me Who I Am Again, The People on the Street* and *The Thoughtful Dresser*.

I first met Beryl Bainbridge not at a literary party but in a minibus en route to Essex in 2002. Also present were her great friend Bernice Rubens, the biographer Michael Holroyd and our publisher Richard Beswick. We were driving to a day for library members to meet authors. At lunch, Beryl ate a few salad leaves and drank a third of a bottle of scotch, which did not appear to impair her in any way. I was perfectly well aware that I was in the presence of greatness. She was a novelist of a generation before mine, whom I had been reading since my early twenties. She had burst out of some territory where the English middle classes seldom went, and her books had nothing to do with sociology. There was a black heart to them, in a comic chest.

On our return, as we sat in the minibus in the car park waiting for the engine to start, Bernice announced that she was looking forward to getting home and having a cup of tea, which Beryl responded to by shouting, 'What a boring thing to say.' Beryl then turned to Michael and asked, 'Any nice soaps on tonight?' Anxious to make a contribution and a good impression, I pointed out that it was Saturday so it was *Brookside* day. Everyone brightened. The conversation turned to *EastEnders*, Kat Moon and sexual abuse; Michael confessed he had shed a tear the previous week. We all agreed that we liked soaps. We drove back into London; Beryl had no idea where she was but

seemed delighted by all of it. 'Look at the lovely fruit and vegetables,' she cried as we drove down Turnpike Lane.

Beryl and I both grew up in Liverpool, both of us were subject
to the then-fashionable elocution lessons intended to free us from
what were seen as the career limitations of our accents. But her
Liverpool was specific to her imagination: she remade it in her
own image. Bainbridge fans divide into those who prefer the later
historical novels and the ones who, like me, believe the earlier
books were where she revealed her genius. I was sorry when she
turned to real people, but she said herself in later life that she had
run out of her own experience to write about.

The chronology of her early work is a little confusing. *Harriet
Said . . .* was the first novel she wrote and submitted for publication, but it was rejected and did not appear until 1972. Her first
published novel, *A Weekend with Claude*, which appeared in 1967,
was later substantially revised and reissued in 1981, so this new
edition is not the one which its first readers saw. Neither of these
are apprentice works, there was nothing for her to be embarrassed
about; she was a fully formed writer from the start.

Harriet Said . . . is set just after the war in a Liverpool suburb
near the Formby sand dunes where Bainbridge grew up – an
unknown part of England, rarely visited, on the outskirts of the
port city. Two girls of around thirteen years old make their way
to the beach during the school holidays where they become
friends with a group of lonely, disappointed middle-aged men.
The degree of freedom the two girls are allowed is unimaginable
today, but reflects the day-to-day life of the war when enemies
were not strangers but aerial bombers, parents were focused on
the war effort on the home front and children were expected to
be self-reliant.

From the first chapter, we understand that there has been

'an incident'. The territory of sexual abuse of children has been worked so hard in fiction and memoir for the past decade or so that it is startling to see such an early novel which undermines what has come to seem a genre. The story turns out to be considerably more complicated than the usual kiddy fiddlers in the guise of uncles scenario. The unnamed narrator's friend is a girl who is knowing, clever and manipulative and with the chilling disdain and ignorance of youth for the complexities of adult life. The men are targeted, even groomed by the girls: 'We took to going for long walks over the shore, looking for people who by their chosen solitariness must have something to hide.'

Bainbridge understood the minds of young girls in the confusion of puberty, but she also understood, through acute observation, the men whose marriages, jobs, homes have led them to the beach, to look out to sea with hope, longing and despair, their backs against the land. Part of what they have lost is their own youth, life has slipped past under bowler hats and heads rested against antimacassars. They are lost and lonely, the girls encourage conversation. Harriet's friend wants to be admired by Mr Biggs, whom they call the Tsar.

The girls have a hunch that there is something in it for them, but they are not sure what it is. Perhaps it is just a desire for transgression; they are flirtatious and innocent at the same time. Harriet's friend is the weaker party, she appears merely to obey Harriet's instructions, but she leads one of the men on to destruction. When the novel was first offered for publication one editor found the characters too repulsive for fiction. Nearly half a century later, they still shock because of their subversion.

On the last page of *A Weekend with Claude*, a photograph is described in which a group of people are posed, two on the ground, a third scowling on a wrought-iron bench and a fourth, 'isolated, hunched ... not looking into the camera. The sun had gone behind a cloud. The three friends posed on, marooned in a summer garden.' Photographs like this, of strangers, incite tremendous curiosity. They freeze time in the moment before or just after a row, or a failed pass, or an opened letter imparting news. Even if we are in the pictures ourselves, we examine them and can no longer remember why one person is not smiling, or looking away, the faces seen only by the eye behind the camera.

Two people have come to buy a desk from Claude, an antiques dealer. They notice a photograph and a letter pushed into the back of a drawer, which Claude reclaims. He tells them a brief version of the story of the people in the picture, which is intercut with first-person accounts of the same events by Lily, Victorian Norman and Shebah. These very disparate characters in both age and background have come together for the weekend. Lily, who thinks she is pregnant by a boyfriend who has abandoned her, is determined to sleep with Edward and fool him into thinking he is the father of her baby.

Victorian Norman, so nicknamed because of the high collars he affects, is a working-class autodidact Communist. Lily has inherited a run-down house in Liverpool in which several of the characters seem to have lodged. She has, according to Victorian Norman, 'left home very early, in a wild stampede of open revolt, splintering in the process the whole framework of her background, so that now she is sad to find that she has nothing to return to but ruins'.

Shebah is a sixty-year-old former actress, tiny, Jewish, resentful and paranoid, filled with fantasies of her own persecution, in exile from her community: ' ... one of those people who once seen are never forgotten. She wears bright red lipstick and her upper lip is quite hairy. Most people refuse to walk down the street with her.'

Apart from Claude, the characters move in a tight orbit around each other, intent on their own minute sensations, grievances and plots for their advancement. It is a claustrophobic novel set in a year, 1960, when the sixties was still a date, not an era half-buried under social commentary. The poverty of the post-war years, of unfit houses filled with Victorian furniture, bathrooms before showers, sex before contraception, is a bleak dream-like glimpse into life on the undocumented margins.

On the novel's republication, the *Sunday Times* described Bainbridge's genius as lying in 'the comic evocation of the flat and mundane life in which her characters are in perpetual and ineffectual revolt'. The weekenders at Claude's might end up as the hopeless cases on the Formby shore thirty years later, tormented by juvenile girls in Spice Girls T-shirts. Beryl Bainbridge was original in detecting what was unusual in the ordinary and overlooked. She did not think like anyone else; perhaps her early years as an actress gave her a heightened sense of the dramatic, but she kept it under control by writing within a limited dimension. There was always comedy in those margins.

The last time I saw her was at the Booker Prize dinner in 2009. I did not know she was ill. She would struggle to complete her final novel, *The Girl in the Polka-dot Dress*, and she died a year later. Rereading these early novels, I realise that she was a great writer from the very start, often overlooked by prize judges, and part of neither a circle nor a movement. She was *sui generis*, one of the greatest.

JANE GARDAM

ON

BARBARA COMYNS

The Vet's Daughter (1959)

First Virago edition 1981

Barbara Comyns was born in 1909. She started writing fiction at the age of ten and her first novel, *Sisters by a River*, was published in 1947. She also worked in an advertising agency, a typewriting bureau, dealt in old cars and antique furniture, bred poodles, converted and let flats and exhibited pictures in the London Group. She was married first in 1931, to an artist, and for the second time in 1945. With her second husband she lived in Spain for eighteen years. She died in 1992.

Jane Gardam is the only writer to have been twice awarded the Whitbread/Costa Prize for Best Novel of the Year, for *The Queen of the Tambourine* and *The Hollow Land*. She also holds a Heywood Hill Literary Prize for a lifetime's contribution to the enjoyment of literature. She was appointed OBE in 2009. Her novels include *God on the Rocks*, which was shortlisted for the Booker Prize; *Faith Fox*; *The Flight of the Maidens*; the bestselling *Old Filth*, which was shortlisted for the Orange Prize; *The Man in the Wooden Hat*; and *Last Friends*. Jane Gardam was born in Yorkshire. She now lives in east Kent.

The Vet's Daughter is Barbara Comyns's fourth and most startling novel. Written in 1959 when she was fifty it is the first in which she shows mastery of the structures of a fast-moving narrative and a consistent backdrop to the ecstasies and agonies of the human condition. It was received with excitement, widely reviewed, praised by Graham Greene, reprinted, made into a play, serialised by the BBC, and adapted as a musical (called *The Clapham Wonder*) by Sandy Wilson of *The Boyfriend*.

But although the book has been kept in print by Virago since 1981 its reputation has faded, probably because the shock of the magical realism of its final chapter has been swamped by the tsunami of fantasy and magic that has almost engulfed the later reading world in the last twenty years. *The Vet's Daughter* is not about 'enchantment', it is about evil, the evil that can exist in the most humdrum people. Without being specifically feminist it describes the evil treatment of powerless Edwardian wives and daughters – a theme in several of her other novels – not as satire, like Stella Gibbons' *Cold Comfort Farm*, not meant to be funny or portentous but as a statement of fact.

Barbara Comyns, like Stella Gibbons, lived in a leafy London suburb for many years, though less quietly! I cannot now remember the year I met her in Twickenham. I lived in Wimbledon, and one morning I walked into the small and excellent private library on the high street where you could borrow a book for sixpence a week (ah, lost world!) and asked the erudite, formidable woman who owned it – we called her the Dong with the luminous nose – if she had any good new novels and she said: 'Certainly not. There hasn't been a good original English novel since *The Vet's Daughter*.' I said that I knew what she meant and she replied: 'So you should. She lives next door to you.'

This was not true for Barbara Comyns had moved by then to either Richmond or Twickenham. Earlier she had lived in Spain with her second husband. I find her movements as hard to track as those of her heroines and in some ways very like them: the adolescent marriages and escapes, the curious jobs, the poverty, the rescues, the bundled-up babies, the messy art-school Bohemianism, the fecklessness and the bravery. And the innocence.

However, the Dong had a telephone number and a young-sounding upper-class voice answered. She didn't ask who I was but she seemed delighted and said, 'Come to tea.' I asked, 'When?' and she said, 'Come this afternoon.'

The impetuous certainty is also like her early fictional heroines. Even in the depths of loneliness and rejection they make lightning and often very unwise decisions. They seem to stem from a perpetual curiosity, an inner observing eye that even death – and there are horrible deaths – can't conquer.

It is hard not to believe that Barbara Comyns's own adventures are entangled in her fiction. *Sisters by a River* which she wrote for her own children and *Our Spoons Came from Woolworths* read convincingly as strongly biographical. Ursula Holden states categorically in her Introduction to Virago's 1984 edition of '*Sisters*', as Comyns called it, 'The events in the book are true.' It is about a long-ago childhood of six siblings who grow up sometimes in heaven, sometimes in hell, always in a lovely landscape, controlled by a savage father and a deaf, distracted unfriendly mother.

When, much later, she published it, it was considered very shocking, but 'true'. Barbara was brought up in the Warwickshire countryside. There was little in the way of education and she was told that the family were poor. In fact the house was large, there were servants (though discontented ones) and beautiful gardens. The landscapes of *Sisters* come into *The Vet's Daughter* too but as a dream of someone else's childhood, the heroine, Alice's mother, who was spirited from its heaven into hell. It seems reasonable to identify this setting as Barbara Comyns's own but the beastliness of the father and the cruelty of the impossible mother are less so, especially as Barbara Comyns's own children do not remember their grandparents as anything of the sort. But it is, I think, true that in all her novels there is a girl seeking sanctuary and in some of them she finds it, often within another family in which she has been absorbed.

In *The Vet's Daughter* though there is no such comfort. The scenery changes. The girl is taken from the countryside to the drab streets of London's Clapham, married off to a monster. In time she tells her daughter of the fairyland world she had had to leave. Alice listens. She listens in the terrible house of her father the demon vet where creatures from the natural world are trapped and doomed. There is a sad little monkey who sits in the hearth wringing its hands (as Barbara's mother's fireside monkey is said to have done) and a screeching parrot inhabits the lavatory. The vivisectionist's rep calls weekly for unwanted puppies. Mother and daughter are helpless; the vet is the demon of fairy tale.

The sense of fairy tale is never far away in Barbara Comyns. Its childhood power never quite left her. In her late novel, *The Juniper Tree*, she writes on the fly-leaf: 'Adapted from a childhood fairy tale of the same name by the Brothers Grimm, which is far too macabre for adult reading' and, over the page:

My mother she killed me

My father he ate me
My sister, little Marlinchen,
Gathered my bones,
Tied them in a silken handkerchief,
Laid them beneath the juniper tree,
Kywitt, Kywitt, what a beautiful bird am I.

Whatever sort of writer was the author of such books?

When I met Barbara Comyns for tea that day in her cheerful house in Twickenham the sun was pouring in through all its bright windows. There was certainly nothing to suggest the macabre. She was merry and welcoming, and I think she was carrying a sweeping brush (when I wrote a short story about her much later I felt I had to give her a stave). She was dressed in light colours and her cheerful paintings – she seemed to think of herself as painter rather than writer – hung all around the hall. I knew that she had been a beauty in her youth for there is a film star-ish author photo on the back flap of one of her last, rather dull, novels *The House of Dolls*, where she looks like Vivien Leigh. The heroines in (I think) all her fiction are obviously – though she never says so – wildly attractive and one sees that she must have been too. They also seem to be attracted to the most terrible men, of all ages.

Her second marriage seems to have put things straight. The delightfully vague-sounding Richard Carr was a senior civil servant who worked in Whitehall.

As I was leaving, she said, 'I expect you've heard that my husband was a spy? He worked in Whitehall with Kim Philby. Oh,

Kim was a *delightful* man. So funny. Always here playing cards. Neither of us had a notion! When he disappeared – to Moscow, you know – they sacked my husband. They said that either he must have known and therefore was a traitor, or that he hadn't spotted it and therefore must have been a fool.'

Perhaps it was after Philby that the Comyns-Carrs went to live in Spain for eighteen years? One thinks of her cooking Spanish dishes – like her heroines she was an excellent cook – among the white almond trees. I feel sure that the terrible juniper tree had withered and died.

As it did, I think, at the end of *The Vet's Daughter* when Alice reached the very depths of unhappiness, without hope of escape or recourse to prayer or divine intervention, comes glorious new knowledge. It is not a promise that her suffering will result in an equal joy but it describes, without reference to a deity, the rapture of acceptance, the giving of the spirit into invisible, all-powerful hands. The gratitude for life itself.

I have no intention of revealing here what happens in the final chapter.

JULIE BURCHILL
ON
JACQUELINE SUSANN

Valley of the Dolls (1966)

First Virago edition 2003

Jacqueline Susann was born in 1918. She left her hometown of Philadelphia in her teens and moved to New York to become an actress. She won the Best Dressed Woman in Television award no fewer than four times. It was, however, the success of her three blockbuster novels – *Valley of the Dolls*, *The Love Machine* and *Once is Not Enough* – that transformed her into the Pucci-clad superstar we remember today, and provided the model for the woman's blockbuster novel. Susann wrote her books on a hot-pink IBM Selectric typewriter and was then the only writer to ever have three novels in a row hit number one on the *New York Times* bestseller list. She died in 1974.

Julie Burchill has written more than a dozen books, with the TV adaptation of one of them, *Sugar Rush*, winning an International Emmy. Her hobbies include spite, luncheon, philanthropy and learning Modern Hebrew. She is married and lives in Brighton.

She has been a journalist since the age of seventeen.

Unlike other things which seemed like a good idea at the time but are revealed as pure folly with the wisdom of age – lovebites and Trotskyism spring immediately to mind – books are becoming at any age. And the thrill of reading a particularly great one, though cheap, doesn't wear off; an old biddy gets the same kick out of the new Mary Wesley as a tot does out of *Can't You Sleep, Little Bear?* But most people have an especially soft spot for the first book they knew they weren't meant to be reading; the book you got your hot little hands on at eleven or twelve, and had to shove under the bed clothes PDQ when your mum put her head round the door to check on your virginal slumber. For earlier generations it may have been *Forever Amber* or *Peyton Place*, but for my generation, those lucky girls who came to maturity (or at least masturbation) on the shimmering sixties/seventies cusp, it was *Valley of the Dolls*.

For a start, what a title! Like *Lolita* and *Great Expectations*, a few tiny words printed in all innocence onto a stack of bound paper would come to cast a giant shadow over the English language, become a part of the frantic twentieth-century slang, the modern Morse instantly understood by millions who had never even seen the book. The Dolls of the title actually refer to the arcane showbiz slang for tranquillizers, uppers and sleeping pills which help the three young heroines – one a model, one a singer, one a sex-symbol and actress – smooth the jagged freeways to the top of their professions, but in the common imagination they have come to represent the actual women; women so bound up in sex and money and performance that they seem in themselves to be some sort of heady, rare narcotic. You can see their echo in the fan magazines of today, in Carmen's eyes, Angelina's lips and Jennifer's BTM; women at once goddess-like and all too human.

Valley of the Dolls can be enjoyed as the ultimate plush, trash human interest story – three decades of gossip columns distilled into one fat novel – but also as a document of some cultural interest, published as it was in 1966 but spanning the years from optimistic post-war 1945 to world-weary pre-deluge 1963. Kierkegaard's theorem that life can only be lived forwards and understood backwards has been used as an excuse to dignify a lot of silly, frivolous cultural frills and furbelows with far greater significance than they actually had – the miniskirt, Barbie dolls, atheism – but the sheer breadth and depth of this particular disco-ball gives it lasting clout. Significantly, it was written by that rare thing, the published novelist not castrated by an extended education (the not particularly talented or attractive Susann left school in Philadelphia at eighteen and went to New York City in order to become an actress, an experience from which she must have emerged, if not entered, in a suitably raw, hysterical state to write this hyperdrama) and thus truly able to write her book for the public rather than her peers and the critics. Hence her book is not a sixties feminist novel, thank God, in the tradition of such souped-up, dressed-down sob sisters as Doris Lessing, Margaret Drabble and Edna O'Brien, who also wrote of young women with an ambitious energy which, due to the stonking gender inequality of the time, they ended up frittering away on destructive love. She had a pizzazz and common touch they lacked. And neither was she a seen-it-all, elegantly shrugging jet-setter along the lines of Françoise Sagan and Jean Rhys, whose wild girls similarly ended up burnt out on the bonfire of romantic illusions. No, there is an indignance and real anger in Susann's writing, a refusal to use irony or education as a wet blanket which might tastefully mute the lurid flames of her outrage over something that is a cliché now but amounted to a denouncement of a good part of the American Dream at the time – the fact that women are valued briefly for their beauty, bought and sold like prime cattle in the meat markets of entertainment, and cast aside when inevitably mugged by gravity whereas men, even in showbusiness, are valued for the sum of their parts rather than some of their parts.

Susann's heroines never acknowledge feminism for the simple reason that, between 1945 and 1963, it just didn't exist; this was a time in which the most rebellious and high-flying job a woman could aspire to was that of air hostess, remember. But their lives, even as they strive and succeed in winning fame and fortune, are miserable because of the bad hand women have historically been dealt when it comes to the balance of power. And they are not shown as being the architects of their own misery for being ambitious; their mothers, traditional housewives who disapprove of their drive and believe that status comes only from making an upwardly mobile marriage, are shown as joyless, bitter parasites. In another subversive sideswipe, the principal men – you couldn't call them heroes – not even Susann's obvious swoon-object, the regrettably named English stud-muffin Lyon Burke – are uniformly vile, weak bullies.

Virtuous women are not rewarded in JackieWorld; the two decent, beautiful, irreproachably feminine heroines – Anne and Jennifer – end the book torn apart in body and soul, one dead, the other defeated, their youthful dreams shattered on the rocks of wrecking-crew male sexuality (as Susann sees it.) But the oft-described 'monster' heroine, Neely – not a beauty, and spiteful, selfish and undisciplined – ends happily in her fashion, because her talent keeps her essentially strong and true to herself. What a very bold, modern message this is – 'guys will leave you, your looks will go, your kids will grow up and everything you thought was great will go sour. All you can really count on is yourself and your talent' – and how refreshing in a period of ceaseless being-a-mother-is-the-most-important-thing-in-my-life guff from the likes of Madonna and the rest of her smug showbiz sisterhood. Like many mainstream entertainments, *Valley of the Dolls* is far more critical of the American Dream than many avowedly 'subversive' projects; as *Dallas* showed American big business as corrupt and filthy through and through, so *Dolls* protractedly and minutely picks apart the 'magic' of showbiz. Broadway, Hollywood, Vegas cabaret and European 'art' films are revealed as glitzy gladiatorial arenas where women pull each other to pieces in search of THAT leading role, THAT modelling contract. Of course, like all the best tabloids, *Dolls* has its cake, eats it too and still has enough to throw triumphantly in the face of the showbiz establishment; the USA is a country where extreme licentiousness and terminal prissiness make strange bedfellows and Susann, like Cecil B. DeMille before her (show lashings of flesh, but then point out that it's happening in Sodom and Gomorrah, and kill the lot of them!), had to make sure that the pursuit of pleasure led to the pincer of pain. Still, it's strong stuff for the sixties – featuring the first mainstream anal sex scene, which mystified me for years – and if the tragic outcomes of various hedonisms are sometimes piled on with a trowel, it still retains its power and a strange sort of accidental integrity. Despite nearly forty years of repeated attempts to castrate it into campness, or kill it with kitsch, *Valley of the Dolls* remains a brave, bold, angry and, yes, definitely a feminist book. All that, and still about the most fun you can have without a prescription!

CARMEN CALLIL
ON
ANGELA CARTER

The Magic Toyshop (1967)

First Virago edition 1981

Angela Carter was one of Britain's most original writers, highly acclaimed for her novels, short stories and journalism. *The Magic Toyshop* won the John Llewellyn Rhys Prize in 1968 and *Several Perceptions* won the Somerset Maugham Prize in 1969. More novels followed as well as her 1977 translation of the fairy tales of Charles Perrault. Angela Carter's last novel was the much-lauded *Wise Children*, published in 1991. Her death in 1992 at the age of fifty-one 'robbed the English literary scene of one of its most vivacious and compelling voices' (*Independent*).

Carmen Callil was born in Melbourne in 1938 and came to London in 1960 where she has lived ever since. A book publisher, in 1972 she founded Virago and ten years later became Managing Director of Chatto & Windus & The Hogarth Press. She is the author (with Colm Tóibín) of *The Modern Library: The 200 Best Novels in English since 1950* and *Bad Faith: A Forgotten History of Family and Fatherland.*

Angela Carter died in 1992, from lung cancer. She was fifty-one. For a good part of her latter years she was one of my closest friends, and for most of that time I was also her publisher. Her photograph sits on the mantel in my bedroom and her sketches are still on my walls; one of them, of sweet peas and marigolds, hangs above my desk and gazes upon every word that I write. There was very little Angie could not do: she drew very well, and loved colour, bold colour, so that everything she created – houses, etchings, writing (and her clothes) – had something of the rainbow about them. Angie was particularly keen on every shade of yellow, and as much purple as could be added to anything. Orange also played a large part in her life.

But these talents were mere coda to what she could do with language, with words, which, after her husband and son, were the joy of her life. It was more than words, actually. The ideas behind the words she chose with such care and enthusiasm were just as important to her. She was such a believer, such a curious, cynical, wicked, robustly unsentimental believer.

What did she believe in? When Angie died, I spoke about her at her funeral at Putney Vale on 19th February 1992.

'Pleasure has always had a bad press in Britain. I'm all for pleasure, too. I wish there was more of it around. I also like to argue. A day without an argument is like an egg without salt,' wrote Angie.

And then I went on to say:

> There are going to be many such saltless days now for those
> of us who loved Angie. What will we miss? We'll miss her
> passionate interest in all of us, her irony, her exotic pleasure in
> everything, her advice, her fabulous imagination, her subver-
> sive irreverence, her anger. Who is there to talk about politics
> now that she is gone? Her long telephone calls: what phone
> bills! What profit for British Telecom! How gratifying it was
> when one's news, gossip or opinions were received with that
> knowing cackle.
>
> (Such was our mutual addiction to these conversations
> that in 1987, when she was on one of her constant travels to
> foreign parts – Angela loved abroad – I sent her a telegram:
> 'Angie, when are you coming home? You are away too much
> and I have gossip one thousand miles long and no address to
> write to you.')
>
> And then: her vocabulary, her cooking, her physical man-
> nerisms, her jokes, her travels, the quality of her voice, her
> writing, her kindness and her compassion; the sheer originality
> of every single bit of her. She was the oracle and guide we all
> consulted, a listener whose eloquent silences kept us hanging
> on every word she quietly and wickedly uttered.

I first met Angela Carter in 1972, at a book launch party of the
1970s kind. Her memory of it was that my first words were 'Don't
you *adore* cabbage?'; mine that she told me that her husband had
thrown a typewriter at her the night before: did I recommend
that she should leave him? She was thirty-one when I met her and
had already written five novels. I had just founded Virago. Angela
went on to become one of the first writers I commissioned.

Commission, however, is the wrong word to use for publishing Angela Carter. She wrote what she wanted to, and to get Virago off the ground, she chose to write *The Sadeian Woman*, a study of women, sexuality and power, which both outraged and alarmed some of the feminists of the time. Angela was a fervent feminist and a determined socialist, but she was a ribald, irreverent and very often a topsy-turvy version of each: and she put up with politically correct nonsense from no one except herself. She wrote to me in 1973:

> Herewith is the Sade book for Virago, who I hope is a healthy child and screaming already. Many apologies for the delay – moving was one thing, and I've been trying to work, which means I go into a kind of self-enclosed capsule, from the centre of which the outside world (when I perceive it) and, also, time, appear to be compounded of porridge. (I don't like porridge either.)

Because Virago was in its infancy she took a peppercorn advance of £400 for this book. Angela was fond of money and the good things it buys, but she never thought the world of it. Over the next twenty years, she continued to produce this and that for Virago. Loyalty was an absolute cornerstone of her personality, and she felt it for all who worked at Virago over the years. As she lay dying in Brompton Hospital, she was fiddling about with a manuscript on her bed: the *Virago Book of Fairy Tales* – 'I'm just finishing this off for the girls.'

For a complicated and formidably original human being, Angie proved to be the simplest person to publish. Everything pleased her. Everything received her attention, from endpapers to the identity of her reviewers. Editorially, of course, there was little to do. She couldn't spell, but apart from that, every word she wrote was chosen with precision, to present with *that* word, and no other, the imagination or opinion she wished to convey. Courtesy was the root of it: Angela was a truly courteous woman. It came from her tremendous interest in, and microscopic observation of, the world about her: she knew what people were worth.

She knew what *she* was worth too. In her later years she became famous herself, the only female in that early gaggle of writers who were, in the 1980s, considered to be Britain's finest – Ian McEwan, Julian Barnes, Martin Amis, and of course, Salman Rushdie. Recognition was slow to come to her; she knew in her bones that her gender had something to do with that. It made her angry, as injustice always did, but that was not the feminism she espoused; hers was of the laughing, ironic and get-on-with-it kind.

Nothing escaped her razor-sharp mind. She was no compromiser and did not cut her purse to fit any pig's ear, but her immense curiosity meant that she took a vast pleasure in everything life had to offer. So while she despised many of the histrionics indulged in by the *glitterati* (mostly male, but neither did she spare such female versions as there were in those days), she was never averse to dabbling her toes in their glamorous pools: good copy for hour-long telephone dismemberment afterwards.

Angela Carter, no narrow Anglophile, was a great traveller and loved America, Japan, Australia, Italy, France. But she was rooted in Britain; in its literature, food, its politics. She was a true child of the last war and the age of Austerity which followed it, and she gave thanks every day of her life to the post-war Welfare State for the good things it gave her. She was an irredeemably radical political animal. Her last years were spent in Thatcher's Britain: 'We're going to hell in a hand-basket' were her words on those years. In this, as in much else, she was the prime representative of a particular British personality which runs a gamut from Shakespeare to Tom Paine to Charles Dickens. She was spared New Labour, Tony Blair, Iraq, George Bush and much else, but she has left behind such a body of work that her views on each require no imagination. More, the language she luxuriated in to express disgust and disdain remain a bible for anyone today who might be lost for words to attack the status quo.

Though she lived in the twentieth century, in fact she belonged to the twenty-first in almost every way. She was fascinated by men, women, children and the beasts of field and sky, but her concentration was on uprooting assumptions about how women live and love, celebrating how they decorate and indulge themselves, and how they hunger for sex. Challenging authority, she stuck a pin into any available literary or cultural balloon, rewriting and reinterpreting fairy tales and myths so that little girls were no longer eaten by wandering wolves, but were given a decent pair of gnashers to do the chewing themselves.

She was the great celebrator of the vulgarian as heroine, and raised her irreverent female creations high, using the fairy tale and the theatrical and music hall images she loved so much. Angie loved the movies, too, everything about them. Popular culture fascinated her. She preceded Madonna and Kylie Minogue, but she prepared us for their arrival. You see them in her heroines as they fly out of her novels and short stories, cursing and sweating, exotic or bawdy, making jokes, using every beautiful word in the English dictionary in magical and exquisite ways, to tell the world to move over, and make way for women.

In that way, she was a seer – an itinerant Pied Piper who travelled whenever she could, doing what she loved to do: teach. She was the Johnny Appleseed of English literature: all over the world are literary incendiary bombs planted by Angela, and in Britain, young writers whom she encouraged.

Virago published *The Sadeian Woman* in 1979. Immediately after that I delved into Angela's suitcases of journalism and in 1982 Virago published a selection, *Nothing Sacred*. Her 'advertisement' for that (Angie never liked to use the word 'synopsis', an insufficiently ebullient word for what was, after all, to become a book) sums up the varied interests of her magnificent magpie mind: 'South London; Venice; Padstow; D. H. Lawrence as closet queen; Red Indians; Health Foods; Underwear; Teddy Bears; Male Nudes.' By this time the Virago Modern Classics list had been launched and Angela, phenomenally well read, was as interested, as critical, and as supportive of that fiction list as she was of everything else Virago did. She read novels for me and became passionate about some of the writers on that list – Margaret Atwood, Christina Stead, Eudora Welty, Elizabeth Taylor, Elizabeth Jolley.

By 1981, she had reacquired the rights to some of her earlier novels. Virago was to publish five of her works of fiction in the Classics list, but the first novel we chose was her second, *The Magic Toyshop*, a perfect introduction to her work. You will laugh on the first page, you will be disturbed by the end of the first chapter, you will soon be transported into mysterious and fascinating places. In her day – and since – Angela Carter's writing has often been categorised as magic realism. Angela herself scorned this description, considering herself a stern realist, and as you follow the story of Melanie in *The Magic Toyshop*, you will see how right she was. You will know what it is like have the body and longings of a young girl, set loose upon a dangerous world. Melanie's adventures, at once charming and unsettling, introduce you to the audacious imagination and fabulous sense of wonder and fun of a great writer. Only the person she was could have produced a novel like *The Magic Toyshop*. You are about to encounter the vibrant and conversational ghost of Angela Carter.

HELEN OYEYEMI
ON
BESSIE HEAD

When Rain Clouds Gather (1968) and *Maru* (1971)

First Virago edition 2010

Bessie Head was born in South Africa in 1937 and is one of Africa's best-known writers. She trained as a teacher then worked as a journalist for *Golden City Post*, a Drum publication, until she left for Botswana. She remained there, with the precarious status of refugee, for fifteen years before she gained citizenship in 1979. *When Rain Clouds Gather* was her first published novel in 1968, followed by *Maru* and her intense and powerful autobiographical work, *A Question of Power*. She also wrote short stories and *A Woman Alone*, a collection of autobiographical writings, and *Tales of Tenderness and Power*. She died in 1986.

Helen Oyeyemi is the author of several highly acclaimed novels, including *White is for Witching* (which won a Somerset Maugham Award), *Mr Fox* and *Boy, Snow, Bird*, and a collection of short stories, *What Is Not Yours Is Not Yours*. In 2013 she was named one of *Granta*'s Best Young British Novelists.

Bessie Head was a witness to the early years of apartheid and its spirit-breaking classifications and restrictions. South Africa's Immorality Amendment Act of 1950, which outlawed interracial relationships, acted as a negation of her very existence. Yet Head was adamant that love affairs are more important than socio-political revolutions. She wrote, 'I have no logical argument as to why these things are more important, except that I believe in the contents of the human heart . . . a silent and secret conspiracy against all the insanity and hatred in mankind.'

In these, her first two novels, Bessie Head makes it understood that love between equals is the only true power in the world. She offers us men and women who are fully alive to each other. They dream the same dreams. Her men, Makhaya in *When Rain Clouds Gather* and the eponymous hero of *Maru*, are intensely perceptive, imbued with a 'feminine sensitivity' that raises them above the level of 'grovelling sex organs' that Head complained African men were traditionally reduced to within their communities. Her women give themselves over to passion that barely stops short at terrible vulnerability. Paulina, Makhaya's lover, strains boldly towards joy, with her colourful skirts and her equally vivid declarations, 'You mustn't think I'm a cheap woman, but I love you.' *Maru*'s Margaret Cadmore, outwardly impassive apart from the occasional tear, has a tumultuous inner life that she finally anchors in her art and the complex ways in which she loves the two men in her life. But the cognitive dissonance involved in falling in love is sometimes almost beyond endurance, even for people as strong as these. In Bessie Head's world, people are 'frightened into' showing each other compassion, and only give way to love 'under extreme pressure and pain'. Head's love stories highlight the great risk of making a gesture of faith in mankind, whose wickedness can be extraordinary. As I read the scene in *Maru* where Margaret Cadmore stands before a classroom full of jibing students, my hands curled up into fists for the harrowing moments that follow as the woman's nerves fray. Her humiliation and the sensation of hatred – her own and that of the children – is scarred onto the page with an authenticity that feels hard won.

Born in a mental asylum in Johannesburg to a white South African mother, disowned by her mother's family and raised in a Coloured family in Natal, Head never knew her black father and confessed to the 'desperate guesswork' of trying to write as what she called 'an African of Africa'. At twenty-seven, she obtained permission to leave South Africa (on the condition that she never return) and spent the next twenty-two years in Botswana; fifteen of those as a refugee while the authorities refused her Botswana nationality. She wrote to friends in England, Norway and America, feverishly making plans to leave for Nigeria, for India, for Kenya – anywhere but this country that didn't want her. Still . . . 'The best and most enduring love is that of rejection,' Head wrote to Randolph Vigne. In another letter she told him, 'You know perhaps nothing about a little village . . . in an African village it's goddam deep and dangerous.' Village children threw stones at Head's young son and called him 'Bushman'. Her neighbours accused her of infanticide and only left her out of their talk once she'd had a breakdown.

Makhaya, the protagonist of *When Rain Clouds Gather*, is a

disillusioned South African activist, newly released from prison
for plotting an explosion; he has just escaped across Botswana's
border fence 'and then on to whatever illusion of freedom lay
ahead'. Golema Mmidi, his adoptive home, is a village at a cross-
roads in its history; its inhabitants submit to the authority of a
chieftain, but the villagers are also receptive to the prospect of
agricultural reform brought by Gilbert, a white British volunteer.
The horror of village life that Head darkly hinted at in her letters
ducks uneasily out of sight on the periphery, only showing its
naked face when Makhaya and Paulina drive out towards the village's cattle post in the drought-parched desert. Then, at last we
see the vultures in the trees, sitting 'full and gorged'. It is then we
see a newborn calf preyed on as it lies beside its dead mother, and
it is then that we see what has happened to Paulina's son, a cheerful little artist who made the best of his solitary existence herding
the family's cattle by making wood carvings with his pocket knife.
We are forced to stand with Makhaya looking in at the door of
the hut, bearing the sight for Paulina, who might run mad if she
saw. Reading this passage brought to mind another meditation on
the death of a child written five years earlier, Ingrid Jonker's 'The
Child who was Shot Dead by Soldiers at Nyanga': 'The child is
not dead . . . / the child grown to a man treks through all Africa /
the child grown into a giant journeys through the whole world.'
Here, however, Head as a narrator makes no attempt to mitigate
the desolation of the scene. It's as if the story is questioning the
technology by which a child becomes a giant, or even a man,
in such a place as Golema Mmidi. And because Makhaya loves
Paulina he takes the loss into himself, 'confused and angry that
there was only this dead, unanswering silence in his heart . . . '
Nini Etlinger, a pen-friend who had loaned Head the money for
a typewriter, advised her, 'You really must not write with your

heart on fire. It's not literature. I really mean it.' Head broke off
all contact with her and never renewed it, despite wholehearted
repentance on Etlinger's part. By the time she was thirteen Head
was already developing an awareness of what a story is able to do;
how it can teach, entertain and propose a wholly new future all at
once. In a short story published in the magazine of the Anglican
orphanage where she received her education, truth features as a
means of crossing a river, a way of moving forward. But the bridge
is built of stones that cannot be walked upon without great pain.

Maru begins so peacefully. The hero comes home to his wife at
the end of a blue-skied day and says to her simply, 'My sweetheart.'
And once you've come to the last page of the novel it is the grace
of that moment that may compel you to reread the first few pages
in a new and triumphant light. The beginning and the end of this
love story slide into each other with ferocious ease, like a snake
eating its own tail. Margaret Cadmore, a San orphan, is adopted
by a forthright English missionary, who has her educated and
sends her away to a Botswana village to take up her first teaching
position. Margaret, made virtually silent and expressionless by a
lifetime of abuse from her peers, is a powerfully disruptive presence in the life of the village, where other San are kept as slaves.
Margaret is not beautiful, but her gaze is eloquent and when
she speaks, something about her voice is enchanting. She wins
the love of Maru and Moleka, bosom friends who become bitter
opponents. Moleka is unable to overcome a dread of breaking
convention to openly proclaim love for a San woman. Maru is a
future chieftain of the village, a man whose eyes are lit with the
conversation of gods. He tests Margaret's dignity and creativity,
taking her bed away from her and giving her art paper, paint and
charcoals instead. And he doesn't claim Margaret for himself

until her heart is completely broken. This is the book that Bessie Head wrote as a response to Hodder and Stoughton's request that she follow *When Rain Clouds Gather* with something like an African version of *The Catcher in the Rye*.

At that period in her life, Head wrote her tales at night in her hut with a candle balanced on her knee. What might she have been if she had been free of Botswana and South Africa? From across an ocean there is a faint answer of sorts. In 1939, two years after Head was born, Billie Holiday wrote that bitter hymn to loneliness, 'God Bless the Child'. Holiday, another extraordinary artist, never knew her father and would have been taken for a Coloured woman in South Africa too. Holiday got forty-eight years out of a life of chequered romance, sorrow, drugs and religious schooling – one year less than Head's forty-nine. Like Holiday, Head brings her grief to her work – and perhaps this is part of what sends a thrill through us readers, who may think that all we have to do is close the book when we no longer want to see into these wounded worlds, these spirited trials at hope.

After reading *Maru*, Megan Biesele, an American anthro-pologist, went to live in the Botswana desert with people of the San tribe (called Marsarwa in the novel), who taught her their language until she was able to read *Maru* aloud to them, chapter by chapter. The San made Head a necklace of shells, seeds and grass and sent it to her, along with their thanks for what she had written. *When Rain Clouds Gather* and *Maru* are fairy tales about the transformations that love can wreak. And they transform love into a force to be feared and a force to be thankful for.

MARIAN KEYES
ON
MOLLY KEANE

Good Behaviour (1981)

First Virago edition 2001

Molly Keane was born in 1904 in Co. Kildare, Ireland, into a 'rather serious Hunting and Fishing Church-going family' who gave her little education at the hands of governesses. Molly Keane's interests when young were 'hunting and horses and having a good time'; she began writing only to supplement her dress allowance. Her novels include *Loving and Giving*, *Devoted Ladies*, *Time After Time*, *The Rising Tide* and *Good Behaviour*, which was shortlisted for the Booker Prize. She died in 1996.

Marian Keyes's international bestselling novels include *Rachel's Holiday*, *Last Chance Saloon*, *Sushi for Beginners*, *Angels*, *The Other Side of the Story*, *Anybody Out There*, *This Charming Man*, *The Woman Who Stole My Life* and *The Break*. She has also published three collections of journalism, *Under the Duvet*, *Further Under the Duvet* and *Making It Up as I Go Along*. She lives in Dublin with her husband.

After the premature death of her husband, Molly Keane abruptly stopped writing. Forever she doubtless thought. But after a thirty-year absence she returned with *Good Behaviour*, a dark, complex, engaging novel, infinitely richer than any of her previous. Clearly, as Keane let herself be persuaded to publish *Good Behaviour* under her own name, and not under M. J. Farrell, her erstwhile *nom de plume*, she intuited that this book was 'the real thing'.

The book documents the dying days of the Anglo-Irish aristocracy. Shockingly, grippingly, it opens with a murder. Aroon St Charles insists on feeding rabbit to her invalid mother. It has always sickened her and it literally kills her to eat it: Aroon, in effect has committed murder. Murder most polite, but murder nevertheless.

But this is no whodunnit; it's much more of a whydunnit and when we return with Aroon to her Anglo-Irish upbringing and see Keane's scalpel-sharp observances thereof, the *why* becomes clear.

The Anglo-Irish are a fast-disappearing tribe but while their rotting world disintegrates, to be replaced by a strange new one, the unyielding codes of Good Behaviour govern their every act. Aroon complains of her Irish servant Rose, 'She has this maddening pretence of deafness.' The irony of which is that the essence of Good Behaviour is assumed deafness, blindness and, above all, *muteness*.

It's a strange world, this crumbling fortress. Young boys are beaten for reading poetry instead of indulging in manly pursuits, such as exercising their ponies. Pet dogs are fed chicken, with the bones lovingly removed, while the Irish servants are forced to eat starch to stave off hunger. A comfortable lifestyle is essential and those Irish tradesmen who threaten it – like the local butcher who had the temerity to submit his bill after giving several hundreds of pounds of credit – are regarded as robbers.

In order that appearances be preserved, fear, affection, grief, even love must all be buttoned down. Aroon's mother was 'gently considerate to all furniture', 'considerate towards all weakness and eccentricity in plant life', but 'she didn't really like children', and handed her own over to a succession of less than competent nannies. (And though she herself was always sickened by rabbit, it didn't stop rabbit stew being one of Aroon's childhood staples.)

Good Behaviour decreed that though one's husband might be casually unfaithful with almost every woman who crossed his path, including the servants, a scene must never be caused. Indeed, when Aroon's mother is told about the inappropriate relationship between her husband and their cook, her cool response is, 'If it gave him the smallest pleasure ... I am only too delighted.' The high-water mark of Good Behaviour comes when the last mourner leaves at the funeral of Hubert, the only son of the family. Up until then Aroon and her parents have behaved impeccably – with gracious manners, without tears. In fact, the bereaved parents hadn't even touched each other. Surely this is when they shut the door on the outside world and indulge in the luxury of their own grief? But no. Once alone, the need for Good Behaviour is heightened, not lessened. It's a terrifying time for them. 'We exchanged cool, warning looks – which of us could behave best: which of us could be least embarrassing to the others . . . '

What's very interesting about the way *Good Behaviour* is narrated is how, even though all events are conduited through Aroon, it's akin to having an unreliable narrator, in that what she tells us is not what the truth is. However, unlike many unreliable narrators, there's no danger of the reader being misled – on the contrary, it's the narrator who is confused. Molly Keane has pulled off the great trick of entering into an alliance, a form of complicity with her readers. In which the truth is revealed, regardless of the spin poor, naive Aroon is putting on it.

Aroon is at her most deluded with regard to her brother Hubert and his 'friend' Richard. The reader discerns almost instantly that Hubert and Richard are in love. When Hubert's father begins to get suspicious, the boys decide to make Aroon their dupe, their smokescreen, and Richard pretends to be in love with her. He even makes a late-night visit to her bedroom, although his behaviour is so half-hearted that even Aroon is barely convinced. 'You have such enormous bosoms,' he tells her. 'Shall I lay my head on one of them just to see what it's like?' 'It's a bit hot,' he says, after a minute. If this was not so tragic, it would be very funny. 'I've had a man in my bed,' Aroon tells us. 'I suppose I could say I've had a lover. I like to call it that. I do call it that.' But we, the readers, know the full, ugly truth of the manipulation. We know better.

Aroon's appearance works against her. She's grotesquely tall with bosoms 'swinging like jelly bags'. 'A swan on dry land,' Hubert calls her. One of the rare times she feels beautiful, her mother withers her with a 'Must you look so majestic?' She's desperate for love but while everyone around her forms alliances, they are never with her. Hubert and Richard, her mother and father, Rose and her father, then – unexpectedly, and across the class divide – Rose and her mother.

Keane tightens the tension by gradually introducing the fact that their money has all drained away. As the bills mount, the mother – who is never hungry – introduces stark economies and proceeds to starve Aroon, telling her, 'They say whales can live for months on their own fat.' And yet, pitiful as she is, Aroon never quite becomes a Cinderella. Keane walks an admirably tight line, holding all the complex aspects of Aroon together. Just as the reader is reaching a peak of outrage at Aroon's mistreatments Aroon turns to us another side of her complex character and reminds us of how arrogant she can be. The humiliation of her night at the Barraway party, having to sit out dance after dance, with her badly judged dress and grotesque body, then discovering, via a magazine announcement, that her beloved Richard is to marry someone else – was anyone ever so piteous?

The book hovers here on the brink of pathos, and Cinderella-style, introduces a potential knight-in-shining-armour in the form of Kiely the solicitor. When he makes his overtures to Aroon, she's looking at a form of salvation – apart from anything else he has money. Her father has already shown willing to pimp her to Richard, so why not sell herself to Kiely, the highest bidder? The *only* bidder. But because he is a 'common little man' she dismisses him with her mother's savage phrase 'You must be out of your mind.'

'In spite of my heartbreak and tears,' she tells us, 'I was, after all, Aroon St Charles, and I felt it too.' Aroon has her Good Behaviour to fall back on. It is both her downfall and her salvation. The rigid codes of behaviour are blocks to happiness, but provide a framework to structure one's life around when all else has failed.

Cruelty begets cruelty. Aroon begins to ape her mother's

mannerisms, the disparaging voice as she dismisses the nurse, the way she offers merely the tips of her fingers to the solicitor. (Not that he accepts them. He grabs her hand and pumps it, one of the many delightful moments of comedy woven through this book.)

Like anything written from a place of decay, there is an inexorable nature to the narrative. From the very first page Aroon and her mother are in reduced circumstances, so we already know that there will be no redemption. Yet Molly Keane writes with such a lightness of touch, and with bursts of shockingly funny black comedy that this book is a joy.

Aroon describes her beloved father, bedbound and semi-mute from a stroke, as he struggles to communicate – '"I say, I say, I say," he was going on like a comic starting his patter.' At the height of her fantasy of living in Africa with Richard, Aroon sees herself in 'a low (though roomy) thatched house in the foothills of Kilimanjaro'.

When she's bored to death by a dinner party companion telling of his lineage, 'I . . . tried out a few "Oos" as he went back through the Crusades, where his forebears had been such career boys.' Though emotions are muted and restrained, the book abounds with sensuality. Aroon describes rustling her hand though bank notes 'like feet in autumn leaves'. Dahlias: 'lately so flaming with life and colour; they were sodden and rotting now, their flowers jelly, their leaves gross and blackening'. Sand is 'sugary', carnations are 'barbed', a window is 'firmly laced with ivy'. Keane's razor-sharp observations are a dream – Breda, the censured housemaid, 'reared her head like an insulted hen'.

And though the zenith of Good Behaviour is the total negation of feelings, Keane's description of emotions is awe-inspiringly perfect. Aroon, describing a moment of unexpected happiness; 'my breath alone could have held me off the ground'.

This book is a wonderful *tour de force*. The ending is as tense and tight and overflowing with reasons to be reread as its beginning was enticement to read on. It was well worth the wait.

NORA EPHRON
ON
Heartburn (1983)

First Virago edition 1996

Nora Ephron received Academy Award nominations for Best Original Screenplay for *When Harry Met Sally*, *Silkwood* and *Sleepless in Seattle*, which she also directed. Ephron began writing for cinema after years as one of America's best-known journalists. Three collections of her essays, *Crazy Salad*, *Scribble, Scribble* and *I Feel Bad About My Neck* have been bestsellers, along with her novel, *Heartburn*. Nora Ephron died in 2012 at the age of seventy-one.

It's been nearly twenty-five years since my second marriage ended, and twenty-two years since I finished writing the book you're about to read, which is often referred to as a thinly disguised novel. I have no real quarrel with this description, even though I've noticed, over the years, that the words 'thinly disguised' are applied mostly to books written by women. Let's face it, Philip Roth and John Updike picked away at the carcasses of their early marriages in book after book, but to the best of my knowledge they were never hit with the thinly disguised thing.

But as I was saying, I have no real quarrel with this description. My second marriage in fact ended exactly the way the one in *Heartburn* does, shortly after I discovered that my husband was having an affair with an unbelievably tall person. In the book, I thinly disguised myself by making myself considerably more composed than I was at the time, and I thinly disguised my ex-husband by giving him a beard that belonged to one of my friends. The unbelievably tall person he had the affair with remained unbelievably tall; it's my experience as a novelist that some things lose everything if they are disguised, even thinly, and that therefore it's best to just leave them alone.

On the other hand, most of the characters in *Heartburn* are entirely fictional, and many of the things that happen in the book didn't happen at all. I made them up. Or I stole them from other people. My therapy group, for instance, was never robbed at gunpoint, but I had a friend whose group was, and the minute she told me the story I stashed it in my 'Use This Someday' file and hoped I would be the first person to take advantage of what seemed to me just the sort of comic, slightly public episode that was destined to be used by someone, sooner rather than later. The world I live in is filled with ravenous writers looking for material, and you have to move quickly if you want to write about even your own life, much less someone else's.

What's more, I am not and have never been a food writer. My mother never ran off and joined a commune run by a man named Mel who thought he was God. There were no pet hamsters named Arnold and Shirley in my first marriage, and my first husband did not talk to me in a high squeaky voice that was meant to be Arnold's, and I did not reply in a high squeaky voice that was meant to be Shirley's. But I do love food and occasionally write about it; it was my sister who ran off and joined a commune run by a man named Mel who thought he was God; and during my first marriage there was quite a lot of talking in high squeaky voices, on account of the cats.

Furthermore, I left out a lot of what happened, but I never get credit for this, especially from my second husband, who ought to be grateful I did.

Everyone always asks, Was he mad at you for writing the book? and I have to say, Yes, yes, he was. He still is. It is one of the most fascinating things to me about the whole episode: he cheated on me, and then got to behave as if he was the one who had been wronged because I wrote about it! I mean, it's not as if I wasn't a writer. It's not as if I hadn't often written about myself. I'd even written about him. What did he think was going to happen? That I would take a vow of silence for the first time in my life?

Here's another fascinating thing about the episode: the

unbelievably tall woman who had an affair with my then husband had a husband of her own – an extremely pompous British civil servant I thinly disguised as an extremely pompous American civil servant – and to this day he constantly takes shots at me for the damage I did to his family. I mean, really! He and his wife eventually divorced, and let me tell you, it was not my fault! And this book had nothing to do with it either! This is the first time I have written about this episode when I wasn't thinly disguising things, and look at all these exclamation points that have just leapt into the text.

My mother taught me many things when I was growing up, but the main thing I learned from her is that everything is copy. She said it again and again, and I have quoted her saying it again and again. As a result, I knew the moment my marriage ended that someday it might make a book – if I could just stop crying. One of the things I'm proudest of is that I managed to convert an event that seemed to me hideously tragic at the time to a comedy – and if that's not fiction, I don't know what is.

SANDI TOKSVIG
ON
FLORENCE KING

Confessions of a Failed Southern Lady (1985)

First Virago edition 2006

Florence King was born in 1936 in Washington DC, which she calls 'a geographical accident for which Granny never forgave any of us, for I was supposed to be an Upton of Virginia just like her'. She worked as a reporter before trying her hand at writing confession stories and pornography. Later she concentrated on writing articles for magazines such as *Harper's* and *Cosmopolitan*, and became a regular columnist for the *National Review*. She published ten books under her own name, a historical novel under a pen name and one ghost job about which her lips are forever sealed. She died in 2016.

Sandi Toksvig went into theatre as a writer and performer after graduating from Cambridge. Well known for her television and radio work as a presenter, writer and actor, she has written more than twenty books for children and adults. She also writes for theatre and television: her film *The Man* starred Stephen Fry and Zoe Wanamaker and her play *Bully Boy*, starring Anthony Andrews, opened the St James Theatre, London in 2012. She was Chancellor of Portsmouth University from 2012 to 2017. In 2016 Sandi took over as chair on *QI*, and in 2017 she started presenting *The Great British Bake Off*. She lives in London and Kent.

The witty woman is a tragic figure in American life. Wit destroys eroticism and eroticism destroys wit, so women must choose between taking lovers and taking no prisoners.

FLORENCE KING

Funny women have an uncomfortable place in society. It is as though being amusing is somehow offensive to femininity. In a historical sense, it is as if Eve got Adam's rib and not his funny bone and that when gender roles were divided up at the mouth of the cave it was men who were tasked as mirth makers. Certainly there is hardly a man in the world who thinks he can't tell a joke and there are very few women who will try. There is, however, a quick sociological test anyone can do to disprove this separation of the female from the funny. At any formal function you might attend, go and spend five minutes outside the ladies' facilities. Each time the door opens the sound that will almost certainly emanate is one of laughter. Then, at the risk of an arrestable offence, spend the same amount of time outside the gents. Here the world is almost silent, bar the occasional mutter – usually about golf. Men are too busy literally sizing each other up to waste time on bons mots and amusing observations.

Being funny about life is absolutely ingrained in women but it is not something generally done for public consumption. One is as unlikely to attend a dinner party that amusingly concludes with a female guest putting a lampshade on her head as one is to hear a risqué joke as the opening gambit to a meeting of the Women's Institute. For most women, finding the humour in life is a secret weapon used to combat the inequities they face and it is utilised daily without too much thought. Gather any three women together and soon they will begin to tell each other stories. Stories that are usually both poignant and comic. This side of humour worries most men in that there is a danger of making some kind of personal revelation that doesn't involve the engine size of their car. Men prefer to engage in something the Americans call a 'joke-off', where they tell one properly formulated gag after another in an attempt to get the biggest laugh. For women humour is a subtler tool that is not about dominating a group through wit, or used to draw attention to oneself. It is not a big leap from the personal to the professional to realise why there are so few women making a living through comedy.

I grew up in the United States in the 1960s and the role models for a fledgling female humorist were slight. If they existed then they tended to base much of their comedy on the fact that they did not fit a traditional woman's mould. There was a sense that stepping outside the bounds of acceptable female behaviour required not a single step but a giant leap. The few comediennes of the time went one of two ways – they either deliberately exaggerated their odd looks for laughs (Phyllis Diller, Lily Tomlin, Ruth Buzzi) or they allowed themselves to be both amusing and pretty by pretending to be stupid (Goldie Hawn, Jo Anne Worley, Judy Carne). Either method had a sort of neutering effect on the comedy and made it all seem much less aggressive.

If there were few funny women at the forefront of comedic performance then there were even fewer in the literary world. Try as I might, I could not find the female equivalent of the sardonic Mark Twain or the observational James Thurber. There were, of course, female authors with wit – Jane Austen, Dorothy Parker, Stella Gibbons and even Jean Kerr, who wrote *Please Don't Eat the Daisies*, but none, it appeared, with (and here the term always used is interesting) the balls to grab life by the throat and wring a laugh out of it. Then in 1985 the American writer Florence King produced *Confessions of a Failed Southern Lady*. Here, for the first time in my literary experience, was a book written by a woman, that ought to be printed with a mechanism for turning down the volume of the reader. It was, and continues to be, outrageous and laugh-out-loud funny.

It was also proof, if proof were needed, that the greatest gift any parent can provide for the putative comic writer is a dysfunctional childhood. *Confessions* has been called both autobiographical and semi-autobiographical. Either term will do as one way or another most writers are economical with the truth about their past. King was born in 1936 and raised by her grandmother in Tidewater, Virginia. It is in this Deep South setting that the book begins. Florence's family provided material that any comic writer would kill for. Her mother 'was a ninth-generation Virginian, the daughter of a relentless memsahib, yet she shrugged off every tenet of Southern womanhood and turned the air blue every time she opened her mouth'. She had smoked since she was eight, preferred baseball to society balls and had resisted every attempt by her own mother to turn her into a lady. 'Granny tried to put a good face on matters by attending a few games so people would think she approved of girlish sport, but the day she noticed a lump in Mama's cheek and realized it was tobacco, she had to be helped from the bleachers and escorted home.' Despairing of her own child, Granny looked around the family for a suitable female that she could mould into a lady: 'someone delicate and fragile in both body and spirit, a true exemplar of Southern womanhood. Someone, in other words, either sick or crazy.' Granny finds her prize in Evelyn, a nervous young thing whose troubles are blamed entirely on her womb and who convinces herself that being 'delicate down below' is part of her charm. Evelyn takes to carrying an empty pickle jar around in case her womb should fall out in public.

Despite not being the marrying kind, Florence's mother does settle down with Herb, an English ne'er-do-well musician. His lack of prospects does not deter Granny: 'He was English. It was all she cared about ... It dropped, like the quality of mercy, into every conversation she had.' When Florence is born Granny comes for the weekend and stays for thirty years in a vain attempt to turn the hapless and hopeless Florence into a lady: 'Expecting Granny to stay away from an unformed blob of female material was like expecting a cobra to stay away from a flute.'

The book is full of fabulous one-liners – 'Like charity, schizo-phrenia begins at home' – and excellent advice for the fledgling Southern belle. We learn that 'silver is the Southern woman's proudest possession' and that 'every decent woman goes to her husband with twelve "covers," and if the knives have hollow handles he'll be running with other women before the year is out, you wait and see. No man respects a woman with hollow handles.'

It's a book that pulls no punches and it is hard to recall that as late as 1985, King's revelation in it of a lesbian affair at college was considered at best risqué and at worst quite shocking. Here, at last, was a woman who wrote with no holds barred. It was gutsy, daring and great. Whether the book accurately portrays her actual life seems unimportant. What matters is that here is some of the best comic writing ever put down on paper.

When Florence King wrote about her foray into lesbianism there were those in the gay rights movement who longed to claim her for their own. In her subsequent life and writing, King has, however, shown no inclination to take up the pink banner. Her author's biography clearly states 'Florence King has never married' but it gives no indication of what else she might have been up to. Nor did she seem keen to march to the drum of the women's movement. When she wrote her first novel after *Confessions* (*When Sisterhood Was in Flower*) she took careful aim at feminists and shot them down in a barrage of lampooning wit. There is, for example, Grace Garrison-Talbot, president of the Birth Bucket League of America, who bemoans the fact that zoo directors won't enter into a meaningful dialogue about supplying crocodile dung to line the buckets to provide a soft landing for the newborn.

In her writing Florence King has always been her own woman and that woman is a product of the conservative Deep South. She has subsequently written many think-pieces for the American right-wing press, including her long-running column, 'The Misanthrope', where for many years in the *National Review* she professed to hate everyone. One can get a sense of the type of journalism she has plumped for by looking online at another conservative publication that has occupied her time, the *American Enterprise*. The advertisements that frame the copy tell you everything you need to know about the target audience. There is GodLovesSoldiers.com – 'a site for soldiers about Jesus Christ' – or ahuracorp.com who sell chemical detectors to 'immediately identify explosives and chemicals used in terrorist attacks'.

There is a modern penchant for attempting to marry up the personality of the author with the product of their pen, which is not always helpful. Learning that Thomas Hardy was brilliant on the subject of 'man's inhumanity to man' but not awfully nice to his wife should not detract from the writing. The fact that the left-wing, liberal lesbian who wishes to embrace Ms King may find some of her later right-wing associations hard to welcome is unimportant. It is Florence's very refusal to succumb to any social pressures that makes her such a wonderful writer. In her collection of essays, *Reflections in a Jaundiced Eye*, she shows a joyous willingness to have a go at anyone. 'We will never have a nation of cultured and reflective citizens as long as the press keeps printing The Sentence: Neighbours described the gunman as a quiet man who kept to himself.' Her work is that of a woman who can't be pigeon-holed and who doesn't give a damn. Thank God.

KATE SAUNDERS
ON
BARBARA PYM

An Academic Question (1986)

First Virago edition 2012

Barbara Pym was born in 1913 in Shropshire and educated at Oxford University. When in 1977 the *Times Literary Supplement* asked critics to name the most underrated authors of the past seventy-five years, only one was named twice (by Philip Larkin and Lord David Cecil): Barbara Pym. Her novels, which include *Some Tame Gazelle, Excellent Women* and *Jane and Prudence*, are characterised by what Anne Tyler has called 'the heartbreaking silliness of everyday life'. She died in 1980. Four of her novels, including *An Academic Question*, were published posthumously.

Kate Saunders is an author and journalist. She has worked for *The Times, Sunday Times, Sunday Express, Daily Telegraph* and *Cosmopolitan* amongst others, and has contributed to Radio 4's *Woman's Hour* and *Start the Week*. She has written numerous books for adults and children, including the bestselling *Night Shall Overtake Us*, and her follow-on to E. Nesbit's Five Children and It stories, *Five Children on the Western Front*, which won the Costa Children's Book Award in 2014. Her latest novel, *The Land of Neverendings*, was published by Faber in 2017. She lives in London.

'Rather to my surprise,' Barbara Pym wrote to her friend Philip Larkin in 1971, 'I have nearly finished the first draft of another novel about a provincial university told by the youngish wife of a lecturer. It was supposed to be a sort of Margaret Drabble effort but of course it hasn't turned out like that at all.'

The novel was *An Academic Question* – witty, sharp, light as a syllabub, nothing like anything by Margaret Drabble and with a cast of typically Pym-like English eccentrics. There is Kitty Jeffreys, who commanded an army of servants on a Caribbean island, until the locals unfeelingly elected an all-black government and forced her into exile. Her son, Coco, is a fastidious bachelor with a passion for gossip; her sister, Dolly, runs a ramshackle second-hand bookshop and obsessively tends hedgehogs.

And these are just the minor characters. In the foreground are the narrator, Caro Grimstone, and her ambitious anthropologist husband, Alan. Caro has a four-year-old daughter and a Swedish au pair, and is longing to find a proper role for herself before the boredom drives her crazy. Other academic wives are 'helpmeets' who type or index their husband's publications and are thanked in the acknowledgements, but Alan does his own typing and is secretive about his work – and he spends a worrying amount of time with his glamorous colleague, Iris Horniblow.

An Academic Question may not be archetypal Pym (no clergymen or 'drearily splendid' spinsters), but it couldn't have been written by anyone else. The freshness, wit and general good nature of this book are all the more remarkable because Pym wrote it without any real hope of getting it published, right in the middle of her fifteen years in literary outer darkness.

By the time she finished the first draft in 1971, the novels Pym had produced throughout the 1950s had fallen deeply out of fashion. Despite her loyal readership and history of decent sales, she had not been published for years, and was beginning to think she would never get back into print. 'It is a wonder to me now,' she wrote sadly in 1970, 'that I ever published anything.'

Even with no hope of being published, however, Pym could not stop being a novelist. As she wrote in her diary, 'It seems unnatural not to be writing bits for novels in one's notebook.' She couldn't sit in a café or walk down a street without putting down some detail that delighted her, such as a man eating his sandwiches with a knife and fork. 'Oh why can't I write things like that any more – why is this kind of thing no longer acceptable?'

It's a famous story now, with a famous happy ending. In 1977 the *Times Literary Supplement* asked various distinguished writers and critics to name the most underrated writer of the twentieth century, and both Philip Larkin and Lord David Cecil chose Barbara Pym. The time was suddenly ripe for her rediscovery, and when Pym's novels were reissued, she found herself a celebrity and a bestseller. In the short time between her rebirth as a published writer and her death in 1980 she produced superb new novels: *Quartet in Autumn* (shortlisted for the 1977 Booker Prize), *The Sweet Dove Died* (1978) and *A Few Green Leaves* (1980).

An *Academic Question* didn't appear until 1986. Shortly after finishing the first draft, Pym had to deal with the major distraction of treatment for breast cancer, and when she took up the story again she had lost heart. 'This draft,' writes Hazel Holt, her friend and literary executor, 'was, she felt, too "cosy" to have any chance of being published ... so she wrote another version ... attempting to make the whole thing more "sharp" and "swinging". But she was writing against the grain.'

Well, yes – and I have to admit that sometimes it shows. Pym can't really write convincingly about motherhood, marriage or sexual politics, and in no sense can she be said to 'swing' (the bare idea is heresy). This final version of the novel is Holt's artful amalgamation of all the available drafts and notes. It is not Pym's masterpiece, but it is filled with authentic Pym wisdom and irony, and is gloriously entertaining.

Caro, the heroine, is a well-meaning young woman, only rather naive and too fond of looking on the bright side. Her favourite word is 'cosy'; she does her best to explain away any kind of friction. 'Oh, Caro,' Alan complains, 'why will you always try to make everything sound so cosy?'

'Cosy' is a word some people associate with Barbara Pym. She writes about a middle-class world that is familiar, comical and essentially safe. Pym is not E. F. Benson or Wodehouse, however, and her tidy suburban gardens usually contain a serpent or two – by the end of An Academic Question, Caro will have seen several of her cosiest assumptions shot down in flames. Her 'adequate' husband will reveal an unknown side of his character, and even her prosaic mother has a bombshell to drop.

This is mainly a comic novel, but I never like to see Pym's brand of comic writing filed away under words like 'gentle', 'quiet' and 'charming'. She can be all these things, but Pym can also be barbed and sour; as pitilessly downbeat as Anita Brookner on a bad day. And she can be seriously, hilariously funny – no other novelist has celebrated our national silliness with such exuberance.

All her admirers have their favourite moments of Pym comedy and I can't resist listing some of mine. In *Excellent Women* (1952) there is a ludicrous argument about hollyhock chintz. In *A Glass of Blessings* (1958), a discussion about the problems of working women includes this Dickensian gem: 'I read in the paper the other day of a woman civil servant who was discovered preparing Brussels sprouts behind a filing cabinet'. I can never think of *Some Tame Gazelle* (1950) without seeing the curate with his combinations tucked carelessly into his socks, and in this novel I love Dolly mourning for a favourite hedgehog: 'my golden Maeve, the ancient Irish queen', while Caro is trying to talk about adultery.

An Academic Question may not be major Pym, but reading it is a major pleasure. Watch out for her Hitchcock moment, when she makes a personal appearance with her sister, Hilary: 'Two women who had just retired from jobs in London came to lunch. They were rather nice, spinster sisters ... Their lives were busy in an admirable way ... They must have loved in their time, perhaps loved and lost and come through it unscathed.'

This is how Barbara Pym saw herself at the time, and the picture seems to please her. She liked to describe herself as 'calm of mind, all passion spent'. Thank goodness it wasn't true.

ACKNOWLEDGEMENTS

Margaret Drabble on Jane Austen © Margaret Drabble 1989
Angela Carter on Charlotte Brontë © Angela Carter 1990
    © The Beneficiaries of Angela Carter 1992
Beryl Bainbridge on Emily Brontë © Beryl Bainbridge 1990
    © The Beneficiaries of Beryl Bainbridge 2010
Maggie O'Farrell on Charlotte Perkins Gilman © Maggie
    O'Farrell 2008
Elizabeth Jane Howard on Elizabeth von Arnim © Elizabeth
    Jane Howard 1985 © The Beneficiaries of Elizabeth Jane
    Howard 2014
A. S. Byatt on Willa Cather © A. S. Byatt 1980
Penelope Lively on Edith Wharton © Penelope Lively 1988
Sarah Waters on Sylvia Townsend Warner © Sarah
    Waters 2012
Jonathan Coe on Rosamond Lehmann © Jonathan Coe 1996
Diana Souhami on Radclyffe Hall © Diana Souhami 2008
Jilly Cooper on E. M. Delafield © Jilly Cooper 2008
Elizabeth Bowen on Antonia White © Elizabeth Bowen 1948
    © The Beneficiaries of Elizabeth Bowen 1973
Mark Bostridge on Vera Brittain © Mark Bostridge 2004
Alexander McCall Smith on Angela Thirkell © Alexander
    McCall Smith 2012
Sarah Dunant on Daphne du Maurier © Sarah Dunant 2003
Rachel Cooke on Stevie Smith © Rachel Cooke 2015
Zadie Smith on Zora Neale Hurston © Zadie Smith 2007

AUTHOR LIST

URSULA HOLDEN
TIN TOYS TRILOGY

WINIFRED HOLTBY
ANDERBY WOLD
MANDOA, MANDOA!
POOR CAROLINE
REMEMBER, REMEMBER!
SOUTH RIDING
THE CROWDED STREET
THE LAND OF GREEN GINGER

E. M. HULL
THE SHEIK

ZORA NEALE HURSTON
THEIR EYES WERE WATCHING GOD

ELIZABETH JENKINS
THE TORTOISE AND THE HARE

MOLLY KEANE
CONVERSATION PIECE
DEVOTED LADIES
FULL HOUSE
GOOD BEHAVIOUR
LOVING AND GIVING
LOVING WITHOUT TEARS
MAD PUPPETSTOWN
TAKING CHANCES
THE KNIGHT OF
    CHEERFUL COUNTENANCE
THE RISING TIDE
TIME AFTER TIME
TREASURE HUNT
TWO DAYS IN ARAGON
YOUNG ENTRY

FLORENCE KING
CONFESSIONS OF A FAILED
    SOUTHERN LADY

ALEXANDRA KOLLONTAI
LOVE OF WORKER BEES/A
    GREAT LOVE

MAURA LAVERTY
NEVER NO MORE
NO MORE THAN HUMAN

MARY LAVIN
MARY O'GRADY

ROSAMOND LEHMANN
A NOTE IN MUSIC
A SEA GRAPE TREE
DUSTY ANSWER
INVITATION TO THE WALTZ
THE BALLAD AND THE SOURCE
THE ECHOING GROVE
THE SWAN IN THE EVENING
THE WEATHER IN THE STREETS

ANNE LISTER
THE SECRET DIARIES OF MISS
    ANNE LISTER

ROSE MACAULAY
CREWE TRAIN
THE WORLD MY WILDERNESS

SHENA MACKAY
A BOWL OF CHERRIES
AN ADVENT CALENDAR
BABIES IN RHINESTONES AND
    OTHER STORIES

LESS THAN ANGELS
NO FOND RETURN OF LOVE
SOME TAME GAZELLE

MARY RENAULT
THE ALEXANDER TRILOGY:
FIRE FROM HEAVEN
THE PERSIAN BOY
FUNERAL GAMES

THE THESEUS NOVELS:
THE KING MUST DIE
THE BULL FROM THE SEA

KIND ARE HER ANSWERS
NORTH FACE
PURPOSES OF LOVE
RETURN TO NIGHT
THE CHARIOTEER
THE FRIENDLY YOUNG LADIES
THE LAST OF THE WINE
THE MASK OF APOLLO
THE PRAISE SINGER

DOROTHY I. RICHARDSON
PILGRIMAGE VOLUME ONE
PILGRIMAGE VOLUME TWO
PILGRIMAGE VOLUME THREE
PILGRIMAGE VOLUME FOUR

E. ARNOT ROBERTSON
ORDINARY FAMILIES
CULLUM
FOUR FRIGHTENED PEOPLE

MERCÈ RODOREDA
IN DIAMOND SQUARE

JANE RULE
DESERT OF THE HEART

ELISABETH RUSSELL TAYLOR
PILLION RIDERS

VITA SACKVILLE-WEST
CHALLENGE
NO SIGNPOSTS IN THE SEA

MARGERY SHARP
THE EYE OF LOVE

MAY SINCLAIR
MARY OLIVER
THE LIFE AND DEATH OF
    HARRIETT FREAN

EDITH SITWELL
THE SELECTED LETTERS OF
    EDITH SITWELL

STEVIE SMITH
ME AGAIN
NOVEL ON YELLOW PAPER
OVER THE FRONTIER
THE HOLIDAY

MURIEL SPARK
A FAR CRY FROM KENSINGTON
LOITERING WITH INTENT
MEMENTO MORI
SYMPOSIUM
TERRITORIAL RIGHTS
THE COMFORTERS
THE MANDELBAUM GATE
THE OBSERVING EYE
THE PUBLIC IMAGE

Lisa St Aubin De Teran
JOANNA

Gertrude Stein
BLOOD ON THE DINING
   ROOM FLOOR

Noel Streatfeild
TEA BY THE NURSERY FIRE

Jan Struther
MRS MINIVER

Jacqueline Susann
VALLEY OF THE DOLLS

Elizabeth Taylor
A GAME OF HIDE AND SEEK
A VIEW OF THE HARBOUR
A WREATH OF ROSES
ANGEL
AT MRS LIPPINCOTE'S
BLAMING
COMPLETE SHORT STORIES
DANGEROUS CALM
HESTER LILLY
IN A SUMMER SEASON
MRS PALFREY AT THE CLAREMONT
PALLADIAN
THE SLEEPING BEAUTY
THE SOUL OF KINDNESS
THE WEDDING GROUP

Angela Thirkell
AUGUST FOLLY
BEFORE LUNCH
CHEERFULNESS BREAKS IN
CHRISTMAS AT HIGH RISING

GROWING UP
HIGH RISING
MARLING HALL
MISS BUNTING
NORTHBRIDGE RECTORY
PEACE BREAKS OUT
POMFRET TOWERS
SUMMER HALF
THE BRANDONS
THE HEADMISTRESS
WILD STRAWBERRIES

P. L. Travers
AUNT SASS
THE FOX AT THE MANGER

Violet Trefusis
PIRATES AT PLAY

Elizabeth von Arnim
ALL THE DOGS OF MY LIFE
CHRISTOPHER AND COLUMBUS
ELIZABETH AND HER
   GERMAN GARDEN
FRAULEIN SCHMIDT AND
   MR ANSTRUTHER
LOVE
MR SKEFFINGTON
THE ADVENTURES OF ELIZABETH
   IN RUGEN
THE CARAVANERS
THE ENCHANTED APRIL
THE PASTOR'S WIFE
THE SOLITARY SUMMER
VERA

Sylvia Townsend Warner
AFTER THE DEATH OF DON JUAN

LOLLY WILLOWES
MR FORTUNE'S MAGGOT
SELECTED STORIES
THE CORNER THAT HELD THEM
THE FLINT ANCHOR
THE TRUE HEART

MARY WEBB
GONE TO EARTH
PRECIOUS BANE

EUDORA WELTY
THE OPTIMIST'S DAUGHTER

REBECCA WEST
COUSIN ROSAMUND
HARRIET HUME
SUNFLOWER
THE FOUNTAIN OVERFLOWS
THE HARSH VOICE
THE JUDGE
THE RETURN OF THE SOLDIER
THIS REAL NIGHT

EDITH WHARTON
ETHAN FROME
HUDSON RIVER BRACKETED
MADAME DE TREYMES

OLD NEW YORK
ROMAN FEVER
THE AGE OF INNOCENCE
THE CHILDREN
THE CUSTOM OF THE COUNTRY
THE FRUIT OF THE TREE
THE GHOST STORIES OF
    EDITH WHARTON
THE GODS ARRIVE
THE HOUSE OF MIRTH
THE MOTHER'S RECOMPENSE
THE REEF
TWILIGHT SLEEP

ANTONIA WHITE
FROST IN MAY QUARTET:
FROST IN MAY
THE LOST TRAVELLER
THE SUGAR HOUSE
BEYOND THE GLASS

AS ONCE IN MAY
MINKA AND CURDY
STRANGERS
THE HOUND AND THE FALCON

CHRISTA WOLF
A MODEL CHILDHOOD

VIRAGO CLASSICS FOR YOUNG READERS

Joan Aiken
THE GIFT GIVING:
    FAVOURITE STORIES
THE KINGDOM AND THE CAVE
THE SERIAL GARDEN

Nina Bawden
CARRIE'S WAR
KEEPING HENRY
THE PEPPERMINT PIG

Frances Hodgson Burnett
A LITTLE PRINCESS
THE SECRET GARDEN

Susan Coolidge
WHAT KATY DID
WHAT KATY DID AT SCHOOL
WHAT KATY DID NEXT

Rumer Godden
AN EPISODE OF SPARROWS
LISTEN TO THE NIGHTINGALE
THE DARK HORSE
THURSDAY'S CHILDREN

L. M. Montgomery
THE ANNE SHIRLEY SERIES:
ANNE OF GREEN GABLES
ANNE OF AVONLEA
ANNE OF THE ISLAND
ANNE OF WINDY WILLOWS
ANNE'S HOUSE OF DREAMS
ANNE OF INGLESIDE

RAINBOW VALLEY
RILLA OF INGLESIDE

THE EMILY STARR TRILOGY:
EMILY OF NEW MOON
EMILY CLIMBS
EMILY'S QUEST

JANE OF LANTERN HILL

E. Nesbit
THE PSAMMEAD TRILOGY:
FIVE CHILDREN AND IT
THE PHOENIX AND THE CARPET
THE STORY OF THE AMULET

THE BASTABLE CHILDREN TRILOGY:
THE STORY OF THE
    TREASURE SEEKERS
THE WOULDBEGOODS
NEW TREASURE SEEKERS

THE RAILWAY CHILDREN

Noel Streatfeild
APPLE BOUGH
CALDICOTT PLACE
CHRISTMAS STORY COLLECTION

Elizabeth Taylor
MOSSY TROTTER

P. L. Travers
I GO BY SEA, I GO BY LAND